MARIA CROSS

Maria Cross

Imaginative Patterns in a Group of Catholic Writers

CONOR CRUISE O'BRIEN

This edition first published in 2015
by Faber & Faber Ltd
Bloomsbury House, 74–77 Great Russell Street
London WC1B 3DA

Printed by Books on Demand GmbH, Norderstedt

All rights reserved
© Conor Cruise O'Brien 1954, 1963
'Conor Cruise O'Brien: An Appreciation' © Oliver Kamm, 2015

The right of Conor Cruise O'Brien to be identified
as author of this work has been asserted in accordance
with Section 77 of the Copyright, Designs and Patents Act 1988

This book is sold subject to the condition that it shall not, by way of
trade or otherwise, be lent, resold, hired out or otherwise circulated
without the publisher's prior consent in any form of binding or cover other than
that in which it is published and without a similar condition including this
condition being imposed on the subsequent purchaser

A CIP record for this book is available from the British Library

ISBN 978–0–571–32358–6

CONTENTS

	Conor Cruise O'Brien: An Appreciation	vii
	Introduction to the 1963 Edition	xiii
	Preface	xv
I	François Mauriac: The Secret Door	3
	1. The Sun and the Rain	3
	2. Women and Boys	12
	3. The Catholic and the Novelist	22
II	The Faust of Georges Bernanos	37
III	Graham Greene: The Anatomy of Pity	57
IV	The Parnellism of Seán O'Faoláin	87
V	The Pieties of Evelyn Waugh	109
VI	The Temple of Memory: Péguy	127
VII	The Rhinegold of Paul Claudel	157
	1. Gold	157
	2. Water	166
	3. Water and Gold	175
VIII	The Paradise of Léon Bloy	189
IX	Maria Cross	209
	Appendix	
	1. A Pillar in the Cloud	243
	2. Mr. Greene's Battlefield	249
	3. Our Men in Africa	252
	Index	257

CONOR CRUISE O'BRIEN: AN APPRECIATION

BY OLIVER KAMM

The last time – literally the last time, when he had an advanced stage of cancer – I visited Christopher Hitchens, we talked about the books and writers that had influenced him. He told how, in 1967, he picked up a volume of essays called *Writers and Politics* by Conor Cruise O'Brien in a public library in Tavistock, Devon. Reading it, he formed the ambition to be able to write like that.

I had a similar experience. I never met O'Brien but he was one of the earliest and most important influences on my political thinking and my wish to be a writer. As an undergraduate at Oxford, I picked up one of his books in the Bodleian Social Science Library. It was a collection of essays and reviews called *Herod: Reflections on Political Violence* (1978). His arguments throughout the book were a different face of O'Brien's politics (though he would certainly have claimed they were the same politics in essence) from his volume of the 1960s. In condemning America's war in Vietnam, he was recognisably a writer of the anti-imperialist Left. In his later volume, encapsulating his experience as a cabinet minister in Ireland's coalition government in the mid-1970s, he wrote of the destructiveness of absolutism.

It's a great book. In it, O'Brien not only denounces IRA terrorism, as you would expect from a mainstream politician, but – in a sense quite different from the rationalisations offered by ideological apologists for political violence – seeks to understand it. I mean, *really* understand it – not extenuate it by equivocation and non sequitur. And his thinking leads him to attack the republican mythology at the heart of the Irish state. Few writers have analysed terrorism so acutely or been as effective in undermining its ideological justifications. Here is how O'Brien recounts his thinking:

> In the politics of the Republic, I was not quite where I was expected to be. In the Congo time, sections of the British press had assured their readers (quite wrongly) that I was motivated by anti-British fanaticism. My career in America had shown me as opposed to imperialism. So I was expected at least to fall into line with the view that the troubles in Northern Ireland were caused by British imperialism. When instead I said that, in relation to Northern Ireland, it was the IRA who were the imperialists, since they were trying to annex by force a territory a large majority of whose inhabitants were opposed to them, my remarks appeared either incomprehensible or outrageous to a number of people who had liked what they heard *about* me much more than they like what they were hearing *from* me.

As a prophet, O'Brien was fallible. He doubted that the Irish constitution, with its irredentist claims to the whole island of Ireland, could be reformed in order to excise those articles. Yet eventually it was, and politics in Northern Ireland became marginally more normal (or at least less sectarian and violent). What was significant, even brilliant, about O'Brien's analysis was its lucidity in exposing cant. He realised that it was an untenable position for democratic politics both to condemn terrorism and to rely on a romanticised view of how the state had come into being and won its independence. O'Brien was repelled by the 'cult of the blood sacrifice' (expressed most eloquently but chillingly by Yeats in his one-act play *Cathleen ni Houlihan*) which underlay republican thinking. Being O'Brien, he didn't hold back in saying so. It took courage – raw physical courage, and not only political heterodoxy – to say such things in Ireland in the 1970s.

O'Brien had many roles in his long and eminent life. He was diplomat, statesman, politician, historian, literary critic, journalist and polymath. But most of all, he was a public intellectual in the best sense of the term. He applied his knowledge and critical intelligence to matters of great public interest, and he expressed his thinking in elegant, spare prose that argued a case with remorseless logic. He was a great man and a great Irishman, and Faber are to be congratulated in reissuing his work.

O'Brien's written output is best represented by his historical studies. Three of those volumes stand out in my estimation. First, *States of Ireland* (1972) remains the finest historical account of how the Troubles in Ireland erupted. It was a seminal revisionist treatment of the myths of Irish republicanism. If, as many of his admirers (including me) thought, O'Brien eventually went too far in embracing the cause of unionism and underestimated the capacity of a constitutional nationalism to reform itself, he did so with an unflinching humane intelligence.

O'Brien's history of the Zionist movement and Israel, *The Siege* (1986), is also a fine work of scholarship whose analysis stands up well in the light of later events. O'Brien was a friend to and admirer of Israel and often a lonely voice in media circles in explaining the Jewish state's security dilemmas. His downbeat but realistic conclusion was that Israel could not be other than it is, a Jewish state, which merited the sympathy of liberals in maintaining its democratic and secular character in spite of being in a state of permanent siege. Devoutly as he wished for a peaceful solution to the conflict in Palestine,

O'Brien believed that a solution was not available. On his analysis, conflicts don't have solutions: they have outcomes. I hope he is eventually proved wrong, and that a two-state solution between a sovereign Palestine and a safe Israel comes into being. But O'Brien's pessimism seems historically well-grounded.

Probably O'Brien's greatest achievement of historical scholarship is his biography of Edmund Burke, *The Great Melody* (1992). Burke is much cited by modern conservatives, and not necessarily accurately. The 'little platoons' that they celebrate aren't what Burke meant by the phrase; he was instead appealing to a notion of a fixed social order, in which each man knew his place. It is far removed from the modern ideals of social (and sexual) equality. Yet O'Brien retrieved the idea of Burke as a Whig of unrivalled historical farsightedness. On O'Brien's telling, Burke foresaw the bloody degeneration of the French Revolution even while celebrating the potential of the American Revolution. Among the gems in the paperback edition of the book is his respectful and affectionate exchange with Isaiah Berlin. O'Brien, as a confirmed Rousseau-basher, will have no quarter with any romantic idealisation of 'the general will.'

O'Brien's was a tough-minded version of liberalism, which stressed the dangers of untrammelled reason. In that respect, he was a worthy inheritor of the tradition of Burke. In his late collection *On the Eve of the Millennium* (1995), he noted that the worst crimes of the twentieth century had been committed by forces that considered themselves thoroughly emancipated from superstition – Nazism and Communism. O'Brien was a man of the Enlightenment, who believed its greatest enemy was absolutism.

His contrarian streak sometimes led him to mistaken and even perverse positions: against European integration; against intervention to stop the aggressive designs of Slobodan

Milosevic; opposition in principle, and not merely pragmatic objections, to the Good Friday Agreement in Northern Ireland; and most notably a deep hostility to the American 'civic religion' that celebrates Thomas Jefferson. His book *The Long Affair: Thomas Jefferson and the French Revolution* (1996) depicts America's third president as (and I don't exaggerate) an ideological precursor of Pol Pot.

It's an extraordinary argument and not, I think, O'Brien's finest. His historical revisionism, so valuable a tool, tended to overreach itself. The strict taxonomy that O'Brien set out – the American Revolution extended liberty, the French and Russian revolutions negated it – was, in reality, fuzzier than he allowed. But, again, O'Brien arrived at his conclusions with an intellectual honesty that caused him not to shirk unfashionable sentiments. The reforms enacted by the Constituent Assembly in France from 1789 to 1791 were quite limited, but went in the direction of secularism and the removal of the hereditary principle. Those who believe, crudely, that the American Revolution was good and the French Revolution bad do have the problem of explaining why Jefferson, as ambassador to Paris, saw these causes as consistent. O'Brien provides his own answer, which may be mistaken (I think it is), but it is an answer: Jefferson's politics were more French than American.

The French revolution of 1789 was admired throughout Europe, including Britain and particularly in Germany, for good reason. It was, like the American Revolution, a historic moment for the cause of reform, secularism and (I use the term without irony) progress. The turning point was war with Austria and Prussia in 1792. This precipitated a second revolution and all that followed: regicide, terror, and the reassertion of autocracy and nationalism. There was no reason that European governments should have sought to undermine the movement of 1789, and in doing so they became steadily more authoritarian at home. The Enlightenment tradition is perhaps more consistent than O'Brien allowed for. But he was brilliant at seeing its darker side. There were idiosyncrasies in his outlook but his was fundamentally an advocacy of a humane and liberal politics. He richly deserves a new generation of readers.

September 2014

Oliver Kamm is a leader writer and columnist for The Times.

INTRODUCTION

TO THE 1963 EDITION

THE linked essays which make up this book were written over a period of five years, from 1946 to 1951. The writer of the essays was in his early thirties; the writer of this introduction is in his midforties; much else has changed.

Some things in the book surprised me when I re-read it. Did I really compare, however guardedly, Evelyn Waugh with Proust? And what are these apocalyptic passages doing here and there, these flashes of certainty about the future, these moments of elegant pessimism? That writer, who used in any case another name, is no longer there to defend these things; his middle-aged successor should neither defend nor attack. Perhaps the sole advantage that one's middle years have over one's youth is that of being able to lecture without reply. It is not an advantage that should be abused. If the younger selves of certain writers had the time-privilege of being able to write prefaces to "the maturer work", they might be harsh from disappointment. In the reverse direction, the temptation is towards harshness from complacency. The reader, being detached, is a better judge in both cases.

Of the writers considered in these essays four – O'Faoláin, Waugh, Greene and Mauriac – are still writing. Mr. O'Faoláin, has not, I think, extricated himself creatively from the situation which I have attempted to describe in the essay on him which follows; I have, in any case, found nothing new to say about him. As for Mr. Waugh his principal work in recent years has been the trilogy *Men at Arms*, which I gave up reading about half-way, feeling hooperish and as if eavesdropping. There is no reason why Mr. Waugh should not talk, in print, to himself and a few friends, but it would be pointless for a critic to comment on the monologue.

François Mauriac's great powers have found expression, in these recent years, not in his novels and plays but in what I have in this book called "journalism", and what I should perhaps have called "the sermon". In some of his political writings – or politico-religious writings – on the back page of *L'Express* during the Algerian war there is a real vein of sacred eloquence such as has not appeared since Bossuet. And also, in some of the same writings, we find traces of the venom of Laclos, the unction of Tartuffe. By becoming a "journalist" the great Mauriac did not become at all less complex, less ambiguous, or less interesting than he was when "personal relations" interested him more than politics – which are, in any case, still personal relations. I worked on an essay dealing with Mauriac as a political writer, but it was a large task and I was distracted from it by other things.

I am glad to have the chance to include, in the appendix, reviews of Mr. Greene's two most recent novels, *The Quiet American* and *A Burnt-Out Case*. The first seems to me an excellent example of the reach of Mr. Greene's immense talent, when he is not cheating, or not cheating more than most writers. The second is one of those metaphysical conjuring tricks which only he either could, or would wish to, perform.

The appendix also contains an article on Claudel, written shortly after his death.

CONOR CRUISE O'BRIEN

Legon, Accra, Ghana
September, 1962

PREFACE

THIS is not a book about Catholicism; it is a book about eight writers who are Catholics. It is not about the lives, or the abstract ideas, or the techniques of these writers, but about the imaginative worlds which their works reveal.

Many great writers have tried to answer the question whether imaginative literature can be Catholic. Cardinal Newman, Léon Bloy, and André Gide leaned to the belief that it could not; M. Jacques Maritain, interpreting St. Thomas, believes that it can. Certainly the imagination of a Catholic will be profoundly affected by his religion, but the manner in which it will be affected is not easy to predict. I have not here tried to predict it, but have followed, as well as I could, the actual patterns of several exceptionally vivid imaginations which are permeated by Catholicism. In my final essay I have set down what these individual patterns seem to have in common. I do not claim that this wider pattern represents a general correlative of Catholicism, or even that anything is proved, in the scientific sense, at all. The writers in question were certainly not picked as a "representative cross-section of Catholic literature" but are simply among the modern Catholic writers who interested me most; the methods I have used in studying their work have no pretension to the uniformity of a questionnaire.

The only requirement of the scientific spirit to which I have tried to conform is that of respect for the facts. Each essay follows the pattern of what seemed to be important in the imagination of the writer studied, and not subordinate patterns which might have been more convenient for a critical thesis. It is quite possible that the living writers discussed will not, if they read the essays on themselves, agree. This need not unduly perturb the critic. G. K. Chesterton, in his introduction to *The Old Curiosity Shop*, gave a valuable definition which has been too little heeded by subsequent Catholic critics. "The function of criticism," he wrote, "if it has a legitimate function at all, can only be one function – that of dealing with the subconscious part of the author's mind which only the critic can express and not with the conscious part of the author's mind which the author himself can express. Either criticism is no good at all (a very defensible position) or else criticism means saying about an author the very things that would have made him jump out of his boots."

C. C. O'B.

Howth, Ireland
January 1952

ACKNOWLEDGMENTS

SOME sections of this book have appeared in *The Bell*, *Hudson Review*, *Irish Writing*, *Kenyon Review*, *Orpheus*, and *Renascence*, whose editors' permission to reprint is gratefully acknowledged. I am particularly indebted to Dr. Owen Sheehy Skeffington, of Trinity College, Dublin, for helping me to avoid, or rather to climb out of, various linguistic and other pitfalls, and also to Professor Liam O'Briain and the Librarian of University College, Galway, for giving me free access to that College's fine collection of works by modern French Catholic authors. My thanks are also due to the editorial staff of the Oxford University Press, New York, for their skill and patience in overcoming the special problems of collaboration at a distance; to Mr. G. E. Hetherington, Mr. Valentin Iremonger and Mr. Thomas Woods.

C. C. O'B.

I
FRANÇOIS MAURIAC

M. François Mauriac (b. 1885) is the author of nineteen novels: *L'Enfant chargé de chaînes* (1913), *La Robe prétexte* (1914), *La Chair et le sang* (1920), *Préséances* (1921), *Le Baiser au lépreux* (1922), *Le Fleuve de feu* (1923), *Génitrix* (1924), *Le Désert de l'amour* (1925), *Le Mal* (1927), *Thérèse Desqueyroux* (1927), *Destins* (1928), *Ce qui était perdu* (1930), *Le Nœud de vipères* (1932), *Le Mystère Frontenac* (1933), *La Fin de la nuit* (1935), *Les Anges noirs* (1936), *Les Chemins de la mer* (1939), *La Pharisienne* (1941), and *Le Sagouin* (1951); four plays: *Asmodée* (1937), *Les Mal Aimés* (1945), *Passage du malin* (1948), and *Le Feu sur la terre* (1950); and several short stories, an important life of Racine (1928), a life of Jesus (1936), and a large number of essays and newspaper articles, many of which have been collected in volume form. There are also four volumes of verse.

FRANÇOIS MAURIAC:
THE SECRET DOOR

I. THE SUN AND THE RAIN

Noble et brillant auteur d'une triste famille,
Toi dont ma mère osait se vanter d'être fille,
Qui peut-être rougis du trouble où tu me vois,
Soleil, je te viens voir pour la dernière fois.

RACINE, *Phèdre*.

THE sunlight pours in "like liquid metal" through the venetian blinds of the room in which a repulsive-looking adolescent, Jean Péloueyre, awakes to consciousness of his condition, and the bad taste in his mouth. The cicadas "light-up" from pine to pine and the sandy coastal plain turns to a furnace under the sun. In some places the forest is actually ablaze and the smell of burning resin reaches a middle-aged woman, Elisabeth Gornac, waiting with a troubled heart for two lovers to return. The sunlight is dirty from the great fire of Mano, as the young Thérèse Desqueyroux watches the drops of poison fall in her husband's glass. Now the air is heavy and electric but, in the near-by city, the two Courrèges, father and son, both intent on Maria Cross, know that, until the last bull has bled to death in the arena, the storm will not break. Over this haunted landscape, through which flows the fiery river of lust, a ferocious but still drowsy beast crouches in the livid sky.

This world in which torrid nature furnishes a lyrical and dramatic commentary (or prompting) to human passion has been a vital expression of Mauriac's imagination; it has also been a source of religious anxiety. In his first mature work, *Le Baiser au lépreux* (1922) – the story of the marriage of Jean Péloueyre – he showed his strange power of transmuting the district round his native Bordeaux, the land of vines and pines, into an enchanted country, an expression and an accomplice of sin. In that novel and in the six that followed (ending with *Destins*, 1928) he used that power insistently, and sometimes to excess. The opening paragraph above – which is built up for the most part of quotations from the novels of this period – gives a general idea of the result, and points to some of the more striking sympathetic movements that occur. It must be emphasized that nature in these episodes is not being used only for effect or with a superficial symbolism. The instinctive meteorology of the Courrèges family (in *Le Désert de l'amour*) would alone make us suspect that something more than a mere extension of metaphor, more even than Baudelaire's "forest of symbols," is involved. But a passage in *Destins* clears up any possible doubts: "She [Elisabeth Gornac] believed implicitly in those stage directions carefully drawn up by the Supreme Being for the lives of each and all of us . . . the soil had to be softened by the storm." From this – for Elisabeth obviously expressed a belief of her creator's – we see that the relation between natural events and human lives is conceived as being of a supernatural, quasi-magical order. In Elisabeth's case the "stage directions" are understood to come from God. In other cases their provenance is not so clear. Who is, it, for instance, that directs the storm not to break until the bull is dead? Or who is the unseen prompter that gives Thérèse her cue in the great fire of Mano? What is the celestial beast whom we glimpse for a moment in *Le Désert de l'amour*?

The diabolical origin of certain of these manifestations cannot be questioned. There is, however, "white magic" as well as black in Mauriac's sultry fairyland. The rain that falls after the storm becomes the sinner's tears of penitence and the cool wind from the ocean is a messenger of God's mercy. And the ocean, always present at the edge of the burning sand, is eternity itself. Yet despite the presence of these elements and the fact that all the novels of this period (except *Destins*) have edifying endings, the total impression left on the reader is of a dominant alliance of carnal passion and southern sun – that "everlasting afternoon" for which poor Elisabeth Gornac envied the doomed lovers. The rain falls seldom and the sea wind easily dies down; the fringe of the eternal ocean can serve to represent not only death but that "annihilation of caresses"[1] which Mauriac compares to death. Grace is remote, and its expressions little more than symbols, but sin is intoxicatingly omnipresent, even in the smell of flowers or of fire. The pagan D. H. Lawrence, who made a cult of sex and sun, never evoked them with anything like the dangerous power of the Christian Mauriac.

Mauriac himself, of course, fully realized that he possessed this power, and in a famous passage he thus defined his use of it: "Thanks to a certain gift of atmosphere I try to make perceptible, tangible, odorous, the Catholic universe of evil." The definition is excellent but it does not cover (perhaps is not meant to cover) the works we are now considering, Mauriac's novels of the 'twenties, where evil is not merely tangible and odorous but often seductive as well. Certainly this last aspect did not escape contemporary Catholic critics. The indefatigable Abbé Louis Bethléem, whose *Revue des Lectures* was presumed to guide the reading of the *bien-pensant* families of France, summed him up, in 1928, as "A rural author, subject to the intoxications of the fields and initiated into the frivolities of Parisian life" and dealt summarily with most of his novels to date:

> *Le Fleuve de feu:* disturbing, unhealthy.
> *Génitrix:* bizarre, morbid.
> *Le Désert de l'amour:* very pernicious.
> *Thérèse Desqueyroux:* morally base.
> *Destins:* very unhealthy.[2]

Nor was the good Abbé alone in this attitude: he was able to call a more scholarly authority, the Révérend Père Eugène Charles, to witness that Mauriac's novels were "steeped in an atmosphere of refined sensuality which penetrates to the marrow of your bones." Many leading Catholic critics, both lay and clerical, concurred in this judgment, and the pious journals of the provinces

---

[1] *Génitrix*. The seashore appears in the description of the unhappy marriage-nights of the Péloueyres and of the Desqueyroux. In the latter case the idea is (in a negative form) as I have stated it (Thérèse is "as if flung back by the sea on to a beach, cold, [her] teeth clenched"), in *Le Baiser au lépreux* the sea seems envisaged partly as a purifying agent, partly as death itself.
[2] *Romans à lire et romans à proscrire* (1928).

were, naturally, more vehement.[1] The young, of course, admired and read Mauriac, but that fact did little to disarm the suspicion of their elders. And the young themselves had a suspicion of what they were up to, as one of them later confessed: "What emotion!" wrote M. René Bady in the *Revue des Jeunes*, describing readings of Mauriac by himself and his friends; "invariably our readings finished in looks shot heavenwards, in stammerings of love, in prayer . . . but all was not always pure in our emotions." Finally the very idol of the infidels, M. André Gide, drove the point home with a graceful flourish. "The object of your novels," he wrote to Mauriac, "is not so much to bring sinners to Christianity as to remind Christians that there is something on earth besides Heaven. . . . Doubtless if I were more of a Christian I should be less your disciple."

Such criticisms as these and his own eventual recognition of their partial truth brought about, towards the end of 1928, a crisis in Mauriac's development – a crisis often referred to as his "conversion," although he had never lost the faith. This "conversion" involved an effort to make his work more positively Catholic, by avoiding the giving of scandal, and by attempting to "purify the source". Most important of all (as regards our present subject, the "climate" of the novels), it meant taking seriously the following dictum of M. Jacques Maritain: "The essential point is to know at what altitude he [the novelist] is when he makes this portrayal [of evil] and whether his art and his soul are pure enough . . . to make it without conniving at it."[2]

The acceptance of the Maritain doctrine, imposing the role

[1] At least one such journal continued to attack Mauriac bitterly long after he had become a highly respectable figure. The following extract, which concerns a book review by Mauriac, I leave in French so as not to falsify its exact degree of malice: ". . . il y a Mauriac dans cette affaire, un Mauriac qui montre le bout du nez, qui laisse entrevoir les mauvais refrains dont il s'alimente . . . [son] appétit de la gloire et des louanges" (*Bulletin des Lettres de Lyon*, 25 Sept. 1936). The writer of this piece wound up by thanking God that "a part of our youth, and that the healthiest, doesn't read at all."

[2] *Roseau d'Or* (No. 30) quoted in *Dieu et Mammon*. M. Maritain adds that "to write the work of a Proust as it should be written would require the interior light of a St. Augustine. Unfortunately it is just the opposite that has happened." This seems to cast new light on the authorship of the *Civitas Dei*.

François Mauriac: The Secret Door 7

of aerial photographer upon the novelist was eventually to dissolve the hot and sensuous world that Mauriac had created. No novel he has written since 1928 contains that combination of qualities previously regarded as characteristic of Mauriac. The direct conspiracy of nature and human love is not found again in his work. But it would be a mistake to assume that he immediately gained "altitude" and has easily maintained it. His flight from the desert, with the aid of M. Maritain's instruments, has been erratic.

The sun did not immediately fade from Mauriac's creation and at first it seemed as if a new cycle was beginning in which the old atmosphere and background would develop in harmony with altered passions. *Le Nœud de vipères* (1932) – the first novel entirely written after the "conversion" – centres round the possession of property. The climate is still the same, stifling and stormy, and the landscape is also the same – old Louis, the hero and narrator, is a rich landowner from near Bordeaux – but it appears in a somewhat different light, because it is conceived primarily as property. The forest of symbols has become "my two thousand hectares of timber."[1] That is not to say that there is no longer any connection between human passion and the visible world, or that the landscape has been turned into an abstraction. On the contrary: old Louis's avarice lends his vineyards and *métairies* and tracts of pine a vivid reality in his narration, and both his avarice and his possessions are forms through which he can express, in hatred against his covetous and expectant family, his frustrated loves of years ago. In fact the love-and-nature collaboration continues, but in a more complex, subtle, and perhaps more beautiful, form. Love appears through a haze of remembrance and nature through a haze of money; the poles are wider apart but the current still spans them. *Le Nœud de vipères* is in itself a very remarkable novel – not far below the previous peaks of Mauriac's achievement, *Génitrix* and *Le Désert de l'amour* – and it seemed to promise even better things: a fruitful phase in

[1] There is a revealing passage in the *Journal* for about this time: ". . . no longer does any symbol spring to me from the slumber of the vines under their sulphate spray; I only try to remember the price of sulphate." *Journal* I (1934), p. 32. Not that the forest had ever been entirely symbolic, or that Mauriac had ever forgotten the price of sulphate.

which the novelist, now older, would be concerned not so much with youthful storms as with the more complicated relations of adults and with the economic and social correlatives of passion. In fact no such development took place. *Le Nœud de vipères* had no worthy successor, and Mauriac's later novels were not much more than vague and inconclusive ruminations of previous themes. I believe that the cause of this break, the second and (so far as I know) unremarked crisis in Mauriac's development, should be sought not so much in his religious attitude – for *Le Nœud de vipères* has been universally hailed as his most Catholic novel and the phase it promised could have been compatible with the strictest Catholicism – as in his attitude to the family and society. In order to understand the disastrous changes that came over Mauriac's world after *Le Nœud de vipères* it is necessary in my view to go back and examine, from the period of his earliest novels, the principal manifestations of his deeply rooted sense of class and family – the two are not easily separable.

Mauriac, the son of a landowning bourgeois of Bordeaux, was sharply conscious from the date of his earliest works of the class to which he belonged, and when he had occasion to present the manners and behaviour of that class, he did so without romantic distortion. Even at the height of his "magical" period, under the livid sky of *Le Désert de l'amour*, the prosaic table of a bourgeois family fills the foreground and the moaning of the storm-wind in the pines does not drown the deft phrases in which Lieutenant Basque decently veils his obsession with promotion, or the lamentations of Mme Courrèges that in her own parish the dead child of an immoral woman should be given an *enterrement de première classe*. It is this realism in romanticism (as if in the middle of a landscape by Van Gogh a window should open on a Dutch interior) that gives Mauriac's best novels of this period their peculiar and unforgettable quality. Earlier still, in his first immature novels, his refusal to idealize the bourgeoisie had gone as far as satire. He had described Bordeaux as "the town with the most conceited and snobbish bourgeoisie in France," and his fourth novel, *Préséances*, developed that description. *Préséances* dealt with the wine merchants, the "Claretocracy" (*aristocratie du bouchon*) who lead Bordeaux society. It gently ridiculed this Anglophile clique with its English Christian names (Harry Maucoudinat, Percy Larousselle, Willy Durand) and showed to what outrageous lengths scions of equally rich but less exalted bourgeois houses (such as that to which Mauriac himself seems to have belonged) were prepared to go in order to break the charmed circle and be elected to the "London and Westminster" Club.

But the satirical vein in *Préséances* rapidly peters out and rarely crops up again in any of the later novels. Mauriac was too intelligent to accept the bourgeoisie of Bordeaux at their own valuation but he recognized that he still belonged to them and was rooted in the same sandy soil. He shared their love of the land, their dislike of the get-rich-quick bourgeoisie of Paris, and their mixed feelings (of dependence and fear) towards their servants. As for the workers, only one representative of that class appears in the pages of Mauriac, and his appearance serves only to reveal the "desert that separates" the consciously bourgeois writer from the proletariat. This worker, Georges Elie, appears in Mauriac's obviously autobiographical first novel, *L'Enfant chargé de chaînes*, and makes the hero's acquaintance as a member of a sort of Christian Democrat party, *L'Union amour et foi:* the hero at first encourages his friendship but soon tires of his banal remarks and of the whole idea of the Union; after returning to his flat from a meeting of this body he gets into "pyjamas of a sombre hue" and takes out a volume of Laforgue, "to deplebeianize himself" ("pour se désencanailler"). The mature Mauriac would not have presented us with that delightful scene, but he would not, I think, disown it either.

The difficulties of Mauriac's position – as a moralist who accepted his class while clearly seeing its vices – were resolved in the splendid years from *Le Baiser au lépreux* to *Destins* by the nature of the subjects that obsessed him. The sin of lust, unlike the sin of avarice, stands in only a contingent relation to the problems of society. As long as the main interest was concentrated on sexual passion, Mauriac could afford to be uncompromising, even harsh, in his portrayal of his class. The portrait was unflattering but it was in miniature and, in the strong light which beat on more exciting things, it did not attract very much attention. That Mauriac would have been unhappy if it had done so is made fairly clear by a preface which he found it necessary to write when the second edition of *Préséances* appeared in 1928: "I do not think I would write this so maliciously today...." he wrote in part. "Since the Tuileries went up in flames the occupation of the nobility is gone: but the *chais* of Bordeaux are eternal and the royal wine of our city may ennoble those who serve it." The greater concern of the mature and established writer for the susceptibilities of the rich was not as yet a menace to his art, but it was soon to become so. The "unregenerate" years ended in 1928 with the publication of *Destins*, and *Destins* ends with Elisabeth Gornac, ageing and balked in love, transmuting her passion into avarice, the sombre and jealous love of pines and vines.

This same transmuted passion – apparently the only possible form in which Mauriac's love-and-nature collusion could continue – is, as we have seen, dominant in *Le Nœud de vipères*, which may be said to take up where *Destins* leaves off. Now *Le Nœud de vipères* is by no means a slashing attack on the bourgeoisie but it has *very near its centre of interest* the same harsh social realism that filled out the details in the previous novels. A series of novels like this, turning round the passion of avarice, would have presented a highly repulsive full-length portrait of what had hitherto been shown in discreet miniature – Mauriac's class, his acquaintances, and, most important, his family.

It was at this point that Mauriac lost his nerve and wrote *Le Mystère Frontenac* (1933), a sort of nostalgic ode to the bourgeois family. He has himself given us an account of this second "conversion." "Last year," he wrote in 1933, "ill and surrounded with affection and kindness, I was afraid of ending on the note of *Le Nœud de vipères*. I thought of the mystery of love which joins together mother, sons, and brothers." This is the mystery of *Le Mystère Frontenac*, a work which (however much we may respect its motive) marks a terrible setback in Mauriac's development as a novelist. There is, fittingly, a change in climate to match the change in purpose: a soft rain is falling most of the time, and "the sleepy whispering of the pines is heard at an infinite distances.'

François Mauriac: The Secret Door 11

The author's tenderness, which excludes all conflict and almost all action, attaches itself not only to the family but unequivocally to the social order that has been so kind to the particular family. In a key passage, one of the characters declares that landed property is essential for the preservation of human personality and grimly prophesies a day when "those below will have triumphed over the human person. No age-old park will any longer stretch its branches over the heads of a single family." It was with reason that a friendly and sensitive critic, M. Jacques Madaule, said of this work, in untranslatable phrases: ". . . ce n'est pas une apologie de la bourgeoisie, c'est une bourgeoisie poétique . . . le bourgeois Mauriac au tombeau de la bourgeoisie accroche cette couronne d'immortelles."

The worst thing about this rather premature wreath was that it represented an apology for *Le Nœud de vipères*, and an implicit promise that such a thing would not occur again – nor has it. The drizzle that set in with *Le Mystère Frontenac* continues to fall in the subsequent novels, accompanied latterly (*Les Chemins de la mer, La Pharisienne, Le Sagouin*) by a thick fog, representing doubt. In this soft air the tensions that held together such works as *Génitrix* and *Le Nœud de vipères* are relaxed and the whole structure sags into shapelessness. Here and there, especially in *La Pharisienne*, an individual scene or character is realized with the old brilliance, but each novel as a whole remains incoherent or has only such meaning as the attachment of an arbitrary "moral ending" can give.

Mauriac is unable to move either forward or back. Sometimes he has taken up again a theme of the 'twenties, as in *La Fin de la nuit*, where he exhumes Thérèse Desqueyroux and tries to make an honest woman of her. Here he fails either to revive the old Thérèse or to convince himself of her conversion. Once – in the scene at the beginning of *Les Chemins de la mer*, where a wily bourgeois mother exploits the stupefied grief of a widow in order to get an I.O.U. back from her – he seems to be continuing the road from *Le Nœud de vipères*, but it turns out to be a blind alley. Often, as in *Les Anges noirs* (an unconvincing tale of diabolic possession), he seems to be attempting the hopeless task of building a novel on an abstraction, the part of faith that is intellectual, not that which is emotional.

The truth seems to be that, by the time he came to write *Le Mystère Frontenac*, he had accepted an intellectual, and therefore false, solution to an emotional dilemma. "It is in proportion," he wrote in his diary, "as *will* enters into my work (through scruple, fear of scandal, et cetera) that I feel myself threatened." He knew in his heart that the heart cannot be "purified." The sun that at last he allowed to be masked with mental fog; the sun that heated all that was living in his work; the "implacable sun" of *Génitrix*, was a continual emotional explosion, a blaze of unresolved contradictions.

We have spoken of an "emotional dilemma" and of "unresolved contradictions." It is time that we attempt to justify this language, by examining the realities that lie behind the "final official version" of *Le Mystère Frontenac*.

2. WOMEN AND BOYS

Sur les soins de sa mère on peut s'en assurer,
Et mon fils avec moi n'apprendra qu'à pleurer.

RACINE, *Andromaque*.

BEFORE Mauriac was two years old, his father died, and he was left to the care of his mother, to whom he was deeply attached. He has told us, indeed, in the one fragment of avowed autobiography that he has published – *Commencements d'une vie* (1932) – that his extreme affection for her was the main cause of the unhappiness of his childhood. It was impossible for him "to live away from what I loved, separated even for a day from my mother. Everything which pertained to her took on in my eyes a sacred character and shared in her perfection – even servants, even inanimate objects. When someone said to me that a dress belonging to an aunt of mine was dowdy-looking, I was astonished that a sister of my mother's could own such a dress." He goes on to tell of his sufferings whenever his mother went away on a visit and he had to stay in school as a boarder. He does not, however, give us – indeed he seems careful not to give

François Mauriac: The Secret Door 13

us — any direct information here about her who was the object of such a cult and the cause of so much suffering. We know that she was pious and wealthy, that she had five children, and that at least one of them felt towards her as an only child is ordinarily supposed to feel. For the rest, if we wish to form an idea of the woman who did so much to shape the future writer, and of the true pattern of Mauriac's childhood, we must go to the novels themselves. At the same time, if we read the novels, or as many of them as possible, with the clue of *Commencements d'une vie* in mind, we are able to understand much that otherwise remains dark. In other words, both the novels and the autobiographical fragment reflect, from different angles, the reality of the writer's life. Mauriac himself has said, "Only fiction does not lie: it opens on the life of a man a secret door through which slips in, altogether unchecked, his unknown soul." Even if that is not altogether true — and I feel that Mauriac in his later novels has kept a fairly strict check on that secret door — we may accept it as relatively so, and as guaranteeing that an attempt to interpret his works by reference to his early life, and vice versa will not be altogether unrewarded.

The most "authentic" portrait of Mauriac's mother — that is to say the most admitted and the furthest from being an unconscious reflection — is to be found in the appeasing and gently reminiscent pages of *Le Mystère Frontenac*. Blanche Frontenac is a young widow with five children, to whom she sacrifices her life, being weary with "the weariness of a mother whose children are eating her alive." Her piety, "somewhat minute and arid" though it was, contained a passionate temperament: "if it had not been for God she did not think she could ever have found the strength to live like this; for she was an ardent young woman." To her children she is strict but loving and to the outer world she is ferocious in their interest, with the ferocity of a rich and warm-hearted woman. This picture which we know to be authentic (for Mauriac scarcely attempts to conceal the autobiographical nature of *Le Mystère Frontenac*) corresponds so very closely to other widowed mothers in earlier novels that we are able to add to it. Mme Thérèse Dézaymeries of *Le Mal*, who considered her widowhood as a state of religion and whose stern piety did so much to cure her son of his infatuation with a dissolute Dublin girl, is the same character as Blanche. It is of her that Mauriac tells us, in a characteristic phrase, that when she kissed her children on returning from early Mass, "her kiss had a taste of church, a smell of fog." We find the same characteristics, in a different context, in Mme de Blénauges, the mother of the villainous Hervé in *Ce qui était perdu*. This poor lady, in her confession, attempts to take her son's numerous and horrible sins upon herself: "You invited me to renounce the world as if it were renunciation to put the whole burden of one's earthly hopes and desires on to a child! ... In a literal sense I burdened my son with all my own concupiscence."

In these three incarnations (Mmes Frontenac, Dézaymeries, de Blénauges) the pious and passionate widow is seen clearly – as an intelligent neighbour might perhaps have seen her – and at the same time accepted. Her son seems to say: "I see now what you were, and why you acted as you did, and I continue to love and obey you." So in *Le Mystère Frontenac* the boy Yves (Mauriac himself), who is first seen, aged ten, clinging to his mother "as if some instinct were urging him to return into the body from which he had been born," still feels at the end equally bound to her after his death, and through her to all his kin, and class. A deep grave, he feels, should be dug at the foot of the pines of Bourideys, where the bodies of all the Frontenacs could be buried in one heap and so remain "embraced forever in their own land which they love so much, while high over the heads of the pines there would pass, closely united for eternity, the souls of the mother and her five children."

The vision of eternal dependence, continuing childhood, is something that recurs in Mauriac's work, but it is not always accepted so calmly. Indeed it is one of Mauriac's vital contradictions that this same vision, Yves' dream of bliss in *Le Mystère Frontenac*, is elsewhere a nightmare. Mauriac's most horrible situations – and he excels in horror – are invariably those in which a parent, almost always a mother, continues to dominate, and begins to absorb, the mind and emotions of a child who, in years, has become an adult. Such a child was Fernand Cazenave, the

François Mauriac: The Secret Door

fifty-year-old "hero" of *Génitrix* (1924), the novel in which the nightmare made its first appearance. We see Fernand living in an isolated sinister house in the middle of the *lande*, with his young wife and his mother, Félicité Cazenave, a massive and terrifying figure. Fernand, a spoiled and pompous elderly boy, is wounded by his wife's failure to give him the same adoration that he was used to getting from his mother, and he joins his mother in a persecution which culminates in the wife's death in childbed, from fever, neglect, and terror. Fernand then, in revulsion, turns against his mother, who slowly perishes from lack of the love she had so fiercely monopolized. After her death, however, Fernand, alone in the haunted house, falls again entirely under her influence and makes her the object of a cult. No bald précis can convey anything of the extraordinarily oppressive quality of this story, in which the intense concentration of the tragedy seems to generate the thunderous heat that fills the air, and the characters, as motionless as if they were besieged, need to be reminded that they are awake and that "it is all true" by a glass rattling on a table as a train goes by.

The great emotional charge of this fearful story would in itself reveal the importance of this dream situation in Mauriac's mind, even if we had no other evidence. But in fact it is not the only, not even the most terrible, version of the dream. For sheer horror *Génitrix* is eclipsed by a fifty-page story of family life, *Le Rang*, which deserves examination, both because of its intrinsic merit and because of the light it casts into the dark places of Mauriac's mind.

A prosperous elderly bourgeois, Hector Bellade, calls on an old and down-and-out cousin, Auguste Duprouy, to condole with him on the death of his sister Emma. Old Auguste, in his shabby but painfully respectable room, talks volubly of his dead relatives, his mother and his sisters Emma and Eudoxia, with whom he spent his life. His mother had been a remarkable woman, pious, strong-willed, and, despite poverty, passionately tenacious of her "position in life" (*rang*). Auguste describes the sacrifice of his own scholastic ambitions to his mother's idea of class, and then the sacrifice of his sister. Eudoxia, occupied with her mother in pious works, had a crisis of melancholia about her thirtieth year. The parish priest had "found a husband for her," but the proposed husband was a mere clerk in a grain merchant's, and the mother, after bitter quarrels, quashed the proposal. Auguste remembered her shouting at Eudoxia: "If you have such instincts you should hide them. No decent girl would admit their existence, even to herself. There's some excuse for common people. But you, a Duprouy!" And she adds: "How frightful original sin must have been to condemn people of the best society to those ignoble acts." Defeated over the proposal, Eudoxia becomes resigned and finally develops cancer. Auguste remembers her last, dying, "hugging the charwoman's baby to her mutilated breast." At this point in his story Auguste breaks down, and confesses that he is starving. Hector takes him to a restaurant and there, slightly excited by food and drink, Auguste begins to talk about himself, reveals that he too had been engaged. His story had been in essentials the same as Eudoxia's; his mother and Emma used to spy on the courting couple through a crack in the floor; finally the mother broke off the engagement by means of an anonymous letter. And now Auguste, furtively looking round the café, asks suddenly: "Is it as nice as they say?"

And his cousin, running his hand over his bald head, replies: "I don't remember."

A few days later Auguste is found dead of hunger in his room. Hector's wife, who had been opposed to giving any help to Auguste, is now conscience-stricken and insists on paying for the transport of his body to the family vault at Langoiran, so that the Duprouys will be again united:

"How happy poor Auguste would have been, if he could have foreseen that he would join his mother, and Eudoxia, and Emma, for eternity!"

The ironic resemblance to the end of *Le Mystère Frontenac* needs no stressing; idyll and horror are very close together, and the real situation which both reflect becomes fairly clear. The mother, for Mauriac, is an emotional storm-centre and an insoluble dilemma. It is she who awakens love and it is also she who restrains and punishes it, with a fury that comes from her own restraint and punishment of herself. The "genetrix" of the *Aeneid*, to whom Félicité Cazenave is compared, was Venus herself, but Félicité is a jealous goddess and will have no rivals. She destroys Fernand's wife, just as Mme Duprouy gets rid of Eudoxia's fiancé, and Mme Dézaymeries "cures" Fabien of his love for Fanny Barrett. And even in the case of the Frontenacs, Blanche's love for her son continues after her death to make any other love impossible for him. He had been accustomed to enter into his mother's love as into the great family park of Bourideys, running down to the ocean, and "henceforth he has to enter into every love with a fatal curiosity to find its limits." In other words she holds him, as Fernand and Auguste are held, in emotional captivity.

He has in the past made efforts to escape. Thérèse Desqueyroux, who burst through "the living bars of a family" by attempting to poison her husband, clearly commanded her creator's not altogether unconscious sympathy. The portraits of Félicité Cazenave and of Mme Duprouy are in themselves acts of rebellion, just as the innumerable scenes of cruelty and emotional laceration – for example the jilting scene in *Les Chemins de la mer*, and the story *Coups de couteau*, in which a husband keeps his middle-aged wife awake all night while he tells her of his sufferings on account of a young girl – seem to be acts of vengeance, for the sufferers are usually women.[1] And there is in most of his work, particularly of the period before the "conversion" of 1929, an undertone of hostility to the family, which betrays his desire to get out of his prison.

But all this is not really very much more than a shaking of the bars. Even Thérèse Desqueyroux is brought back into the family circle to die (in *La Fin de la nuit*, 1935) and none of Mauriac's other heroes or heroines ever made such a break as Thérèse. The characteristic pattern of a Mauriac novel is one of "temptation and renunciation," and the "renunciation" almost always involves a

[1] It is not clear, however, whether the vengeance is directed against the mother, or against women who have failed to take the mother's place, or both. Old Louis, the vindictive hero of *Le Nœud de vipères*, certainly revenges himself against his wife for her failure to take the place of his adoring and indulgent mother.

log-like acceptance of some family obligation. So Elisabeth Gornac (of *Destins*) continues to manage the family property; Noëmi Péloueyre (of *Le Baiser au lépreux*) devotes herself to the memory of a husband whom she did not love, and the heroes of *L'Enfant chargé de chaînes* (1913) and *Les Anges noirs* (1936) enter into virtuous marriages which consist of sharing stuffy, over-furnished bedrooms with women whom they don't much like. And even the sensual temptations through which such characters pass carry within them, powerful though they are,[1] a germ of disgust which guarantees their transience. Daniel Trasis, the libertine of *Le Fleuve de feu* (1923), is typical. Daniel strongly desires Gisèle de Plailly but just as strong as his desire to corrupt her is his "thirst for limpidity," which makes him desire her to be virtuous. His discovery that Gisèle has already had a child makes him burst out crying. He ends by renouncing her.

The tears of Daniel Trasis are revealing enough in regard to the sort of horror that accompanies sexuality in the Mauriac pattern, but a scene in a much later novel, *La Pharisienne* (1941), is almost explicit on the point. The great set piece of this novel is an improbable and unforgettable scene in which a boy, Jean de Mirbel, who has cycled miles through the night to see his mother, arrives outside her hotel at the moment when she appears at a bedroom window with her lover.[2] The boy watches them for a while, and hears their conversation, and the course of his whole life is deflected by what he sees and hears. The Comtesse de Mirbel is one of two maternal figures in this novel. The other is Brigitte Pian, the "woman of the Pharisees" herself. Brigitte is as anti-erotic as the Comtesse is erotic and by preventing Jean from

---

[1] The strength of such feelings is revealed in the following un-English passage: "He must think of asking her did she play tennis; it should be easy to find two racquets. Games light up young bodies like candles . . . and he imagined her burning on the court, got up, filled his tooth-glass with water, swallowed an aspirin, waited for sleep." (*Le Fleuve de feu.*)

[2] This scene, which Mauriac handles so brilliantly as to make credible, is grotesquely foreshadowed in one of his early and immature novels: "One day in a suburban street where I chanced to pass I saw my uncle, clad in violet pyjamas, on the balcony of a red-brick *maisonnette*. Beside him a woman with her hair down was watering geraniums; by the artificial tints of hair and cheeks I knew the lady was of easy virtue." (*La Robe prétexte.*)

seeing a young girl who loves him she completes the ruin brought about by the Comtesse. Brigitte also ruins other lives, those of a teacher, M. Puybaraud, and his wife Octavia, and her own husband's, by her malevolent prudery which she identifies with virtue and religion. Her attack on Octavia during the period of the engagement is a refined and canting version of Mme Duprouy's denunciation of her daughter Eudoxia: "You must not think that I am hostile *in principle* to these promptings of nature . . . it may be that the intentions of the Almighty on your behalf have made necessary this deviation of Monsieur Puybaraud from a higher vocation. I realize that he may have to be humbled if you are to be saved." She then causes M. Puybaraud to lose his job.

The most interesting point in all this is the attitude of the narrator Louis, Brigitte's stepson, with whom Mauriac clearly identifies himself. Louis, who in retrospect sees so lucidly the evil results of Brigitte's actions, was in fact himself a collaborator in these actions. He was a sneaking schoolboy who betrayed both his teacher, M. Puybaraud, and his sister, Michèle, to Brigitte – the former out of curiosity and the second out of possessive, almost incestuous, affection.[1] He confesses that "The Brigitte Pian type appealed to me. I found it beautiful . . ." and, even in retrospect, he shares her contempt for the Puybarauds and her view that their marriage was a falling-off from a higher state. He does not turn against Brigitte until, in her latter years, she herself loses her vigour, becomes remorseful, then soft, then engaged, finally a spiritualist. In this long decline the narrator follows her with a contempt worthy of her own great days.

And yet he is not really Brigitte's son, and his real mother was, as he discovers, much less like Brigitte than like the erring Comtesse de Mirbel.

Keeping in mind Mauriac's previous work, we can see clearly in *La Pharisienne* a sort of prismatic diffraction of a beam that

[1] Long before this, in *Ce qui était perdu*, Mauriac set out to treat an incest theme, and the results should have been extremely interesting if he had finished the novel on the lines originally proposed. But the "conversion" took place while he was writing, and the "secret door" of which he speaks elsewhere was hurriedly battened down.

had before been intensely concentrated. The mother-who-sinned-long-ago, the mother-who punished-sin, the mother-found-in-sin, the mother-suffering (Octavia), all different characters, are all at the same time not so much aspects of the one jealous and passionate mother (Blanche Frontenac or Félicité Cazenave) as a set of abstractions from the conflicting emotions set up by such a mother in a sensitive son. This was not, of course, the first time that Mauriac had made such abstractions – in a sense his work consists of little else. But hitherto in any one novel he had focused attention on only one "mother." In *La Pharisienne* we are confronted at every turn by a "mother." It is as if Mauriac were desperately trying to enlarge the place of his captivity by burning different effigies of his jailer in remote and improbable corners. Perhaps at the same time, irritated by those critics who affect to consider him unimportant because his novels are short, he felt obliged to undertake a work of considerable bulk, and then found it hard to fill it. But I think the main cause of the diffusion lies in the difficulty in which Mauriac, as a writer, finds himself since the double "conversion" of 1930–3. He has been forced by his religious "conversion" and consequent fear of scandal to keep some sort of watch upon that "secret door" and that alone would prevent any deeper development of his theme. At the same time he shrinks (since *Le Nœud de vipères*) from any sustained realistic treatment of the environment he knows best, for, given his temperament, such treatment would have seemed a harsh satirical attack (which he does not consciously want to deliver) upon his family and class.[1] Thus unable to go deeper down or further out, he can at best perform only ingenious variations upon his theme or (putting it more harshly) give his work a spurious extension by disguised repetition. The fact that *La Pharisienne* includes two "boys" and four "mothers," instead of one "boy" and one "mother," does not really make it a greater novel than *Génitrix*.

---

[1] Those of his stories and scenes that reveal hate of "the mother" tend also to be attacks on bourgeois values. Compare *Le Rang*, where the mother's half-crazy puritanism and her exalted sense of class are closely related, with the powerful scene in *La Pharisienne*, where Brigitte terrifies the pregnant (and dying) Octavia by denouncing her fecklessness in hiring a piano while she depends on charity.

François Mauriac: The Secret Door 21

It is true that other novelists, even such a "neurotic" as Proust, can multiply their own experience in a convincing work of great scale. But those who have succeeded in doing so have always been completely undeterred by any fear of giving scandal, social or moral, and their experience has been less specialized and ingrowing than that of Mauriac. The population of Mauriac's small, brilliantly lit world cannot expand, for that world lacks an essential element of reproduction, a father. The men that play prominent roles in his work are almost always adolescents (usually in love with older women), and the few men of mature years that appear (Fernand Cazenave in *Génitrix*, Louis in *Le Nœud de vipères*) are usually seen, from the inside, as merely oldish small boys, spoiled by indulgent mothers and wizened by spite at the cessation of their mother's care. There is hardly a male figure in the novels at all comparable to the formidable female objects round which the whole work turns in awe.[1] The father is usually simply not there, with something slightly ignominious about his absence; he left behind a bowler hat, he was an anticlerical, he committed suicide. Sometimes he remains alive, even more ignominiously, as an impotent and dominated being (Octave Pian of *La Pharisienne*; Symphorien Desbats of *Les Anges noirs*). Such, in Mauriac's latest novel, *Le Sagouin*, is Count Galéas de Cernès, the degenerate father of a retarded youth, the "sagouin" of the title. In this autumnal work, in which the simplicity if not the intensity of the earlier period returns, the heroine is the wife and mother, "the Gorgon" who drives father and son to drown themselves.

They are nearing the moist borders of that kingdom where the mother, where the wife, will torment them no longer. They are going to be delivered from the Gorgon, they are going to sleep.

* * *

This matricentric world is the creative inheritance which came in the fullness of time to that little boy to whom "pious

[1] Virelade, the possessive father in the play *Les Mal Aimés*, is only an apparent exception to this. His possessiveness directed towards a daughter is only a disguised form of the familiar pattern.

and aged ladies, altogether unlyrical, had, without knowing it, taught poetry." The poetry they taught him seems to obey the magical law that it is valid and true only so long as the learner remains within the narrow circle where it was taught; and the pious ladies, not all very aged, and bearing a remarkable resemblance to the Furies, seem willing to continue their lessons forever. And they not only taught him poetry, they heard him something much more important, which we have not yet considered, his catechism.

3. THE CATHOLIC AND THE NOVELIST

Armez-vous d'un courage et d'une foi nouvelle,
Il est temps de montrer cette ardeur et ce zèle
Qu'au fond de votre cœur mes soins ont cultivés,
Et de payer à Dieu ce que vous lui devez.
Sentez-vous cette noble et généreuse envie?

RACINE, *Athalie.*

MARGARET of Cortona, a thirteenth-century Franciscan saint, had been a great sinner and was the mother of a son. When, after her lover's murder, she became converted and entered upon a life of sanctity, she treated this son with an extreme harshness which excited horror and pity among the villagers of Cortona. It was believed for a while that the boy, in despair at his mother's treatment of him, had thrown himself down a well. This story was untrue; he lived to become a friar, although apparently a somewhat refractory and tormented one.

Mauriac, Saint Margaret's biographer, and himself the son of a pious widow, sees this boy as being saved almost against his will, certainly without the exercise of free choice. "Dragged in the wake of his mother's heavenward movement," he writes, "ravished from the earth, he followed from afar, consenting to everything. Was he not both a child of guilty love and son of a holy woman – born of the two loves which had possessed Margaret, torn between the inclinations of an ardent nature, and the demands of that terrible grace to which his mother was a prey and which, through her, reached himself and wrenched him from the world?"

It is clear that Mauriac is here interpreting the young friar's mind in the light of his own religious education and experience. He had not been free to choose or reject Catholicism for he was born a Catholic. He has expressed envy of converts like Psichari for whom Catholicism had been a matter of choice; the faith had reached him principally through a mother who was a formidable emotional force; he, too had been torn between "the inclinations of an ardent nature" and grace. Further the grace that reached him through his mother did indeed deserve the adjective "terrible." "We know what it is," he has written in his life of Racine, "to live from our first years in a sort of familiar terror, in the presence of a God whose eye pierces even into our dreams. . . . Jansenism . . . which accustoms the young to live in fear and trembling, has left more traces in our provinces than is generally thought." And we know that this semi-Jansenistic piety which he absorbed regarded all carnal love, even in marriage, as guilty,[1] so that he could in his heart apply to himself the words "a child of guilty love and son of a holy woman."

For the child Mauriac the Catholic religion was not merely something taught and accepted, a system of rules and lessons, as it is for so many children. He was one of those rare people who from the beginning are incapable of drawing any dividing line between their religion and their emotional lives, or even between the supernatural and the mundane. On the one hand the faith penetrated deep into his life; in particular, the practice of frequent examinations of conscience[2] brought his intellect completely and forever under the sway of Catholic morality as it was taught to him in his mother's home. On the other hand his

[1] In his life of Racine he speaks of "that certitude fatal to human happiness, that carnal love is Evil, Evil which we cannot help committing." And in *La Pharisienne* the narrator agrees with Brigitte's view that "all the miseries of our human state come from our inability to remain chaste." In many places he quotes Pascal's definition of marriage as, "The lowest of the conditions of Christianity, vile and prejudicial in the eyes of God."

[2] Examination of conscience was encouraged by many pious practices in his mother's home. In *La Robe prétexte* he mentions a preciously bound "moral account-book" given to him on the occasion of his first Communion, and elsewhere he tells us that each child could expect to receive at Christmas, along with his present, "a letter in which God himself was believed to have written our besetting sin." (*Conte de noël*.)

faith itself became at once a solemn apotheosis of the life of his home, and a sanctuary for emotions for which that grim home could tolerate no other outlet. For him as for the tormented hero of *Génitrix* there existed "a kingdom of love and silence where his mother was an altar."[1] In that kingdom of bearable meanings, Mauriac reconstructed the home of his unhappy childhood.

School might have been expected to break up the childish synthesis, in which feelings about mother and beliefs about God formed a continuous whole. God as praised in most of the best schools, whether run by English clergymen or by Jesuits, is sharply opposed to everything that is maternal and "soft," to "feelings" in general, and especially to an emotional interest in the liturgy of the Church. For better or for worse, however, the Marist Fathers of Bordeaux, who gave Mauriac his schooling, did not adopt this view of God. They were gentle pious men, not remarkable for theological scholarship, and they did not exert themselves either to harden the boy (a practice in any case not so much in vogue in France as in England) or to substitute a more virile and intellectual Catholicism for his sensitive religiosity. Home, not school, and mother, not headmaster, remained the dominant influences in his formation, and the emotional pattern of his childhood continued into his adolescence with only a biological transmutation, not a violent break.

Mauriac himself in later years – after his "conversion" – reproached his early teachers for their failure to give him adequate theological instruction, and for the indulgence they showed towards his emotionalism. When he left school he was, according to his own account, incapable of replying to any of the main arguments which were then, at the beginning of this century, being advanced against Catholicism. His theological reading, unsuperintended, had strayed to the slippery edges of orthodoxy: Pascal, Lamennais, Lacordaire, and, worse still, Father Tyrrell and the Abbé Loisy. He liked the prose style of these writers,

---

[1] Compare the passage in *Le Baiser au lépreux* about the religious feelings of the orphaned Jean Péloueyre: "La Vierge héritait de cette dévotion qu'il eût vouée à sa mère selon la chair."

François Mauriac: The Secret Door 25

and certain of their ideas, those that were dramatic and uncompromising, rationalizing the stern practices of his mother's home, as well as those that laid indiscriminate stress on love. But fundamentally he was not theologian enough to be either an apostate or a heretic. Father Tyrrell could not deflect his faith any more than Nietzsche, the leading antichrist of that time, could destroy it, for it was based not on brittle syllogisms, but on love and fear. He obeyed the Church as he would have obeyed his mother and he was not going to hell for Father Tyrrell.

In essential results, then, the good Marists of Bordeaux were more successful than, for example, the learned men who at about the same time were giving James Joyce such a thorough theological grounding. But although the faith, in the form in which Mauriac had kept it, was itself proof against intellectual attack, it was not a reliable defence against temptations of the flesh. Even if the "Catholic revival" of the 'nineties, in which tapers, incense, and church music played so large a part, had not influenced the young Mauriac, the unchecked emotionalism of his childish piety would quite naturally have taken a sensuous turn in adolescence. The youth for whom the intoxication of the natural world was only increased by the sense of an immanent spiritual world[1] scarcely needed the superficial stimuli of Huysmanesque Catholicism in order to become confused about the object of his raptures. For a long time, indeed, sensuous piety might repel temptation. Jean-Paul Johanet, the hero of Mauriac's first novel, *L'Enfant chargé de chaînes* (published when he was 28), makes this clear when he exclaims: "... much will be forgiven to me because I have *not* loved much; between God's Justice and me are all the tears of my adolescence." But an alert Catholic friend later points out to him: "You are turning even the purest emotions into sensuality, Jean-Paul. You cannot serve two masters." This was the essence of the reproach which Catholic critics were later to address more vehemently to Mauriac himself when his writings, while remaining

---

[1] Compare *Le Jeudi saint* (1932): "Christ tells our souls that he is the vine and we are the branches, but Cybele teaches the same lesson to our bodies." Mauriac has been accused of pantheism as well as of Manicheism and Jansenism.

Catholic, began to show an alarming degree of insight into the psychology of carnal love.

It is no wonder that the repentant Mauriac of later years, contemplating the ease with which sensuous piety had given place to ordinary sensuality, speaks of this type of piety with extreme severity. The protagonist of *Les Anges noirs*, who is a debauchee, a pimp, a blackmailer, a sadist, a murderer, and a familiar of the Devil, is made to ascribe his downfall in great part to an early education that was too indulgent to his excesses of religious emotion. It is plain that Mauriac, although his career has been considerably less picturesque than that of Gabriel Gradère, had his own education in mind, and that he feels that his teachers should have sternly thwarted the natural line of his development and turned him into a different type of person. A recent and sympathetic writer on Mauriac, Father Emile Rideau, apparently shares this view, for he suggests that Mauriac would have been a healthier person in every way if he had joined the Boy Scouts. ("Que n'a-t-il fait partie d'une patrouille scoute?") This suggestion makes a pleasing mental picture (a wizened melancholy figure in shorts and wide-brimmed hat, the Hemingway of the *Académie Française*), but the attitude it represents is a meaningless one. The combination of sensuality with religious feeling is at the centre of Mauriac's peculiar greatness: if it had been possible to eliminate it, by woodcraft or otherwise, the magnificent works of his maturity from *Le Baiser au lépreux* to *Le Nœud de vipères* would never have been written.

It is true that many Catholic critics think that this would have been a good thing. The great period that begins in 1923 (ten years after the publication of his first novel) is, in the eyes of many, one of sin and collusion with sin. In the four early novels the air of sensuous religiosity was more sickly than dangerous, but now the sensuality becomes overtly sinful in character, the religion appears to embrace elements of nature worship, and the mixture is made dangerously explosive by the writer's extraordinary evocative talent. We have seen how fiercely certain Catholic critics assailed him on account of these characteristics, and how, eventually, he conceded the position to them. But in the meantime, while, without ceasing to be a Catholic, he continued to write books that exhaled the very scent of sin, how did he justify himself?

There is some evidence that in his own heart he did not attempt to justify his activities of this period. Poetry is more frank in these matters than prose, and Mauriac's last book of verse, *Orages* (1925), seems to me to shed a good deal of light on his real attitude at this time. "Le regret du péché," one of several more or less erotic poems in this collection, contains the expressive lines:

> *Ah! tant qu'un autre en moi me laisse de répit*
> *Les paumes de mes mains suivront tes jambes pures.*

This provisional voluptuousness, this postdated check in favour of God, is too simple and disreputable not to be authentic. Mauriac here expresses what all believing sinners have felt, and we need hardly doubt that his latent repentance applied to much of his work of this period.[1] But, in the harsher light of prose and in the face of bitter polemics, other arguments had to be used, sincerely no doubt, yet not with absolute candour.

Two main arguments were used by Mauriac and his apologists. The first was comprehensive and effective but specious. It consisted of an appeal to the virtue of truth. Truth being of God, objectivity was its own justification and it was wrong to accuse a novelist of immorality simply because he depicted the evil he saw. "It is impossible," wrote Mauriac towards the end of this period, "to reproduce the modern world as it exists without there appearing a broken holy law." The trouble with this argument, which was also used by Mauriac's admirers Charles du Bos and Gabriel Marcel, is that the claim to objectivity is unjustifiable. The Catholic writer must hate sinful acts. He may love them too. In any case, however carefully he picks his words when describing them, his tone will reveal that he is not an impartial witness. The

---

[1] He certainly regarded his work at this time as being a transition through fires, whether of Purgatory or Hell he hardly knew. "I must pass through this fire, cost what it may," he wrote in *Insomnie* (1927). "I shall travel round this ravaged universe until I reach the point from which I started; my childhood, the evening prayer with my forehead against my mother's bed, the preparation for death."

real charge against Mauriac was that his tone, and the images he evoked, suggested a secret sympathy, a connivance with sin, instead of the uncompromising detestation of sin which Catholic critics felt they had a right to expect from a Catholic novelist. As he said himself, he "depicted evil with a secret collusion, because he was describing attractions which he felt."

The second argument is on an altogether different level. Indeed it is more than an argument; it is a philosophical formula which covers everything that is valid in Mauriac's work. This is the doctrine of Lacordaire that all love is fundamentally the same, that there are "no 'loves,' only one love." The love of a woman, the love of a cause, the love of your mother, are all, in so far as they are love at all, the love of God. This theory, theologically unassailable if strictly interpreted, yet possessed enormous flexibility. It accorded perfectly with Mauriac's predispositions, for it is in practice impossible in describing the behaviour of fallen man to disentangle pure love from the various and frustrated lusts of the flesh. This theory, therefore, enables a Catholic novelist to pass almost imperceptibly from one plane to another, from the physical to the spiritual and back again, through many gradations of consciousness and a shimmering veil of confusion. The process sounds dishonest but, unlike the first argument I have mentioned, it is not so at all. The confusion was not an attempt to deceive, but represented the genuine state of mind of one who was primarily a feeling rather than a thinking being and who could never completely separate the spiritual from the sensual. It was, artistically, a beneficent confusion, far more fruitful than the thorough and logical application of some rigorous principle: a confusion of strong emotions which, allied to an acutely sensitive perception, enabled Mauriac to give us what still remains his masterpiece, *Le Désert de l'amour*. This novel is worth examining in a little detail as an example both of Mauriac's art and of the singular quality of his thought.

"For years," the story begins, "Raymond Courrèges had cherished the hope of meeting again that Maria Cross upon whom he ardently desired to revenge himself." Now he sees her in a Paris bar, and suddenly he is back in the Bordeaux of years ago, coming back from school in the ill-lit evening tram, watching a woman. From this point and through his recollections, moving erratically in time, we come to perceive the main figures: Raymond himself; his father, Dr. Courrèges; and Maria Cross. Maria is an object of scandal, a kept woman, the mistress of the wealthy wine merchant, Victor Larousselle. In this capacity she attracts the interest of young Raymond, smutty minded and sex-starved. At the same time and in a different way, Raymond's father, her doctor, falls in love with her, starting from the point of seeing in her a wronged woman and a sorrowing mother (her son, François, had died shortly before). Maria herself is neither lust incarnate, as Raymond thinks, nor yet the noble figure of his father's vision. She is self-dramatizing, romantic, indolent, and above all dissatisfied. She for her part has an equally incorrect impression of the two Courrèges. The Doctor for her is a good old bore, whose solid worth she values, but whom she never for a moment imagines as capable of being in love. And when she sees Raymond watching her in the tram, his young beauty, which she is the first to perceive, leads her to associate him with her dead son, and with fabulous dreams of purity and love. It is this misunderstanding between her and Raymond that leads to the decisive events of the story. Raymond, thinking she is leading him on – which is partly true (she scarcely knows what she is doing herself) – forces himself to make advances to her which are so crude and brutal that she repels him in disgust. In the horror of awakening from the illusion about Raymond which had come to dominate her mind she attempts to commit suicide: "that the desert within her might lose itself in that of space." And afterwards in the excitement of fever she tells Dr. Courrèges, who attends her: "Not loves but only one love in us. . . . We take the only road we can, but it doesn't lead towards what we're looking for. . . ."

This summary of the main elements in the story does not give even a faint idea of its complexities. It gives no hint of the strange lyrical and nostalgic quality of Raymond's recollections: the way in which he evokes at the same time the secure environment of boyhood, the massiveness of objects, the suburban garden, the prosperous table, and also the inner storm of anarchy and eroticism, the turbulent mind for which a passing tram, with its lighted windows, is "like the Titanic." For it must not be forgotten that the story is told from Raymond's point of view, from the point of view of the smutty schoolboy, the middle-aged debauchee, the lover, the son. And the summary also omits the base of the triangle, the relation between father and son, which is in many ways the most interesting aspect of the book. Raymond and his father are members of a family that lived together "as mingled and as separate as the worlds which make up the Milky Way." No communication is possible between them until they realize that they are suffering on account of the same woman. They are "related through Maria Cross." That is to say, father and son are related through their feelings about a woman who is for one of them a sexual image, for the other a sorrowing mother, and who is herself directed, unawares, towards God and who bears the name, consciously or unconsciously symbolic, Maria Cross.

The balance of emotion that produced *Le Désert de l'amour* was of its nature impermanent. Despite the argument of "objectivity" and the theory of "un seul amour" Mauriac himself fully perceived the "impure" element present in this work and all his work at this time. It was inevitable that, with advancing age, the balance should move in the direction of austerity. Mauriac has always been acutely, painfully, conscious of the action of time on the body. His characters leave the "ephemeral springtime of the flesh" to sustain "the scar of the thirtieth year," until their forties "stretch the skin, begin a dewlap." He has written of "that torture, the *approach* of old age, even when old age is still distant." Meditating on Lawrence he has thought of writing "a terrible novel, *The Old Age of Lady Chatterley*." And writing of Racine, whom he resembles in so many ways, he expresses surprise at the way in which biographers cast about for the reason why Racine, approaching forty, became converted: "For the fact that he was approaching forty is in itself sufficient." And he points out that "what we call humanism suits only one moment of our lives."

It is not surprising then, that Mauriac, who was forty when *Le Désert de l'amour* appeared, should before long reconsider his position and that the latent repentance of *Orages* should become overt and dominant. Yet this did not take place without a struggle and even an acute crisis of doubt and semi-revolt. He came to feel, certainly, that his peculiar alliance of sensuality and religion was no longer possible, but for a time it did not seem quite certain which element he would retain. *Destins* (1928), his last unregenerate novel, is also his most deplorable from a Catholic point of view; it contains an unqualified defence of carnal love and its only Catholic character is shown in the most unfavourable light possible. And in the same year he published *Souffrances du pécheur* (November 1928), an essay full of anguish, ostensibly Christian but revealing in every line the sense that Christianity is not a practicable religion. This essay begins with the words: "Christianity makes no allowances for the flesh: it abolishes it," and it takes as its text the words of Bossuet concerning ". . . the deep and shameful wound of nature, that concupiscence which joins the soul to the body with such tender and violent bonds." And the most vivid passage in this little work, so rigorous and uncompromising, deserving more than anything else he has written the epithet Jansenistic, is the description of how he imagines that Bossuet's famous sermon, "A grave opened before the Court," must have affected some of its hearers: "with what increased frenzy must certain courtiers, leaving the chapel, have hurled themselves on a prey destined to perish and, for so short a time, still beautiful, living and full of blood!"

That was the last cry (though there have been echoes) of the old Mauriac, the instinctive and contradictory, the gloriously confused and Protean author of *Le Désert de l'amour*. In April 1929 appeared *Bonheur du chrétien*, sequel and refutation to *Souffrances du pécheur*. This essay breathes acceptance of Christianity, as much as its predecessor breathes rebellion, and it bids farewell, without a qualm, to the flesh, quoting Pascal: "What pleasure is greater than being disgusted with pleasure?" The change is as dramatic as it is obviously sincere. The writer of *Bonheur du chrétien*, stammering and incoherent as it is, is obviously, as he himself says, "foudroyé par la grace."

Dramatically, the story should end there. As Mauriac said of one of his own friends who became a compiler of edifying stories, "Holiness is silence." But in his own case holiness was garrulous. After the "conversion," and after the social reconciliations which followed naturally though not inevitably on conversion, Mauriac wrote as fluently as ever, and on similar subjects. But now, although he accepted (*Dieu et Mammon*) Gide's view that no work of art could be produced without "the collaboration of the Demon,"[1] he had to try to get on without his old collaborator. And although he also agreed with Gide that a novelist should not try "to prove anything," the burden of proof was placed upon him.

The predominantly "intellectual" and "moral" novels which resulted from this situation are a depressing series, *Le Fin de la nuit* (the problem of liberty), *Les Anges noirs* (the problem of evil), *Les Chemins de la mer* (the problem of vocation, and miscellaneous allied subjects). One of these prefabricated edifices, *La Fin de la nuit*, has been taken to pieces with great care by Jean-Paul Sartre ("François Mauriac et la liberté," *Nouvelle Revue Française*, February 1939). M. Sartre stresses the God-like manner in which Mauriac intervenes in and interprets the action of his characters and deprives them by his definitions of all liberty. "In a true novel," he says, "as in the world of Einstein there is no place for a privileged observer.... M. Mauriac preferred his own way. He chose divine omniscience and omnipotence.... God is not an artist; neither is M. Mauriac." This little essay, and especially this easily memorized ending, completed the ruin of Mauriac's reputation among the younger generation. His work since then has done little to restore that reputation. *La Pharisienne* (1941), although it contained – as we have seen – a few startling flashes of the old intensity, was on the whole a laborious and dreary failure; the narrator, as if in a pathetic attempt to clear the author from Sartre's charge of "omniscience," produces an extraordinary array of "diaries," "testaments," and "confessions," which reveal with much literary eloquence the inner motivations of all the characters. *Le Sagouin*, his latest novel, seems no more than

[1] Maritain, however, has stigmatized this as "a Manichean blasphemy." (*Art and Scholasticism.*)

an attenuated echo from the haunted past. Even his reputation as a playwright, founded on the considerable technical skill with which in *Asmodée* (1937) and *Les Mal Aimés* (1945) he dramatized characteristic Mauriac situations, has declined; his comedy, *Passage du malin*, fell completely flat on its presentation in Paris in 1947, and its successor, *Le Feu sur la terre*, in 1950 did not make a much greater impact. Altogether he seems to have lost his power to dominate. A disciple of Sartre or Camus could say of him as he once said of Anatole France: "On n'en parle plus."

And yet one need only read the body of his work to be convinced that his present relative eclipse is merely temporary, a conviction that deepens on a reading of those French writers who are most admired today. Sartre and Camus are now, of course, producing far more interesting work than the declining Mauriac. They are also better-equipped philosophers than he ever was, more acute moralists, cleverer men altogether. They excel just where he has always most lamentably failed, in the intellectual development of a theme, what he, though not they, would call a "problem." But, logical exponents of irrationality that they are, they lack just that irrational instinctive force whose explosion made the greatness of Mauriac's prime. They handle sordid and terrible themes, but they do so with rubber gloves, and have, one feels, thoroughly disinfected their minds before each artistic operation. They are *avertis*, they have read Freud, although they prefer to talk about Heidegger. If they have their own personal obsessions they do not reveal them; they try to observe not themselves but the external world. In their most important works – Camus' *La Peste* and the three volumes that have so far appeared of Sartre's *Les Chemins de liberté* – they deal with the action of many men. Sartre indeed, with an "omniscience" which puts Mauriac altogether in the shade, enters, in *Le Sursis*, into the minds not merely of a middle-aged philosophy teacher and his circle, but also of a provincial haberdasher, an illiterate peasant, a paralytic patient, and a perambulating Mahometan. Camus, more modest and more convincing, realizes the limitation of objectivity. The narrator of *La Peste*, speaking of himself in the third person, says: "In general he has made it his aim not to report more things than he has actually been able to see and not to lend to his companions of the plague year thoughts which, after all, they did not necessarily think. . . . He has maintained a certain reserve, as befits a good witness." Different though their methods are, however, Sartre and Camus both produce effects of intellectual abstraction rather than of creation. They take as their subject a stimulus of high historical generality, the impact of the plague or the threat of war, and then they examine, very carefully and subtly, the reactions of a rather large number of human beings, who, despite emphasis laid on their biological variety and differing functions, retain in common a certain algebraic quality.

Mauriac on the other hand was, at his best, the least cerebral of writers; he was incapable either of the reserve of Camus or of the spiritual mass-radiography of writers like Romains and Sartre. He knew, effectively, nothing of science, history, philosophy, or psychoanalysis; the wall of his family property formed, one might say, the boundary of his mental and emotional world. That circumscribed world was not perhaps what Toynbee would call "an intelligible field of study," but it was a powerful generator of contradictory passions. Works like *Génitrix* and *Le Rang*, to take the most clear-cut examples, give dramatic form to these passions in a manner that is neither distorted by knowledge of Freud nor deflected by a will to theorize; Catholicism for Mauriac at that time was not a theoretical system, but a passion and a circumscription. The horror in these stories is real because it is personal, not conjectural; some hypnotic inward power fixes physical environment with intense and unnatural clarity and turns an incipient shriek into the carefully balanced cadences of a metaphor about the sea. Sartre composes, as Zola did, on a large scale, with a wide historical perspective and in the light of the most advanced ideas of his day, but Mauriac wrote, like Dostoevsky, out of his own inner torment, and his delight therein. The power of transmuting such torment and delight into a communicable form is very rare, and those who possess it will find readers and admirers as long as humanity continues to enjoy tormenting itself. That will perhaps be longer than the theoreticians of "anguish" can hold their large but restless audience.

II
GEORGES BERNANOS

Georges Bernanos (1888–1948) wrote eight novels: *Sous le Soleil de Satan* (1925), *L'Imposture* (1927), *La Joie* (1929), *Un Crime* (1935), *Journal d'un curé de campagne* (1936), *Nouvelle Histoire de Mouchette* (1937), *M. Ouine* (1944), and the posthumous *Un Mauvais Rêve* (1951). He also wrote many polemical works, of which the two most important are *La Grande Peur des bienpensants* (1931) and *Les Grands Cimetières sous la lune* (1938).

THE FAUST OF
GEORGES BERNANOS

Augurs and understood relations have
By maggot-pies and choughs and rooks brought forth
The secretist man of blood.
                                    SHAKESPEARE, *Macbeth*.

"Do you believe in hell, Pernichon?" asked M. Guérou, a character in Georges Bernanos' second novel, *L'Imposture*. And he goes on: "Look, you need go no further; my house is a hell."

Poor Pernichon, a wretched little man on the brink of suicide, who has come to Guérou as his last hope may well believe him. The house of M. Guérou as Pernichon finds it on his last desperate midnight errand is not a comforting place. The host is stretched out in his bed "like a corpse in its shroud of fat," his eyes half closed and his mouth drawn inward by impending paralysis. Lifting his hand in a gesture of benediction, he greets Pernichon with ferocious irony, and offers him instead of help a bundle of compromising letters with which to ruin his enemies. To get the letters he has to rise from his bed, or rather to be lifted out of it by his nurse, Jules, "a burly fellow in blue overalls, with a thick jet-black moustache, his sleeves rolled up over enormous hairy arms." As this retainer lifts M. Guérou from his couch, the frightened Pernichon can discern on his swelling biceps a complicated tattoo mark, imperfectly obliterated with acid – the sign of a stay on Devil's Island. Jules departs and M. Guérou, the sweat running down his face, talks on, with the sole and gratuitous purpose of reducing Pernichon to despair. He is interrupted by a cry, followed by an apparition.

"Here I am, Sir," said a strange voice behind him.

A Thing had appeared which is seldom seen by day, in bright light, in a fashionable flat. Perhaps it was this incongruity alone that made the sight so strange. But the contrast was too much, and rent the heart.

M. Guérou's neck turned dark red, and his lips pale.

"Get out! Who sent for you? Get out of here, I say!" he cried in a voice of thunder.

To escape the faster the little girl jumped over the low tea-table, showing an emaciated leg in a filthy stocking. Pernichon saw her pitiful face with its dead skin and eyes shining with terror. Was she ten years old? Was she fifteen? She disappeared....

Jules, whose negligence was responsible for the apparition, volubly defends himself. There's no controlling her since the bachelor flat in the rue d'Ulm was shut; he never touched her, that's all lies; she ate the half of a pound of sugar, et cetera. Tired out, the invalid sends him away again. This, he explains to Pernichon, is only one of a thousand such episodes in a house that has become a hell. Since his illness, "this poor life of mine all comes up to the surface again, like a choked sewer.... And the letters I get, my friend, the atrocious letters!"

Saying these words, M. Guérou's great head rolls round on his shoulders and he falls to the ground in an apoplectic seizure. Jules proceeds to revive him with blows of a wetted towel, which he also uses at intervals to wipe away his own tears as he recalls the former prowess of his master, the days before he let himself be destroyed by "females, those bitches." As for Pernichon, he slips quietly away, to die, as we learn much later, by his own hand.

2.

Of this particular hell-house we catch only a brief vertiginous glimpse. The whole episode of Pernichon with M. Guérou takes up less than fifteen pages, and the main narrative then leaves both characters behind. Yet this brief scene not only darkens the whole novel and prepares the mind for other horrors; it is a summary statement of the novelist's obsessive vision of life. Bernanos sees the modern world as a organism in visible rapid decay, pullulating with evil. The life of M. Guérou, that regurgitating sewer, is man's life today; the house of M. Guérou, with its com-

The Faust of Georges Bernanos 39

fortably furnished living-room and the nameless things going on in the basement, is our civilization. For Bernanos this is not just an opinion or even a conviction; it is an *évidence*, something directly and physically manifest, like maggots in meat. All his novels, with increasing intensity, tell of this loathsome vision; two of them, *La Joie*, the sequel to *L'Imposture*, and *M. Ouine*, concentrate it in the same symbol of the hell-house. This apocalyptic dwelling so dominates his imagination – in a sense it *is* his imagination – that it is the true starting point for an inquiry into his work.

The whole action of *La Joie* is laid in a house not perhaps so dramatically sulphurous as that of M. Guérou but, in the long run, just as fatally stifling. The distinguished Aynard de la Clergerie is not an actively wicked man, but that does not prevent his home from becoming the seat of evil. Indeed his mediocrity, his spiritual lifelessness, call down, like vultures, a series of satanic beings; the Russian chauffeur, Fiodor, who combines drug-taking and homosexuality with a sort of epileptic mysticism; the mad doctor, La Pérouse, who profits by the weaknesses of the chauffeur, and who teaches that health is an illusion and that "life has neither method nor principles, nothing but an ignoble persistence"; finally the impostor himself, the Abbé Cénabre, the priest without faith or hope or charity. Through the corridors wanders old Mme de la Clergerie, clutching her keys, a prey to avarice and hate, pursued by servants' insults, which she cannot quite distinguish from her own hallucinations. "This house is rich," says the illuminated chauffeur, "and it looks respectable, but the insects have begun to eat it."

The castle of Néréis, abode of the principal characters in *M. Ouine*, is equally corroded by sin. An odour of rottenness and stagnant water comes from the walls; the dirt oozes out between the flags of the floor; the crazy châtelaine known as "the ghoul" makes murderous sorties; and the dying teacher, M. Ouine himself, exercises a general vocation of corruption. "A fire!" says the village doctor to the ghoul, "Do you hear, my pretty? A fire is what's wanted to do away with your nest of lies and frogs." But the corruption of the castle permeates the whole village. The boy Steeny, turning in disgust from the Lesbian couple of his mother and his governess, comes under the even more unhealthy tutelage of M. Ouine; the Mayor's hypersensitive nose takes on an obscenely independent life and destroys his mind with obsessions of impurity; a murder is followed by anonymous letters which cause a double suicide and a lynching. By the time the inhabitants of the castle are dead, the whole village is morally in ruins.

3.

The bachelor flat in the rue d'Ulm, the country house of M. de la Clergerie, and even the castle of Néréis are not startling, for quantity and degree of vice, to any reader of modern French novels. The sins of M. Guérou, though they might have shocked Zola, come as no surprise after *Sodome et Gomorrhe*, and admirers of Céline or Aragon or Sartre will find Bernanosian depravities distinctly provincial. The novel-reader becomes so accustomed to conventional crapulousness and routine horror that he experiences no emotion even at such an episode as that in M. Marcel Aymé's *Le Chemin des écoliers* where one of the protagonists makes a black-market coup during the war-time meat shortage by murdering aged prostitutes and selling them by the pound. *Le Chemin des écoliers*, like *Voyage au bout de la nuit*, is a serious novel; M. Aymé is no more a James Hadley Chase than he is a daring innovator. He is merely a conscientious worker in a well-established tradition; his over-emphasis on private horrors is a conventional representation of the general collapse.

Bernanos, too, works, in part, within this convention. It is obvious, for example, that the decay of the village in *M. Ouine* may be taken as a symbol of the decay of the modern world. Yet the decay that he sees so directly and with such loathing is not part of a literary algebra, such as theorists like Aragon employ. In Bernanos' vision the world and the village are one monstrous entity, sick with the same evil principle. His whole career as a novelist, from *Sous le Soleil de Satan* to *Un Mauvais Rêve*, has been a long effort, often hardly coherent, to convey to his readers his own burning conviction of the existence and power of the Devil. The hells of his novels differ from those of more conventional writers in that they invariably contain a satanic

The Faust of Georges Bernanos 41

person, through whom the power of evil irradiates the whole scene. The nature of that person is worth examining, for it expresses an important part of that dark romantic philosophy which joins Catholicism in Bernanos' mind.

If we consider the dominating figures of the three hells we have briefly inspected, we shall find that they have a great deal in common.[1] Of the three – M. Guérou in *L'Imposture*, the Abbé Cénabre in *L'Imposture* and *La Joie*, and M. Ouine – the fat and licentious M. Guérou is certainly the most earthy and therefore the least satanic. Yet even M. Guérou is no mere vulgar voluptuary. He is, like most Bernanos villains, a distinguished literary man; in his works, "intellect, turning on itself, devours itself, like a fabulous beast." The principle of his life is curiosity, a curiosity variously described as "pitiless," "fantastic," and "hideous." It is this curiosity which leads him to give banquets where the guests are subtly provoked into vile altercations; this which makes him experiment with Pernichon's despair, to find the suicide point; this which makes him – very characteristically – delight in the society of certain ecclesiastics.

"The mediocre priest, my boy, has a sort of fascination for me. The idea of such a being tickles an appetite in me. It excites a brain which is probably by now no more than a little ball of fat."

His taste for infant prostitutes and moustachioed masseurs is merely an expression on a lower plane of that curiosity. The "choked-up sewer" which Pernichon beholds is the remnant of a life in which curiosity has finally revealed itself as hate. As M. Guérou, ever lucid, himself explains, "the best thing about vice is that it teaches you to hate mankind. That's all right until one day you begin to hate yourself."

M. de la Clergerie, the owner of the country house in *La Joie*, is not – although a literary man – a diabolic figure, but his intellectual snobbery places him under the ascendancy of a great and

---

[1] There is a fourth hell-house, the home of the "devouringly curious" writer, M. Ganse, in *Un Mauvais Rêve*. Ganse, however, is little more than a mechanical amalgam of earlier characters, principally Guérou and Ouine.

evil mind, the Abbé Cénabre. This priest, who dominates both *L'Imposture* and *La Joie*, is a much more important character than M. Guérou, and his vice is of a more exalted sort. He is a Canon, widely revered because of his learning, and an authority on the mystics. Yet he is an impostor. He "no longer believes," as he once, in a great crisis, admits. But it is not primarily against faith that he sins, and he is far from the "music-hall materialism" of such a man as Renan. The truth is that pride and curiosity have taken the place of the love of God in his heart.

The Abbé Cénabre never denied miracles, and he even has a taste for the miraculous. Only in a reverent spirit does he approach the great souls of whom he writes, and his very curiosity has such *élan* that it might be mistaken for love. His real gift, however, is to conceive a spiritual order robbed of its crown of charity.

He has reached this strange state by means of a persistent refusal, by murdering charity in himself. The grace of God can still at times be revealed in him, but only "like the face of a corpse at the bottom of the water, like a plaintive cry in the fog." Pride alone makes his outward behaviour impeccably priestlike for he despises "ex-priests." He makes full and regular confessions, omitting nothing "except the perverse and diabolic refusal which was petrifying him," and carries out the penances enjoined on him. At Mass he even says the words of consecration "not through a secret taste for sacrilege but because he thought it would be unworthy of himself to deceive the old women who would be kneeling a moment later at the altar rails." Pride has in fact become "the foundation of his whole life."

The Abbé Cénabre's decision to continue acting as a priest is a fatal one, for himself and many others. On the purely human level, his loveless curiosity makes him mortally disruptive as a director of consciences. The opening scene of *L'Imposture* shows him beginning the ruin of that same Pernichon whom we have seen, towards the end of his life, as a client of M. Guérou. The Abbé Cénabre is the first to force Pernichon to see himself as he is. When the religious journalist confesses that he is "sorely tried

The Faust of Georges Bernanos

by sensual temptations," the priest overwhelms him with penetrating scorn: "No experienced priests – in spite of the usual prejudice against us – attach more than a symptomatic value to sexual behaviour.... In your case, your interior life bears a minus sign... only by keeping up, with difficulty, a few little vices can you manage to give yourself the illusion of life." With such words as these he breaks down the barriers of Pernichon's artificial personality; and gives him nothing in exchange. The suicide, of which we learn in the closing sentence of the book, has been prepared.

While his victim is sinking, Cénabre himself degenerates. His dominant passion, curiosity, once so loftily intellectual, takes a compulsive and slightly indecent form. He wanders idly in the crowd, greedily staring; he grows dirty and lazy, through desire to explore these forms of disorder; he deliberately puts a greasy thumb-mark on the flyleaf of one of the rarest of his beloved books; he pursues a half-starved mountebank through the streets of Paris, bribes him to reveal "his most secret thoughts," and harasses him with searching questions until the poor man falls down in an epileptic fit. But the final catastrophe comes not from his degradation of others or of himself, but from the necessity for his spiritual redemption by the sacrifice of a saint. The girl Chantal de la Clergerie, in an ecstasy, perceives his state as that of Judas and offers up her life for him. This offer is immediately followed by her rape and murder by the chauffeur Fiodor. The Abbé Cénabre, when he sees her body, loses his reason and regains his faith.

Far more formidable than either M. Guérou or the Abbé Cénabre is the "hero" of *M. Ouine*. This little retired teacher of languages, slightly ridiculous in appearance with his red wig, his bowler hat, and his buttoned cardigan, is in reality supremely and purely satanic. He is not humiliated, nor does he degenerate in any way, but preserves to the end – and beyond it – his lucid, empty mastery. When the boy Steeny first meets him, in his ascetic cell in the foul castle of Néréis, he recognizes in a flash "the predestined companion of his life, the initiator, the hero pursued through so many books." And at the same time he senses the shadow of death on the house.

M. Ouine teaches him to love death, and a sort of death in life. "After a few useless experiments – for which of us has not gone looking for the lost sheep, or brought back the lamb on his shoulders? – I will never go looking for anything again. Like one of those living jellies at the bottom of the sea, I float and I absorb."

This, however, is less than the truth, and M. Ouine is preparing a last experiment: the murder of the little cowherd. This murder, which occurs on the night of the conversation with Steeny, and which is never "solved," has no easily recognizable motive. It is apparently a gratuitous act; its real motive is curiosity. "Certainly," as M. Ouine later explained to his parish priest, "the village of Fenouille had long been deeply demoralized. All that was needed was a commonplace crime – or was it a crime? who knows? – to give that demoralization an intolerable character." The wave of calumny, panic, and despair that engulfs the village is the calculated result of M. Ouine's experiment in "commonplace crime." The experiment is successful, the precipitation completed, and M. Ouine can die, not indeed in peace, but in a strange self-perfection. On his deathbed (and when, according to the doctor who arrived later, he was already dead) he gives his young disciple the true key to his actions.

"Life passed through me as through a sieve ... I opened and dilated, I was nothing but orifice, aspiration, swallowing, body and soul, yawning on all sides.... Curiosity devours me ... hunger for souls. ... The security of humble souls was in my hands, and they didn't know.... I played on their clumsy security as a man might play on a delicate instrument, I drew from it a special superhuman harmony, I enjoyed the pastime of God. ... That was what my work was in this old house which must preserve my memory, for every stone of it is saturated in my pleasure. Yes, out of an ordinary sticky mixture I made something lighter, more impalpable than a soap-bubble. ... I now return into myself for ever."

4.

Marlowe gave us the Faust of the Renaissance, Goethe the Faust of the Enlightenment, Bernanos gives us, in Cénabre and Ouine, the Faust of the Collapse, who is a Catholic Faust. We are back again at the medieval starting point, where Faust is a bad man who has committed the most terrible of sins. Stripped of the glory that surrounded him in the centuries of hope on earth, he now appears as a fatal insect, the moth who has corrupted the treasury of faith. The soaring pride of intellect, the spirit of scientific inquiry, the abstract Socratic love of truth for its own sake, are here reduced to a sinister and obscene curiosity. This itch for knowing, the essential Faustian characteristic, is a deadly infection carried primarily by a small group of the *élite* but spreading rapidly under certain conditions and finally causing a general paralysis of the whole community. Bernanos does not conceal his personal hatred of those whom he regards as the carriers, the Faustian avatars. In his first novel, *Sous le Soleil de Satan*, he devotes the last forty pages to a savage caricature of Anatole France under the name of the Academician St. Marin, the "hideous old man," inquisitive and debauched, than whom "no thinking being ever deflowered more ideas or wrecked more hallowed words." M. Guérou is again obviously a literary portrait, although I do not recognize the model, and M. Ouine has also, I think, a great prototype in the world of letters. It is hard not to see in that fastidious teacher, with his epicene disciple, his zoological metaphors, his infinitely subtle curiosity and his use of the so-called "gratuitous act," a hostile portrait of M. André Gide. "Je me penche vertigineusement sur les possibilités de chaque être et pleure tout ce que le couvercle de mœurs atrophie." The words are Gide's but they could have been spoken by M. Ouine. The difference is that while Gide only deplores "the lid of morals," M. Ouine takes it off. Bernanos is not a mere writer of *romans à clef:* a Gide or a France is to him not an individual but the mask of a particular form of evil; his novels tear the mask to leave it ineffective but recognizable. The true enemy is not any person but the Faustian intellect, the disguise of the devil. Indeed the brain itself is at fault.

"What's the use of thinking?" thinks a good old man in *M. Ouine*. "All the harm comes from the brain, always at work, the soft, shapeless, monstrous animal, like a worm in its cocoon, pumping tirelessly away."

But if the evil reaches us through the intellect, that does not mean that its original source is in the intellect. The devil, with whom Faust made his pact, is a person, with his own ideas, different from those of Faust. Faust wishes to know; the devil wishes only to destroy and not to be. The devil, "with whom no human thing can be compared, save perhaps atrocious irony," both encompasses and penetrates mankind. The hatred which is his essence seizes on human souls mainly in the form of the two intellectual sins, pride and despair. It is pride, taking the form of overweening curiosity, that determines the fatal pact: "Connaître pour détruire – ô soleil de Satan!" The pact once made, despair begins to take a hand. Faust, the natural intellectual leader, exerts himself to destroy the faith in others. The results are terrible. Even the words of Musset to Voltaire,

*Il est tombé sur nous cet édifice immense
Que de tes larges mains tu sapais nuit et jour*,

do not express the full horror of the catastrophe, which is that Christianity turns cancerous. In the climate of despair, discarded virtues and half-rejected beliefs become a guilty ferment in the unconscious mind of the people. The nasal hyperaesthesia of the Mayor of Fenouille is a morbid expression of damaged purity. The Lesbian woman who pretends to be a priest, in *Un Crime*, is actually reliving, one by one, the hallucinative images born of her mother's remorse, for her mother was a nun. Mme Alfieri of *Un Mauvais Rêve* is "a kind of saint" but one whose sanctity is so "poisoned, rotted, liquefied," by a boredom which is in fact despair, that she becomes a pathological liar, a drug addict, and finally a cold-blooded murderess.[1] "Man," as the saintly Abbé Chevance explains, "has sullied even the very substance of the divine heart: pain. The blood which flows from the Cross can kill us." The whole procession of suicides – there is at least one in every novel by Bernanos – of sexual perverts, drug addicts,

[1] Mme Alfieri's regeneration was apparently envisaged but Bernanos was not able to carry it through further than the words, "one hope remained perhaps ... to admit defeat. ..." As Mauriac confessed: "I could not *see* the priest who was to receive Thérèse's confession." Mr. Greene, in *The End of the Affair*, was more sanguine, or less scrupulous.

The Faust of Georges Bernanos

vampires, brain-sick doctors, alcoholic peasants, sadistic servants, conceited literary men, and theological murderers, winds round in a modern *danse macabre* of despair. And yet most of these are only on the fringe of things, and merely glimpse "brief flashes of the inaccessible storm." To only the few, the saints and the possessed, is it given to feel the storm's full force, Satan's direct attack. The possessed – Mouchette in *Sous le Soleil de Satan*, the Abbé Cénabre, M. Ouine – are marked out by a sort of inner quietude, " a dumb solitary icy peace," by a *volonté d'avilissement*, a will for self-degradation, and by a laugh, which is the clearest outward sign: the hysterical laughter of Mouchette; the "vulgar laugh" which the refined Cénabre is astonished to hear coming from his own lips; the "trickling limpid laughter" of M. Ouine on his deathbed. Laughter, the purest expression of intellect, marks the meeting place of pride and despair in these chosen souls; it is the triumph of inhuman hatred through the operation of the human mind.

5.

It would be wrong, however, to suppose that Bernanos has consistently depicted this triumph as complete, the world entirely given over to the demon. He has his saints – the Abbé Donissan in *Sous le Soleil de Satan*, the diarist of *Journal d'un curé de campagne*, Chantal de la Clergerie in *La Joie*, the Abbé Chevance in *L'Imposture*. These humble, childlike people have the power of saving the souls of the proud; the "country priest" heals the squire's wife, and the "servants' priest" and his pupil redeem the great impostor, Cénabre. Their heroism is as great as their simplicity. Donissan, who also tries to raise the dead, would offer his own salvation in exchange for that of his parishioners: "If I could do it without hating Thee, I would damn myself for these souls." Chantal offers her life for Judas. These challenges, chivalrous rather than purely Christian in spirit, are taken up by the powers of hell. The Devil, who appears, disguised as a horsedealer, to Donissan on the road to Etaples, attacks with the weapon of despair the souls whom pride cannot tempt. "I do not want glory!" cries Donissan, "I do not want joy! I do not want even hope!" Each of the others in turn is tried by a similar distrust of Grace, a sort of voluntary acedia. They do not finally succumb; they save themselves and even others, and yet we know that the demon has attained a great part of his objective. "The world," as M. Ouine pointed out, "ferments around an innocent being." The hatred which holiness evokes foams around them, like a sea from which they are able to rescue one or two of the shipwrecked, while scores are left to drown. The Bernanosian "saint," half-paralysed by a form of despair, is inadequate to deal with the amount of evil in the Bernanosian world. Therefore that world has itself grown darker until at last the evil is intolerable and without relief. The Jesuit reviewer who exclaimed "What a gloomy sort of Christianity!" on reading Bernanos' first book would hardly recognize the last novels as Christian at all, so unrelieved is their pessimism. "Evil," says the hero of the relatively happy *Journal d'un curé de campagne*, "is only beginning." Bernanos' whole work testifies to his agreement with this statement, to his apprehension that evil is historically cumulative while good is static. In the hopeless world of his later novels, despair itself almost ceases to have any meaning, dissipating itself into a vague, dumb loneliness. The young heroine of *Nouvelle Histoire de Mouchette*, who lives with her drunkard father and dying mother in a half-abandoned hamlet "on the edge of a festering pond," is raped by an epileptic and commits suicide. At no time does she receive any help, hope or consolation from anyone. All those around her are either themselves hopelessly oppressed, like her mother, or vicious, or deranged. It is a world in which the only gleam of virtue is the inarticulate humility of the oppressed. In *M. Ouine* – written earlier but published later than the *Nouvelle Histoire* – there are virtuous characters, but they are, so far as one can discern, completely defeated. The priest of Fenouille is a good and holy man of the type of the Abbé Chevance, but unlike Chevance (who in his simplicity overthrew and humbled the Abbé Cénabre) he is defeated at every turn by his diabolic parishioner, whose wickedness he does not even perceive. "There are only the two of us here," says M. Ouine to him, "who take any interest in souls." The poor priest, who takes

The Faust of Georges Bernanos

this sort of remark at its face value, confides in his strange collaborator:

"I am, indeed, quite alone," said the priest of Fenouille.
"More alone than you think, perhaps," went on M. Ouine with a painful grimace.

And when at the end of their long interview, the priest, beside himself, tries to explain what he sees as the real trouble of his parishioners, the devil's advocate has again the last word:

". . . They want to be delivered from their sins, that's all . . ." [said the priest].
While he was talking M. Ouine, bowing and scraping, was backing towards the door. At the priest's last words he stopped suddenly.
"The last ignominy of man," he said, "is that evil itself bores him."
He rubbed his hat with the back of his sleeve, bowed profoundly and left.

6.

When Léon Bloy despaired of civilization in the midst of the progress and complacency of the late nineteenth century, his despair was a valuable though little-heeded warning. But what are we to say of one who, in a time of despair, prophesies disaster and teaches despair to a despairing people? Is not Bernanos himself, like Cénabre with Pernichon, one who wantonly tears the wretched bandage from the spiritual wound and can administer no help? Is he any better than a guide who loses his nerve at a difficult part of the ascent? I think that in so far as we accept the metaphors of teacher, surgeon, and guide – and Bernanos himself might accept them – we cannot answer these questions in a way favourable to the novelist. But, if, having noted that Bernanos is, in his own way, just as dangerous to mankind as he thinks Gide is in other ways, we pass on to consider what importance, other than a simply didactic, directive, or medicinal one, a philosophical or religious novelist can have, then we at once discern where

Bernanos' real greatness lies. He does not teach anything, but he does express something. He speaks things which no one else has spoken, and which form an important part of the collective conscience of ordinary European people today. In Europe, which according to Mr. Belloc "is the faith," part of the faith has only a faint or suppressed existence and part is violently, and consciously, alive. The part that is suppressed is the whole supernatural element in Christianity, including the belief in a personal God and in the immortality of the soul; the part that is active is an ethical part, the emphasis on the equal importance of every individual and on the iniquity of the rich. This situation, itself widely recognized, leads inevitably to consequences that have not been thoroughly explored but might be stated as follows: first, a passionate belief in the achievement of happiness on earth; second, a sustained, determined struggle by the disinherited to attain this happiness for themselves; third a craving for some dogmatic system to replace the Christian theology both in support of equalitarian ethics and as a general source of reassurance, for the old supernatural beliefs, although not intellectually held, are still a source of profound emotional disturbance; fourth, the finding of this system in a political creed like Communism or National Socialism; fifth, agonies and convulsions in society, as a result of the unresolved and undeflected class struggle; sixth, despair and mental and moral anarchy as the people discover that happiness on earth must be, at best, postponed. The actual sequence of political events is not, of course, nearly so simple as the logical series, consisting principally of emotional events that have happened to many, but not to all. Nor does the whole terrifying situation give any sign of the truth or lack of truth of Christianity; the fact that many people, believing that "pie in the sky" is a fictitious commodity, have caused great anguish and danger to themselves and others by their impatient quest for "pie on earth" proves nothing in a religious sense. Yet the emotional events have taken place, and in order to interpret them in their inner being it is necessary to have a Christian conscience, since their beginning is rooted in Christianity. It is also necessary to be subject to despair, since their end, for the many who have undergone them, has been despair. One might almost say that, just as the Black Mass must always be said by an ex-priest, so only some kind of warped Catholic can express the tormented unconscious mind of modern ex-Christendom. Bernanos, who is the Catholic warped by despair, would not state the problem in this way. He believes, perhaps rightly, that "systematic philosophizing is a form of insanity," but his emotional response to the problem is the source of his power. He is sensitive, for example, to the strange mental vibrations that went to make up Nazism and he reacts sympathetically to many of them. His quite unorthodox antirationalism often takes the Nazi form of baiting intellectuals and Jews (he wrote a book, *La Grande Peur des bien-pensants*, in homage to Drumont, the father of modern anti-Semitism); he has a special cult of those who died in the 1914-18 war and believes that their useless death may be the "cause of the general disorder"; he hates the rich, violently and without theorizing, in the manner of the Brown Bolsheviks; he is a strong racialist and speaks confidently of "petty, envious, ill-conditioned races like the Italians"; he was, to say the least of it, not repelled by Hitlerite anticlericalism, and usually spoke of Hitler himself with a certain respect; above all, he desires, and believes that the people desire, a society in which a "realism" based on economic rewards will not be supreme, and in which the call to honour and the virtues of the soldier will not be greeted with laughter. I think it probable that if he had been a German (and he often writes more like a German than a Frenchman) he would have been, for a time, a Nazi. That is to say, Nazism purported to answer certain real needs and gratify certain real hates and Bernanos was one of the few articulate among the millions who shared and still share those needs and hates. But, however great his sympathies with certain of the driving forces of Nazism, he was too honest to have accepted the Nazi answer for long. He spat out with contempt the "realistic" and "intelligent" Fascism of men like Maurras in his own country; hated Mussolini for attempting to revive the antique oppression of the Roman Empire, "beloved of pedants"; and, in *Les Grands Cimetières sous la lune*, the most eloquent and courageous of all his books, denounced Franco for bloody crimes committed in Majorca.¹ This potential Nazi was in fact one of the most effective literary adversaries of all kinds of Fascism, including Hitlerism. But he saw their cause as he saw the cause of Communism (which he attacked also, in *La France contre les robots*) in "the deficiency disease of the democracies ... the unemployment of the heart." Reason had dried up the fountains of honour and love, belief in the Christian God and the Christian king, and there was nothing left to hope for. "The peoples," he wrote in 1939, "have made a God out of their despair, and adore it. We have lived to see despair made flesh – *et incarnatus est*. We shall perhaps live to see it die and rise again on the third day."

7.

A Marxian critic would say that Bernanos was one of those feudal reactionaries whose attacks on the bourgeoisie are useful at a certain stage in the class struggle. A Spenglerian, if any now exist, would see reflected in his work the madness and suicide of Faustian man. A disciple of Toynbee would label him as a member of the "internal proletariat" (which would, in Toynbeean terminology, include French Catholics and Monarchists), protesting against the no longer creative "dominant minority" and playing a part in the evolution of a new Church or the transformation of the old one. The three methods of definition are all relevant and useful. Each furnishes an agreed vocabulary, a means of relating the writer schematically to his environment. But the danger – and this applies to all the "historical" and "environmental" approaches, which are at the same time the only ones capable of yielding any clear results – is one of excessive simplification and abridgment. The boy-scout Marxism of official critics like Ehrenburg can tell us no more about literature than can the Middletown Behaviourism

¹ This book was generally attacked in the Catholic press, but some French reviewers were more honest about it than some English ones. In the French Jesuit periodical, *Études*, Father Henry du Passage wrote: "We are obliged to believe this man's story and it is our duty to say that these facts are abominable." "These facts" were the murders which Bernanos said he saw committed by Franco's forces in Majorca. In the English Jesuit periodical, *The Month*, the reviewer (Fr. Brodrick, S.J.) could bring himself to say no more than "It remains an open question whether the Nationalist authorities were not excessively Draconian. ..."

The Faust of Georges Bernanos

of the Watson school. The "frames of reference" of such critics exclude from "the environment" factors that belong to it but are inconvenient, such as the influence of the dead and the inadequacy of words. Some of them, in their eagerness to deny the "eternal values" postulated by the religious, write as if moral ideas had little more than the life-span of a single individual; as if something called "bourgeois morality" had been invented by M. Thiers in 1830, and had been neatly replaced in 1917 by a "proletarian morality" having nothing in common with anything that had gone before. Severances, abrupt breaches of continuity, syntheses from inadequate material, refusal to allow for the existence of the unknown: these are the fatal aberrations of the critics who put a writer "against the background of his time" – and leave him there.

In defining Bernanos, then, as expressing the despair of the men of his time, we may still not have said everything or even the most important thing about. him. What sort of man is it that can not merely feel, but also express, a fundamental inarticulate thing? What sort of novelist is it that seems to know none of the tricks of novel-writing, whose plots are almost unintelligible, whose themes erupt rather than develop, and whose dining-rooms are as devoid of furniture and food as they are filled with violent talk? What sort of thinker is it that hates the brain and all its works and pomps?

Plato, who very sensibly banished a certain class of citizens from his rational Republic, could have supplied the answer. Bernanos on his highest level is a poet; not a verse-writer but a special kind of being. like William Blake, who tries to use words to communicate a vision, or rather to infect others with the possibility of seeing a vision. His fantastic eloquence, his successive gales of wild images, his dramatic enormities and frenzied caricatures are intended not to much to express anything as to rip usual words off the truth to blow away the accepted and habitual ways of thinking which shelter people from such a vision as his. Like the visionary hero of his first book, he "knows nothing of the detours of a form of thought which follows the rhythm of words." That is to say, he rejects ordinary logical thought as presumptuous and absurd. Words are instruments of emotion and extralogical revelation. To freeze them into systems and believe that they "prove" or "disprove" things is a radical misuse. Even as means of reference they are misleading. Bernanos constantly emphasizes the interpenetration of states and things for which we are accustomed to use separate words. He shows pride turning first into curiosity and then into sexual aberration; he hints at the "secret relations" between madness and lust, between hatred and fear; he says that "what we call sadness" and "the soul" may be one and the same thing, and that there is perhaps "only one sin." The most valuable use of language is in emotive imagery, clearing the way to a fundamental identification, transmitting power from one unconscious mind to another. Here is described the mental collapse of that great reasoner, the Abbé Cénabre:

> As on a night of insurrection you my see rise up on every side forgotten men, disgorged by cellars and prisons, and now, dazzled by the light, cautious and furtive, hastening with silent steps towards the clamour and the fire, so the Abbé Cénabre might have recognized and numbered, one by one, the thousand faces of his childhood. In that predestined soul, pride and ambition had established their empire too soon; the inflexible will had not vanquished its ghosts but pushed them back, left them in the shadow. All the dark corners were pullulating with a fierce embryonic life – thoughts, desires, and covetings, half-evolved, reduced to their essential, asleep but living in the germ. And all this monstrous little people, suddenly dragged from the limbo of memory, tottered to the edge of consciousness, as hard to know and name as those middle-aged sexless dwarfs which haunt the imagination of certain painters.

The "forgotten men" of the Roosevelt era, the oppressed and inarticulate members of a cerebral and industrial society, are here identified with the emotional elements which a rational mind does its best to suppress. The disorder of an individual soul and the disorder of society are envisaged in the same terms, perhaps as being in truth the same thing. Cénabre in his collapse becomes not merely Faust, but the world in which Faust is dying. The poet's long, barbaric metaphor is at the same time a shout of triumph over the double defeat of reason and servitude, and a cry of impending doom.

III
GRAHAM GREENE

Mr. Graham Greene, who was born in 1904 and was converted to the Catholic Church in 1926, is the author of thirteen novels, of which the most important are: *It's a Battlefield* (1934), *Brighton Rock* (1938), *The Power and the Glory* (1940), and *The Heart of the Matter* (1948). He has also written a number of short stories, critical essays, and film scenarios.

GRAHAM GREENE:
THE ANATOMY OF PITY

> No man that ever I heard of, ever committed a diabolical
> murder for sweet charity's sake.
> HERMAN MELVILLE, *Bartleby*.

PITY is an equivocal and often impure disposition. It descends from piety, is inspired by charity, and is said to mean *compassion*, the ability to suffer a fellow-creature's hurt. Yet the verb betrays the cloven hoof: a pitying glance, a pitying tone, assaults from above upon the personality. "Sometimes implying contempt," says a standard dictionary definition. It is perhaps a form of love, but not a form of which anyone wishes to be the object. Charity is not puffed up, but he who is addicted to pitying others may be exalting himself above them. Were one – monstrous operation – to remove the element of love from pity, one would be left with a hybrid vampire emotion, compound of pride and parasitic insecurity and looking singularly like cruelty.

> *The load of their loveless pity*
> *Is worse than the ancient wrong.*

Yet pity is hardly ever altogether loveless: it is, even more than most abstractions of human feeling, an indication of a frontier between conflicting states of mind. And both frontier and conflict are peculiarly the creations of Christianity, the religion that exhorted its followers to love without the aid of admiration or desire. Christ told men to love; the most they could manage was pity: it was something.

Now that the impossible orders, never obeyed, are more than half expunged, it is likely that our future society will be as innocent of pity as was classical Rome. We shall have an intelligible and practicable code: desire that which is desirable, hate your enemies, repair or destroy the sick, admire your leader, obey the sanitary laws. This is a possible programme; no need here for ambiguities and subterfuges and the collective nervous breakdown that is hidden at the heart of a word like *pity*. Man is perfectable, provided he sets his own standards of perfection.

That is before us; that is what we see from the edge of the plateau. But we still belong ourselves not to a Christian but to a Christ-pervaded culture. The corrupt and shifty pity that permeates our laws, disarms our governors, and exposes us to our successors is the soul of our dying society. It is the merit of Mr. Graham Greene that he, more than any of our other writers, has sensed the importance and expressed the essence of this dissolving pity. *The Heart of the Matter* is a novel about the progress of pity; it exposes, not always consciously, the complex state of mind of two of the last inhabitants of Christendom, the police-officer Scobie and Mr. Graham Greene.

2.

In structure – or rather, divisional nomenclature – the three-hundred-page novel is highly elaborate: it is based on over fifty short scenes, chapter-sections of five or six pages. The nineteen chapters formed of these units are grouped into nine "parts," three of which make up each of the novel's three "books." Such an organization, more hierarchical than that of *War and Peace* or *Remembrance of Things Past*, seems altogether disproportionate in so short a work; it is as if the events described were taking place in some vast structure that had crumbled and caved in: so in a sense they are. As far as the narrative is concerned, the only consistently meaningful divisions are the scenes – the brief dissolving bubbles through which the story is exhaled – and the "books," which present the three stages in the destruction of the protagonist, Scobie. The other divisions, "parts" and chapters, are for the most part arbitrary and, one suspects, nostalgic – an effort to restore a framework of order and impose a discipline on the uncontrollable flux.

The scene is West Africa, a port of exile, "foothold on the very edge of a strange continent." It is a place of open and manifest corruption: the black schoolboys lead the drunken sailor "towards the brothel near the police-station as though to a nursery"; a vulture clangs down on the corrugated-iron roof. Human nature is naked, one knows the worst; only for a moment in the evening the laterite roads turn pink and there is the illusion of beauty. The people are a mixed population – European, Syrian, native – uniform only in untrustworthiness. The time is war-time, the war being felt as an isolating factor and a guarantee that life is evil also outside the colony.

Wilson and Harris prepare the scene for the arrival of Scobie. Wilson is a stranger, immature and ignorant, as innocent of the ways of the colony as of the ways of life, but ready to be moulded; he is at heart a lover of romantic poetry and by profession, a detective. Harris is a case of arrested development, a melancholy, middle-aged, minor-public-school boy, full of ugly hates. He explains the country and points out, with hatred, Scobie. "A vulture flapped and shifted on the iron roof and Wilson looked at Scobie."

The hero introduced by this sinister and childish chorus is a middle-aged police-officer. Scobie's life has been devoted to the application of the law among a population that rejects it, flinging up a barrier of endless lies and evasions. To this Scobie has opposed the austere routine of his own integrity. His office is as bare as a cell, its only emblem being "some rusty handcuffs hanging on a nail." Here he applies the meaningless regulations to the uncomprehending and untrustworthy people: he is the responsible man. But the responsibility of this policeman goes beyond the law. "It had always been his responsibility to maintain happiness in those he loved" – and this applies to his wife, Louise, whom he no longer loves and who is unhappy. This exigence, the compulsion to achieve the impossible, is symbolized by a broken rosary in the drawer of his desk, for this policeman is a Catholic. The outward responsibility is the exact compliance with possible, if meaningless, human standards – what is called integrity. The inward responsibility is compliance with a superhuman standard, the attempt at love and the achievement of pity. The two compulsions, potentially explosive with contradictions, are for the moment stuck together with a sort of dry decay they have in common: the handcuffs are rusty and the rosary is broken.

Scobie has learned that he will not succeed the retiring Commissioner of Police and he must break this news to his place-conscious wife. She is asleep; his pity is perceptive. "Her face had the yellow ivory tinge of atabrine: her hair which had once been the colour of bottled honey was dark and stringy with sweat. These were the times of ugliness when he loved her, when pity and responsibility reached the intensity of a passion." Then she wakes up and pity gives a sudden flick of its claws. "His wife was sitting up under the mosquito net and for a moment he had the impression of a joint under a meat-cover. But pity trod on the heels of the cruel image and chased it away." He tells her the news, endures her disappointment, partially soothes her, finally succeeds in getting her to come down and have something to eat. "A vulture flapped heavily upward from the iron roof and down again in the yard next door. Scobie drew a deep breath; he felt exhausted and victorious: he had persuaded Louise to pick a little meat."

This scene sets the note that will be maintained. Pity is the condition of all relationships, but it is an unreliable climate. The pity that is directed at Scobie's hosts is a humiliating one: Louise is shown as hateful and compared to carrion and to carrion-fowl. One is never quite sure whether the evident waves of hate are coming from Scobie or from some hidden source playing around him — perhaps the same source that emits in the narrative a constant hum of tender approbation for Scobie himself. The reader is invited to add contempt to the pity Scobie feels for Louise, and to experience, for Scobie himself, a more exalted kind of pity, tenderness bordering on admiration. The outlines are blurred by a sort of imperfect subjectivism, but the general shape is clear enough: Prometheus stroking his vulture's raw, red neck.

A party at the club introduces the officials of the colony. Louise is affected, Scobie sensitive — "he was bound by the pathos of her unattractiveness" — but Wilson is attracted to Louise; they discuss poetry. We see, among the officials, the artificiality and snobbery of the colony's life; then its corruption is displayed in the encounter of Scobie with Yusef, whom he meets on leaving the party. Yusef is a fat Syrian, a smuggler and black-marketeer;

he has a sincere respect for Scobie because he knows that Scobie is too honest to frame him, and the evidence to secure a legitimate conviction does not exist. They discuss the diamond smuggling, which is the main concern of the authorities; then the police black-market in the staple food, rice. Scobie reflects: "There was a retort in this colony to every accusation. There was always a blacker corruption elsewhere to be pointed at. The scandalmongers at the secretariat fulfilled a useful purpose – they kept alive the idea that no one was to be trusted. That was better than complacence. Why," he wondered, swerving the car to avoid a dead pye-dog, "do I love this place so much? Is it because here human nature hasn't had time to disguise itself?"

Before going home Scobie inspects the quayside. Among the fat water-side rats and the unseen – human – wharf rats he finds a planted bottle and opens it. "It was a dimpled Haig and when he drew out the palm leaves the stench of dog's pizzle and nameless decay blew out like a gas-escape." His black policemen look on disapprovingly, for this was native-medicine – a charm directed at an enemy, "but now that its contents had been released it was as if the evil thought were left to wander blindly through the air, to settle maybe on the innocent."

Scobie goes home; he has cut his hand on a splinter, it is dripping with blood. Louise is reading poetry to Wilson; she can't bear the sight of blood and neither of them does anything to help. Scobie goes to the bathroom, "the room where he had always been alone," and there, sitting down on the edge of the bath, from which he has disturbed a couchant rat, he feels, as in his office with the handcuffs, "the sense of home." Here Ali tends him – Ali, his trusty boy – capably, tenderly, with "gentle clucking sounds of commiseration." When he comes down Louise kisses the clean white bandage and leaves "a little smear of orange lipstick."

That night in bed he is wakened by his wounded hand to find that his wife beside him is crying. " 'Darling,' he said, 'I love you.' It was how he always began. Comfort, like the act of sex, developed a routine." Louise can no longer bear the colony since Scobie has been passed over for promotion. She must get away – away to South Africa. He has not got the passage money, or any

idea how to get it, but, since he must comfort her, he promises
" 'Yes, dear, I'll manage somehow' ... She was asleep before
he had finished his sentence, clutching one of his fingers like a
child, breathing as easily."

3.

By now all the main characters save one – and she the detonator –
are introduced, and all the elements are in place. The central
figure is the policeman, the responsible man, the protector. Mr.
Greene, like other modern English writers – witness Miss Rebecca
West's controlled infatuation for elderly and well-born judges –
has a tendency to idealize the instruments and symbols of the law,
the blue uniform or the wig. The policemen – the Commissioner
in *It's a Battlefield*, the junior officer in *A Gun for Sale*, even to
a limited extent the Communist lieutenant in *The Power and the
Glory* – stand up like rocks in an ocean of childish irresponsibility,
knavery, and untrustworthiness. Untrustworthiness, unreliability
– this is a key concept and the words are constantly recurring:
servants, witnesses, drivers, guides, strangers, friends, each main
character in turn, almost all are, or seem at some time to someone
to be, untrustworthy. This is so of all Mr. Greene's work and
especially of *The Heart of the Matter*: the whole currency of the
colony seems counterfeit. Only Scobie is sterling, the archetypal
policeman: he can be trusted.

Yet – and this is what makes *The Heart of the Matter* more
interesting than any of Mr. Greene's relatively simple and static
earlier novels – Scobie really cannot be trusted at all, by anyone.
There is something wrong with Scobie, of which the germ is
already visible in his affinity with the colony and his broken
rosary. The watching vulture whom he comforts, the pariah dog
before his car, the fat rat whose seat he takes in his bathroom
"home" – these half-obscene creatures are very near to Scobie. It
is true that, like the buzzards of Mexico and the seagulls of
Brighton – "half vulture and half dove" – these are the normal fauna
of Mr. Greene's universe. Zoological metaphor, akin to the symbolism of the medieval bestiaries, is congenial to Catholic writers:
Bloy's anger swells into bisons, hippopotami, and thirsty lions;

Péguy praises the visceral in terms of a herd of four-stomached ruminants; Mauriac's Mediterranean insects rear stiffly and hieratically, displaying their wing-cases in some arid and fatal sexuality. Mr. Greene's carrion birds and beasts are normally conventional symbols of the corruption that waits upon the flesh and the horror of a world without God. But here, in *The Heart of the Matter*, they are something more: they have moved, as it were, closer to an organism whose impending dissolution is more apparent. For Scobie, Louise is both vulture and carrion (the joint of meat) and he, by implication, is to her carrion and vulture. The rat – "like a cat on a gravestone" – whose place he takes "on the cool rim of the bath" is nearer to him than Wilson reading poetry in the drawing-room. What makes the bathroom "home" is its rattishness, its resistance to the improvements that Louise has tried to introduce: "the tin bucket under the lavatory seat emptied once a day: the fixed basin with another useless tap. . . ." He is drawn to the carrion creatures by an obscure sympathy – disgust, which is one of the faces of pity: ". . . this was the life he would have chosen again to live . . . the rat upon the bath, the lizard on the wall, the tornado blowing open the windows at one in the morning, and the last pink light upon the laterite roads at sundown." It is this quality in him which makes him, despite his rectitude, untrustworthy. This policeman has friends among the underworld: the story tells how he is sucked down by that undertowing friendship: that and something more.

Scobie has now to keep his promise and find the money for Louise's passage. This will be hard – he has really assumed an extra and incompatible responsibility – and as, meanwhile, he carries on his daily police-work, he finds that also becoming infected by this climate of pity. One of his duties is to search neutral shipping for smuggled goods and infringements of the navicert regulations, including letters addressed to people in enemy territory. Searching the Portuguese ship, *Esperança*, he discovers such a letter, concealed in the lavatory cistern. The letter is from the Captain to his daughter in Leipzig; it is Scobie's duty to report the incident, and forward the letter unopened to his authorities. But the Captain "kept on wiping his eyes with the back of his hand like a child – an unattractive child, the fat boy of the school. Against the beautiful and the clever and the successful, one can wage a pitiless war, but not against the unattractive; then the millstone weighs against the breast." Furthermore this Captain is, like Scobie, a Catholic – "they had in common the plaster statues with the sword in the bleeding heart: the whisper behind the confessional curtains: the holy coats and the liquefaction of blood: the dark side chapels and the intricate movements and somewhere behind it all the love of God." The letter is touching and obviously genuine. Scobie himself had lost a daughter: the daughter is "the turning point"; Scobie destroys the letter and sends no report. He feels in his heart at one with the policemen who were broken for bribery: "They had been corrupted by money and he had been corrupted by sentiment."

Sentiment at the same time involves him still deeper in his commitment to Louise. He has found that he cannot borrow the money from his bank, he knows no other way of raising it, yet he repeats his promise, knowing how far it may carry him. "Despair is the price one pays for setting oneself an impossible aim. ... Only the man of good-will carries always in his heart this capacity for damnation."

One glimpses part of an obscure allegory. The policeman searches a ship named *Hope*, commanded by a weeping child, and finds only despair.

4.

Immature, uncertain, Wilson is spying on Scobie, and is in love with Louise. He hunts cockroaches with the lonely Harris, in Harris's bedroom. He accepts an invitation from Scobie; Scobie has to go on a journey and Louise asks Wilson to leave, but first to "go upstairs and see whether there's a rat in the bedroom." There is no rat. Wilson stands in the bedroom, observant and utterly confused. He is a trained spy "but his employers had never taught him that he would find himself in a country so strange to him as this."

All this, with its familiar elements, is no more than an interlude before the great theme of despair reappears, in an episode that

Graham Greene: The Anatomy of Pity

seems like a digression but is really central and decisive. Scobie has to go down to a remote jungle station, Bamba, where the District Commissioner, Pemberton, has killed himself. The journey to Bamba is broken by sleep, obsession, and the coming on of fever. In a dream "a small green snake" slid up his arm and "touched his cheek with a cold friendly remote tongue." The figure 200 – the sum of the passage money – goes round in his head. Ali nurses him. They cross a "dark Styx-like stream" and come to Bamba. At Bamba, with the priest, Father Clay, he sees Pemberton's body. "When Scobie turned the sheet down to the shoulder he had the impression that he was looking at a child in a nightshirt quietly asleep: the pimples were the pimples of puberty and the dead face seemed to bear the trace of no experience beyond the classroom or the football field. 'Poor child,' he said aloud. The pious ejaculations of Father Clay irritated him. It seemed to him that unquestionably there must be mercy for someone so unformed." Wondering how the picture-rail and cord sustained the weight of the hanged body, "he remembered a child's bones, light and brittle as a bird's." There is a letter ending: " 'It's a rotten business for you but it can't be helped.' The signature was 'Dicky.' It was like a letter from school excusing a bad report." Father Clay and Scobie differ in regard to whether Pemberton is damned or not.

"The Church's teaching . . ."
"Even the Church can't teach me that God doesn't pity the young . . ."

Later Pemberton takes a place in Scobie's fevered dreams. Sometimes he is Louise, sometimes Scobie himself under the nickname "Ticki," which his wife used for him. "There was someone he had to save, Louise or Dicky or Ticki; but he was tied to the bed. He is writing a letter ending: 'Your loving husband, Dicky.' He tears up the letter, calls frantically for Louise, and then a key turned and the door slowly opened with a sense of irrecoverable disaster, and he saw standing just inside Father Clay who said to him: 'The teaching of the Church . . .' Then he woke again to the small stone room like a tomb."

The image of the spotty boy hanging from the picture-rail will return again, long afterwards, when Scobie himself is near to taking his own life. "Christ had not been murdered: you couldn't murder God: Christ had killed himself: he had hung himself on the Cross as surely as Pemberton from the picture-rail." And later still, hearing "the Pemberton case" casually discussed, he makes the same august comparison: "Through two thousand years, he thought, we have discussed Christ's agony in just this disinterested way."

Pemberton and the Captain, two ungainly children, attractive *only* through pity, prevail against Scobie's integrity. The Captain had made the first breach; now Pemberton, "obscurely linked" with Louise, makes the second. As Scobie watches Louise writing a letter, he decides to get her passage money by compromising himself: he borrows money from Yusef, the only man who will lend it. At the rumbling of the luggage "the vultures took off from the roof, rattling the corrugated-iron roof"; Louise leaves for South Africa; Scobie is alone, already well advanced in pity. As he returns from seeing Louise off, he catches sight of Wilson, watching the ship. "Scobie paused. He was touched by the plump and boyish face. 'Sorry we didn't see you,' he said and lied harmlessly. 'Louise sent her love.'"

5.

The second book begins, as did the crucial episode of the first, with the crossing of a river. But this is not the death river, dark and Styx-like with its "bank where life ended," which led to the land of Pemberton. This "wide passive river" which separates the colony from Vichy-held territory is in a sense a river of birth.

The survivors of a sinking, brought ashore in French territory, are being sent across the river to the colony. Scobie watches them come in: old men, an elderly woman hysterical with exhaustion, children. A little girl is dying, having survived forty days in the open boat. A young woman, Helen Rolt, is brought in on a stretcher; her husband has been drowned. "Her arms as thin as a child's lay outside the blanket and her fingers clasped a book firmly. Scobie could see the wedding ring loose on her dried-up finger." The book contains stamps: Mrs. Rolt is little more than a schoolgirl. "Scobie always remembered how she was carried into his life on a stretcher, grasping a stamp album, with her eyes fast shut."

Brooding over the disaster, Scobie feels the weight of all this suffering on his shoulders as a new responsibility: there is no comfort in the feeling that responsibility for suffering is shared with all human beings, "for it seemed to him that he was the only one who recognized it." He hears that the child will die and he thinks of Pemberton, and of the absurdity of expecting happiness in a world so full of misery. The lights in the hospital give an appearance of peace and security, just as the stars do. "If one knew," he wondered, "the facts would one have to feel pity even for the planets? if one reached what they called the heart of the matter." At the bedside of the dying child he thinks of his own child, whose death he had missed. The child calls "Father" and dies. Mrs. Rolt is asleep in the same room, still grasping the stamp album. "It was the stamp album and not the face that haunted his memory, for no reason that he could understand, and the wedding ring loose on the finger, as though a child had dressed up." Later, still in the temporary hospital, he takes down a book for a small boy:

"Just begin it," the boy pleaded.
"Yes, begin it," said a low voice from the other bed, so low that he would have discounted it as an illusion if he hadn't looked up and seen her watching him, the eyes large as a child's in the starved face.

Days later the African rains have begun – falling "in interminable tears" – and Scobie on his rounds enforcing the blackout knocks at a Nissen hut. Helen Rolt is there. They talk, about net-ball, paper chases, trigonometry, the French mistress: they avoid the shipwreck and the dead husband. They feel happy and secure in each other's presence, divided by so many years. Scobie promises to bring her some stamps for her album. When he comes back with the stamps, they talk more seriously: she of her dead husband, he of his dead child. Scobie explains why we do not suffer for the dead as we do for the living. It is a singular explanation, coming from a Catholic: "When they are dead our responsibility ends. There's nothing more we can do about it. We can rest in peace." She has been down at the beach, not knowing how to talk to people; Bagster, an R.A.F. officer, stroked her leg. Scobie visualizes her on the boat, then with the stamp album, then with Bagster.... "Sadly like an evening tide he felt responsibility bearing him up the shore." He feels responsible towards her, "this stupid bewildered child," as he would never feel towards "the beautiful and the graceful and the intelligent." The native boy who waits on her was Pemberton's boy. Her hollow face, and the rat's tail down the nape of her neck, her childish ugliness are "like handcuffs on his wrist." He feels safe with her, feels not desire but sadness and affection and "an enormous pity ... the terrible promiscuous passion that so few experience."

Then Flight-Lieutenant Bagster, apparently in a less involved state of mind, knocks on the door and calls, pleading with her to "be a sport." She is terrified, like, in Scobie's mind, a hunted animal; she stands close to Scobie, not answering.

"When the sound of Bagster's feet receded she raised her mouth and they kissed. What they had both thought was safety proved to have been the camouflage of an enemy who works in terms of friendship, trust, and pity."

They sleep together. When he wakes up, she is lying "in the odd cramped attitude of someone who has been shot in escaping." It occurs to him that she looks like "a bundle of cannon-fodder." He feels responsible again as he lies looking out at the grey sea. "Somewhere on the face of those obscure waters moved the sense of yet another wrong and another victim, not Louise, not Helen. Away in the town the cocks began to crow for the false dawn."

6.

This scene, surely the most lugubrious seduction in literature, has about it something of the same confused lighting as bathed the interludes with Louise. We are told, in detail and with considerable repetition, of what Scobie's feelings are to Helen: responsibility, pity. The background is of childhood – that sempiternally

Graham Greene: The Anatomy of Pity 69

symbolic stamp album – and of death: the deaths of Helen's husband, Scobie's daughter, and Pemberton. We are not given the slightest hint that there is anything of what the French understand by *trouble* in the relationship: on the contrary we are assured that "his body in this climate had lost the sense of lust." His feelings for Helen are apparently the same as his feelings for his dead daughter. Then Bagster knocks on the door and the two of them tumble into bed. One presumes that his constitution had recovered from the climate or their condormition would scarcely have inspired so theological a hangover.

It is salutary, I think, in dealing with this scene to employ a certain cynicism, for here more than anywhere else there is a lack of candour. The elaborate apparatus – the rain of pity and the handcuffs of responsibility – seems disposed so as to give Scobie a flattering background: or at least if Scobie is flattering himself, the writer does nothing to let him down – one of the difficulties with Scobie is that one can never be sure whether the narration represents what he feels, or what he admits to himself that he feels. There seems to be, in any case, an intention of proof: we are shown to what a pitch of contradiction and guiltiness a good man can be brought simply by pity and responsibility. This point is made more explicit later, when Scobie, wishing to go to confession, remembers that the priest will only tell him to avoid the occasion, not to see the woman again, in fact not to commit adultery. Then: "Helen – the woman, the occasion, no longer the bewildered child clutching the stamp album, listening to Bagster howling outside the door: that moment of peace and darkness and tenderness and pity 'adultery.'" The reader can hardly help reflecting that not on pity alone is adultery committed, in any climate: not, that is, unless by pity something more psychologically complex is intended than *The Heart of the Matter* admits. Something is left out – out of Scobie or out of "pity." The reader who feels that a theological-emotional sleight of hand has been practised on him can hardly be blamed if henceforth he looks for the missing card elsewhere than in the pack dealt by, or for, Scobie.

The chapter immediately following reveals, possibly, a certain sense of the incompleteness or idealization in the scene between Scobie and Helen. Wilson and Harris – the introducers of Scobie – are sitting in another Nissen hut, reading. The rain falls on the roof and some drunken R.A.F. men pass by, shouting. Harris feels a sense of comradeship and extraordinary peace. "Sometimes his eyes strayed to the walls seeking a cockroach, but you couldn't have everything." He turns the pages of his old school magazine, for he "felt the loyalty we all feel to unhappiness – the sense that that is where we really belong." Wilson, for his part, has contributed a romantic poem – about Louise – to the magazine and fears that Harris will find it. He is full of self-disgust and feels re-engulfed in his schooldays: "It was as if the hideous years had extended through the intervening mist to surround him again." He strolls to the door and sees Scobie go by between the huts. Scobie says he can't sleep; he has been taking a walk. Wilson, seeing through Scobie, feels towards him as an "old lag" might feel towards "a young crook." They are at different stages of equivocation. On the following day, in his office, Wilson is distracted from his task of spying on Scobie: "Naked to the waist a young girl passed gleaming through the rain and Wilson watched her out of sight with melancholy lust." When this spectacle has repeated itself, Wilson decides to go to the brothel. He is not a reliable driver and he has to wipe the windscreen with his handkerchief. On the way he passes "a dead pye-dog . . . with the rain running over its white swollen belly." He feels depressed with a premonition of the sadness of the aftertaste. The brothel itself is not an exhilarating place: rat-holes, pencil-scrawls, dirty shifts. Wilson tries to get away, but is coerced; the place reminds him of a newly opened vault. "A grievance stirred in him, a hatred of those who had brought him here. In their presence he felt as though his dead veins would bleed again."

The inversion in the endings – Scobie conscious of being an executioner, Wilson of being a victim – not only serves to bring out the relation between the characters. Wilson and Harris, with him, are commentaries on Scobie. Harris's lonely return to unhappy schooldays, his craving for beetles; Wilson's duplicity, his romanticism, his melancholy lust, above all his self-pity – these characteristics are necessary to Scobie and would complete him as a credible person. They are projected on the simplified and sordid personalities of Harris and Wilson for one purpose: the sanctification of Scobie.

Scobie's love affair meanwhile draws him into new entanglements. Helen rags him about his wife, his religion, his secrecy; she is beginning to turn into Louise and he now pities her in that capacity. "Pity smouldered like decay at his heart.... Nothing ever diminished pity. The conditions of life nourished it. There was only one person in the world who was unpitiable – himself." They quarrel and this pity drives him on to commit himself to her as absolutely as he can. He writes her a letter: "I love you more than myself, more than my wife, more than God, I think." He himself, as he drops in the letter, is not sure why he had to write "more than God." "The sky wept endlessly around him: he had the sense of wounds that never healed." The priest, Father Rank, calls on him – the rain is now falling "in grey ecclesiastical folds" – but Scobie is unable to ask his help, for he cannot look after his own soul at another's expense. "How can one love God at the expense of one of his creatures?" But he feels at heart that he has nothing to share except his despair: he wants peace, to be alone; he is beginning to think of suicide. "Christ had killed himself."

Events are, in any case, closing in on him. He gets a telegram: Louise is coming home. At the same time his letter to Helen has been stolen; Yusef has it through Pemberton's boy and is blackmailing him – Scobie must help Yusef to smuggle out a package of diamonds, or Yusef will hand the letter to Louise. Pity for Helen, pity for Louise: Scobie accepts. He smuggles out the diamonds by the Captain of the *Esperança*, whose cabin he has to search. As he searches, he catches sight of a face in the mirror – "a fat sweaty unreliable face" – which for a moment he does not recognize. Then he knows it for the Captain's, changed only by an unfamiliar expression. "He thought: am I really one of those whom people pity?"

7.

The end of the rains marks the beginning of the third and last book. Flies settle everywhere in clouds and Louise comes home. It is, naturally enough, a cheerless return as far as Scobie is concerned. The picture of the dead daughter, in her Communion veil, is back on the dressing-table. The mosquito net – formerly, as we remember, the "meat-cover" for the joint that was Louise – now hangs "a grey ectoplasm over the double bed." Decay is perceptibly more advanced.

Louise urges Scobie to come to Communion with her on Sunday; we learn later that this is a test, for she suspects the truth about Helen. Scobie is now in his last dilemma. He cannot go to Communion without sacrilege, since he is in a state of mortal sin: he cannot be absolved of his sin unless he repents and breaks with Helen, destroying his pattern of pity and abandoning her, as he believes, to Bagster and despair. At the same time if he does not go to Communion, Louise will know the worst. Someone must suffer, God or Louise or Helen and, in any case, also Scobie. "His automatic terrible pity goes out to any human need and makes it worse. . . . Any victim demands allegiance." Both his victims are merciless; Louise pushes him to the test and Helen doesn't see the test at all: "It's all hooey to me." For the time he manages to evade the test, feigning illness and need of stimulants. As he watches Louise at Communion, Scobie is aware of the sense of exile. "Over there where all these people knelt was a country to which he could never return. The sense of love stirred in him, the love one always feels for what one has lost, whether a child, a woman, or even pain."

The same themes occur again at a lower level: Wilson calls on Louise to read her his love poem. She is not interested, does not believe in his love, calls it just Coast fever. Angry and unstable, he taunts her with Helen Rolt, and she hits him on the nose. His nose begins to bleed and he has to lie down on the floor "between the table and the meat safe among the ants." In this position he has to continue his part of the dialogue of love. She stands over him as "though he were a corpse" and the room is "as close and intimate and airless as a vault" when Scobie returns and cures Wilson of the nose bleed.

Love, exile, pain, death; Scobie and Wilson again shade into each other, but this time there is a strange theological overtone. For is not Wilson, the rejected lover, stretched bleeding and humiliated on the floor, a grotesque image of the Redeemer? As Bloy says, it is impossible to strike anyone, even the most wretched creature, without his face becoming for that moment and for that purpose the face of Christ. So Scobie, through whom Wilson is hurt and by whom Wilson is healed, is seen to stand in this double relation to Christ himself; a dim perspective of hope is opened up. Very dim; for here again the intention is uncertain; all that one receives certainly is the impression of Wilson, the immature spy, as a sort of scapegoat carrying the defects of Scobie and perhaps, in a sense, the sins of the world.

Scobie cannot go on evading his decision indefinitely. He prays, seeing as he prays not Helen "but the dying child who called him father: a face in a photograph staring from the dressing table: the face of a black girl of twelve a sailor had raped and killed glaring blindly up at him in a yellow paraffin light." He cannot persuade himself that he is more important than that child – who is now specifically Helen – he cannot be absolved. He dreams that he is a decayed body drifting down an underground river, and wakes to find that he is going to his sacrilegious Communion. "He was desecrating God because he loved a woman – was it even love or was it just a feeling of pity and responsibility?" He kneels by Louise's side "like a spy in a foreign land" and is aware of "the pale papery taste of his eternal sentence on the tongue."

Being now "of the devil's party" and therefore a success, Scobie learns that he is, after all, to succeed the Commissioner. He begins quietly to prepare for an orderly suicide: he studies the symptoms of angina. The charnel fauna – vultures, pye-dogs, lizards, moths – pullulate around him more abundantly, and his weary character conspicuously goes to pieces. He has "lost the trick of trust," since he knows himself to be untrustworthy, and begins to suspect his faithful servant, Ali of spying on him. In a pity-inspired panic –

"he could ruin them" – he confides in Yusef, the only person who already knows the worst about him. Yusef, corrupt as he is, really loves Scobie; he promises to "look after" him. This in itself is a moral catastrophe: the breakdown of the policeman. Having so abdicated, Scobie seems to pass into a curious state of mental or moral coma: "a kind of nursery peace descended." Although he is touched by uneasiness at Yusef's offer of help, he does what is asked of him, gives Yusef a token which will make Ali follow his messenger. The token is the broken rosary. Yusef is away a long time, and Scobie sits vaguely uneasy but paralysed by despair. "God was lodged in his body and his body was corrupting outwards from that seed." Yusef returns and they drink together, Yusef evading his half-hearted questions, talking about Shakespeare. Scobie is still a victim of his strange lethargy, or consent. "When I was born I was sitting here with you drinking whisky, knowing . . ."

Their talk is interrupted by a cry, and Scobie goes out to find the corpse of Ali on the wharf. He looks for the broken rosary and comes to see Ali as part of it, the image of God. " 'Oh God.' he thought, 'I've killed you: you've served me all these years and I've killed you at the end of them.' God lay there under the petrol drums and Scobie felt the tears in his mouth . . . 'I loved him,' Scobie said."

There is about this scene, as about much else that concerns Scobie, a curious kind of ambiguity: not the enriching ambiguity in which possible meanings are superimposed and intermingle, but an ambiguity of irresolution. Did Scobie know that Ali was to be murdered? The passage about "knowing . . ." certainly strongly implies it and so does his final self-accusation. Yet it is later suggested that he could not have known anything of the sort. On the following day, when Helen questions him about the murderer, he reduces the accusation against himself to "he died because I existed." He does not know who did the murder and even tends to exonerate Yusef: "We will never prove anything. I doubt if Yusef intended it." Now clearly – and there is no suggestion here that Scobie is concealing anything – if Yusef did not plan the murder, or even if Scobie can, after the event, doubt whether he

Graham Greene: The Anatomy of Pity

planned it, Scobie's responsibility is of a very different kind from the somnambulistic collusion suggested earlier. In one view Scobie is an accomplice in intention; in another he is simply a suffering and scrupulous man, guilty only in virtue of his distrust and premonition. The reader is left to choose whichever interpretation he prefers, for this is not, or is only to a small extent, a psychological ambiguity *in Scobie*: it is an ambiguity in the facts as presented. This ethical sliding scale makes acceptable the idea of the innocent-guilty man. Pity, pure pity, can lead a man to acquiesce in murder. At the same time a man so compassionate cannot really acquiesce in murder. These two propositions, necessary to the Scobie theorem, are reconciled by leaving open two interpretations of what actually happened. So Scobie is corrupted and left intact at the same time. Just as he committed adultery without lust, so he commits murder without intending violence. A large part of his personality and story is rigidly unreal, fixed in a plaster of paradox.

To achieve the demonstration it is necessary that he commit the greatest crime of all. Before he kills himself he has a dialogue with God, for whom his love is tinged with pity: "even God is a failure." Scobie is committing suicide, indeed, out of pity for God, on whom he is inflicting sacrilege. "You'll be better off if you lose me once and for all." God urges him to break with Helen; or, if necessary, to go on living with Helen but without lies any more; or, at worst, to go on with the lying and the sacrilege – anything rather than the ultimate act of despair. But Scobie, caught in the conflicting currents of his pity, cannot do anything but go down: "That's impossible. I love you . . ."

After he swallows the overdose of sleeping tablets, he tries to say an Act of Contrition but his clouded mind cannot "remember what it was that he had to be sorry for." Yet he feels that someone, perhaps Ali, is seeking him, calling him. "Automatically at the call of need, at the cry of a victim, Scobie strung himself to act. He said aloud, 'Dear God, I love . . .' and died."

We feel that he is saved, that his suicide, like his murder and his adultery, has not been a real one.

The book ends with three dialogues: Wilson and Louise, with

Wilson about to replace Scobie, and with "the vultures clambering on the iron roof"; Helen and Bagster, with Bagster withdrawing and the suggestion that, in Helen's case, it will be God who will replace Scobie; finally Louise and Father Rank. Louise, who has learned from Wilson the truth about Scobie, believes that he is damned, but Father Rank will not condemn him.

"Father Rank said, 'It may seem an odd thing to say, when a man's as wrong as he was, but I think from what I saw of him that he really loved God.'

"She had denied just now that she felt any bitterness but a little more of it drained out now like tears from exhausted ducts. "He certainly loved no one else,' she said.

" 'And you may be in the right of it there too,' Father Rank replied."

8.

In the theological sense, the sense of its intent, the story of Scobie is the record of an attempt to imitate Christ. Scobie's "pity," his assumption of responsibility for all suffering, is a simulacrum of the Passion. "Any victim" demanded his allegiance: he saw the lineaments of Christ in any suffering human being – Pemberton, Ali, the Captain, Helen, Louise. But because of the discrepancies of this world of appearances – and this is the importance of the curious emphasis on the "unreliability" of people – he becomes caught up in a contradiction. His "pity" for creatures is really charity – the love of God – but it can only exercise itself blunderingly in action among fallen human beings and brings about in fact the very thing from which it most shrinks: the increased suffering of God. This situation of anguish is progressive and reaches its culminating point in the act of despair, suicide: the wounding of God because of love. Yet we know that Scobie will be saved since love was the motive of his misguided actions. His last words are not an Act of Contrition but an aposiopetic Act of Charity: "Dear God, I love..." The morality is the same as that expressed by the Angels in Yeats's myth on a similar theme, *The Countess Cathleen*:

*The Light of Lights
Looks always on the motive not the deed
The Shadow of Shadows on the deed alone.*

When Father Martindale described the *Heart of the Matter* as Christlike and as satisfying Maritain's fundamental requirement for the Catholic novel – compassionate understanding of the sinner without collusion with the sin – I think the scheme he had in mind must have been that which I have outlined: that which Mr. Greene seems to have intended to present. This scheme is entirely based on the unstated equation: "pity" = charity.

Now one factor in this equation is "known." "Charity" is one of the three theological virtues: it means the love of God. The other factor, Scobie's "pity," is "unknown" and requires analysis, not just vague assent, before the equation, and with it the theological scheme, can be accepted as valid. Does the equation, to begin with, stand up to the crudest and simplest test, that of explaining the motivation of Scobie's actions? Scobie's "pity" impels him to the following infringements of his code:

1. Breach of regulations (opening and destroying the Captain's letter).
2. Professional indiscretion (borrowing from Yusef).
3. Adultery.
4. Corrupt practice (smuggling for Yusef).
5. Complicity (?) in murder (Ali).
6. Sacrilege.
7. Suicide.

How far could charity, pure love, have motivated these actions? It could certainly have motivated the first two; and as for the fourth, only the most impenetrable Protestantism would maintain that smuggling was necessarily evil. In these three actions he breaks his own rule – the rule by which the policeman lived – but his sole and adequate motive was the desire to accept suffering in order to spare others: pure charity. But for his other actions it is hard to accept pure charity as the cause. I have discussed already the dubious nature of "pity" in the adultery scene:

we could only accept that particular "pity" as charity by embracing (*inter alia*) one of the more ebullient Eastern heresies. Nor could charity have dictated any complicity, however vague and elastic, in murder. As for sacrilege, the idea of charity as the motive is here so wildly paradoxical that it almost becomes plausible. Scobie "offers his own damnation" in order to save others, including God, from suffering. He does what Countess Cathleen, under other symbols, did and what Péguy's Saint Joan aspired to do. Yet this romantic form of sanctity, appropriate to Yeats's semi-Christianized creature of faëry or to the untaught and rebellious Joan of the early Péguy, does not seem to fit Scobie. Scobie is represented as a stolid, intelligent, elderly man who knows his catechism and takes rules seriously: he knows that to damn himself is the greatest injury he can inflict on God – an injury in comparison with which any hurt he can give Louise by abstaining from Communion is insignificant. His sacrilegious Communion therefore appears forced, imposed from without for an extraneous purpose; or else proceeding from some streak of histrionic perversity in the man's nature which the narrative does not adequately reveal. The same considerations apply to the suicide: charity – the desire to avoid causing pain to Helen, to Louise, and to God – cannot be taken seriously as the motive for an action that inflicts pain on all three.

"Pity" is clearly not the same as charity, and if it is not, the elaborate theological *tour de force* cannot be sustained. What then is left of the novel? And what is "pity"? These are not easy questions to answer, for both the story and the nature of "pity" are obfuscated by the insistence on identifying, for an ambitious paradox, this ruinous "pity" with the love of God. To come at the heart of *The Heart of the Matter* the augur must cut through much fatty tissue: it is worth the attempt, for if ever a heart was ominous, this heart of "pity" is surely so.

9.

"Pity" – and this is its clearest aspect – is the form of Scobie's relationship with those around him. This solitary tentacle of his takes hold only on children, or on adults who appear to him in the

Graham Greene: The Anatomy of Pity 79

guise of children. His wife, his mistress, his enemy are for him rather unattractive fumbling children. If they leave that role for a moment and appear as more or less competent adults – as Louise does when she thinks she is to be the Commissioner's wife – the tentacle relaxes its hold until "the child" reappears. The people who touch him must be immature and helpless: he alone is responsible, the policeman, the father. The relationship seems sometimes incestuous, as with Helen, sometimes parasitic, as with Louise – that blood-bank of pathos – but the initial pattern is constant: pity generating responsibility, the child as father to the man. For Scobie cannot be a man, cannot emerge from the solitude of his bathroom "home," until he has reduced others to the status of moribund children, imposed on them the image of his "dead daughter, Caroline." Then he can be for them the adult he is so conspicuously dressed to resemble.

"Pity" generates "responsibility"; that is, pitying others is necessary to Scobie in order that he may play his part as a grownup, or have any sort of intercourse with other adults. Is "pity," then, only a means, an offensive weapon, a stupefying liquid with which he drenches his victims? It cannot be, for it is "pity" which in the end kills its child "responsibility" (*ô lueur dans le gouffre!*) and wrecks Scobie's professional career and his whole life. "Pity" is not merely a self-flattering discernment of childishness in others: it is a deep sympathy with childhood, inimical to maturity. This is most remarkably apparent in the crucial Pemberton episode.

Scobie crosses a river, a river of death prefiguring a river of birth, to come to the land of his own childhood, a horrible empty jungle. There he finds himself as a hanged boy:

Dans ton île ô Vénus je n'ai trouvé debout
Qu'un gibet symbolique où pendait mon image.

This boy had refused to accept responsibility at all: he had killed himself rather than grow up. On him, that is on Scobie himself as he might have been – on Scobie *as he will be* – the priest prepares to pronounce the ultimate censure. But Scobie interposes "pity": "Even the Church can't teach me that God doesn't pity the young." And the image of his hanged self is already in his dream not only himself but the present overt object of his "pity," Louise. And it will become the ultimate object and source of all "pity," Christ himself.

"Pity," then, in Scobie, is an emotional loyalty to his own childhood, as well as a generalization of that loyalty by an ability to discern and cherish childhood subsisting in others. But the generalization, the transfer to others of that ardent and arrested self-loyalty, produces only a painful and precarious adulthood. He is still at bottom the small boy whom Mr. Greene described in his most sincere story, *The Basement Room*: the boy on whom grown-up passions and demands had intruded too soon. "A kind of embittered happiness and self-pity made him cry; he was lost; there wouldn't be any more secrets to keep; he surrendered responsibility once and for all. Let grown-up people keep to their world and he would keep to his. . . ." Scobie, it is true, accepts responsibility, but his "responsibility" is only a spurious maturity, dependent, in effect, on a continual external re-creation and cherishing of his childish self. This is his life and his religion: Helen, Louise, God. But since this "responsibility" is not at all a reasoned acceptance of duties and liabilities but the outward form of an emotional craving, it is essentially unreliable and irresponsible. Since the craving of "pity" is insatiable – for how can Scobie be a child again? – the "responsibility" is irresistibly driven into bankruptcy, accumulating moral liabilities which it cannot hope to meet in full. The only possible conclusion is suicide, the outright rejection of the grown-up world and the final act of self-pity. It is the act foreshadowed by Pemberton, by the images of death in all the love-making, and by the carrion beasts and birds that accompany Scobie everywhere. It is the death of Ali, for if it is himself he loves in the boy, it is to his own death he gives assent. The sacrilege also, the form of self-damnation, is a rite preliminary to suicide, and the adultery itself is suicidal: he sees Helen at first as a child and afterwards as one dead: "shot trying to escape."

This interpretation, unlike the superficial theological one, has the merit of explaining Scobie's actions: or rather it contributes what is necessary, in addition to the overt commentary, for an

Graham Greene: The Anatomy of Pity

understanding of these actions. The portrait that bears the name of Scobie is idealized and flatteringly lit: but we get elsewhere – in the self-pitying Wilson, in the school-fixed Harris, and above all in Pemberton – some of the missing elements which, together with undeveloped hints in the portrait, enable us to reconstitute something of the true Scobie, the potential hero of what might have been a great novel. Yet even as it stands, marred by sentimentality and moral juggling, *The Heart of the Matter* tells more about the people of our time than do many more honest books. Indeed, its intellectual dishonesty, its ellipses of approximation and selective omissions, as well as its fragmentation of character are themselves a part of "pity," for the novel is soaked in the element it attempts to describe. The true story of Scobie *together with* the narrative's tricks of perspective form a half-allegorical tale composed of the very stuff of our society, the "pity" and "responsibility" which are all that remain of the Social Contract.

10.

Superficially, one of the most curious features of *The Heart of the Matter* is its almost complete lack of social interest, or rather its implication of social stasis. We are told that the colony's population is of mixed origin and "unreliable": that the unreliability of native witnesses is their defence against an alien and incomprehensible system of law. This situation is fixed. A native boy – represented as being unusually bright – "realized that a Syrian might one day go home to his own land, but the English stayed." The only non-Europeans who have individual parts in the story are two Syrian black-marketeers and the boy Ali, a sort of Nephew Tom. There is no tension between European and non-European, no apparent sense of history. In marked contrast with most intelligent modern novels on any kind of colonial life – E. M. Forster's *A Passage to India*, for example, or George Orwell's *Burmese Days* – the centre of interest is not the interaction between colonists and colonized but simply the relation between the colonists themselves. The colony is apparently little more than a backdrop, or a reserve of suitably repulsive fauna.

In reality, however, the sense of history is present, but, according to the classical mode, compressed into the personal relationships of a few people. Scobie's relations to his pity-group are very much those of a colonizer to the natives. He is "responsible," sees himself as assuming the burdens of these undeveloped people. At the same time they are in fact necessary to him *because of* their undeveloped state. It is this – their "childishness," the cheap labour of the heart – which temporarily saves him from disintegrating. He feels guilty – "he had formed her face" – because he knows that although the whole significance of his work is supposed to be development – "charity" – what he really depends on is relative underdevelopment – "unhappiness," "unattractiveness," a state resembling the "childhood" of the exploiting group. His "pity," his relation to those whom he exploits, is composed of a genuine acceptance of the imperative to help – the Christian imperative – and an equally genuine compulsion to do nothing of the kind. In this dilemma, the imperialist can either abandon his Christian pretensions or cease to be: in fact he does both, as Scobie's action depicts. Scobie's sacrilegious Communion is the rejection of the impossible code: here he mimes the apostasy of the rulers of Christendom. Like Christendom he cannot escape the tension of guilt: in killing his God he has begun to take his own life. "Responsibility" goes bankrupt: Scobie cannot meet the moral and emotional commitments he has incurred, any more than the imperial powers can meet their financial liabilities. Like them he reacts with violence: the scene in which the honourable policeman more or less knowingly assents to the murder done in his interests by the gangster Yusef has obvious analogies with the rise of Fascism, as well as with less publicized events in respectable "dependencies." This attempt at a solution leaves things worse than before and Scobie, utterly demoralized, destroys himself: but, almost in the very act of doing so, he returns to the God whom he had abandoned. There is no need to point the moral here.

None of this is probably intended at all, and *The Heart of the Matter* is certainly not a neat ballet with each movement corresponding to a stage in the decay of monopoly capitalism. It is primarily a personal tragedy but it corresponds in a startling way

Graham Greene: The Anatomy of Pity

to the tragedy of a class. The place, selected for its nakedness – "the place where one knew the worst" – is the raw spot of the capitalist world: the colony. The symbols of decay are not solely those that might refer to mortality alone – the vultures – but also symbols of failing faith and power – the rusty handcuffs and the broken rosary. And even the way the story is told, with its evasions and its apologia, is part of our climate of fear and guilt, where it is hard for a man of good-will, lacking good actions, to see straight or to speak plain. The personal tragedy is in the womb of the general one and pity is their common blood-stream.

It would be easy, too easy, to regard this pity as simply a hypocritical veneer of sham Christianity over the realities of personal and social exploitation. It is much more than that: it is the warped and tortuous response of humanity – or rather the section of humanity that is conscious of having some degree of control over its own destiny – to the infuriatingly impractical command "... and thy neighbour as thy self." Now this response may be no longer needed, since the command is to be expunged and replaced by a practical philosophy. The citizen of the new republic will be encouraged to contemplate the worker in the forced-labour camp not with love or its ersatz pity, or even with hate, but with blank complacency. He will regard these and other unfortunates much as the devout of certain Eastern religions are said to regard women – as creatures whose debased condition is inseparable from their peculiar sinfulness. The strong will exploit the weak efficiently and without queasiness, for – if once there is equality of opportunity – what have the weak got to whine about? It is reasonable to guess that the morality of public life will – as it does in our own society – enormously affect personal relations also. Between the limits of high sensibility and extreme brutality – either of which would adversely affect production – the State could tolerate a wide range of domestic conduct. In the absence of a transcendent ideal, and with the example of the police, humanity would certainly approximate the lowest permitted point. Complex states of mind would be rare indeed. As a de-Christianized policeman, Scobie could keep all his pity consciously for himself, bully his wife to his heart's content, and love Helen – and leave her – without remorse. The moral air becomes cold and clear, and objects are seen to be quite different from what they appeared in the extraordinary sunsets of the last years of Christendom.

IV
SEÁN O'FAOLÁIN

Mr. Seán O'Faoláin (b. Cork, 1900) is the author of three novels: *A Nest of Simple Folk* (1933), *Bird Alone* (1936), *Come Back to Erin* (1940); three books of short stories: *Midsummer Night Madness* (1932), *A Purse of Coppers* (1937), *Teresa* (1947); four biographies: *Constance Markiewicz* (1934), *King of the Beggars* (1938), *Eamon de Valera* (1939), *The Great O'Neill* (1942); a play: *She Had to Do Something* (1938); two travel books: *An Irish Journey* (1940) and *A Summer in Italy* (1949); an outline history: *The Story of Ireland* (1943); and a historical essay: *The Irish* (1948). He has also written an unpublished play about Parnell.

THE PARNELLISM
OF SEÁN O'FAOLÁIN

– O he'll remember all this when he grows up, said Dante hotly – the language he heard against God and religion and priests in his own home.
– Let him remember too, cried Mr. Casey to her from across the table, the language with which the priests and the priests' pawns broke Parnell's heart and hounded him into his grave. Let him remember that too when he grows up.

JAMES JOYCE, *A Portrait of the Artist as a Young man.*

THERE is for all of us a twilit zone of time, stretching back for a generation or two before we were born, which never quite belongs to the rest of history. Our elders have talked their memories into our memories until we come to possess some sense of a continuity exceeding and traversing our own individual being. The degree in which we possess that sense of continuity and the form it takes – national, religious, racial, or social – depend on our own imagination and on the personality, opinions, and talkativeness of our elder relatives. Children of small and vocal communities are likely to possess it to a high degree and, if they are imaginative, have the power of incorporating into their own lives a significant span of time before their individual births. Such a power has informed the greatest Irish writers: Yeats with his mysticism of tradition; Joyce, in whom the idea of a continuous flux of life broke down the conventional structure of language. The "realists" of today, although inclined to revolt or grumble against the rule of the past, have also a powerful and often creative sense of tradition. In the case of Mr. Seán O'Faoláin this sense is especially, perhaps morbidly, acute. It has animated some of his best writing with the mass-emotion of living history; it has also often fallen like an antique blanket smothering the life out of the beings he has created. It is my object here to study the action of this peculiar traditionalism in his work and in particular to examine how it affects him at the points where, as an Irish Catholic and writer, he can be compared with European Catholic writers.

His first two novels, *A Nest of Simple Folk* and *Bird Alone*, are situated almost entirely in the shadow of preceding generations: a penumbra of folklore and historical conjecture in which, however, the living figure of a hero is clearly visible. Leo Foxe-Donnel, the central character of *A Nest of Simple Folk*, was born about the middle of the last century, of mixed parentage, his father being of the people, an O'Donnel, and his mother one of a Protestant landlord family, the Foxes. Leo is his mother's favourite, as she discerns aristocratic traits in him, and she tricks his dying father into leaving him the best part of his property. From this time on Leo is outcast from his father's people and begins to live the life of "a gentleman" (although continuing to be brought up as a Catholic) in the pretentious squalor of a fantastically decayed Ascendancy family. This environment also rejects him; he fails to fit himself for a profession and proves a thoroughly incompetent gentleman-farmer. His life is now that of a "desperate character"; he gets a girl with child and then disowns her; he is regarded as a menace to the girls of the district; finally his name is read from the altar of the local church. This is the low point of his career; he has achieved nothing except disgrace and has no purpose in life. It is just at this point that he meets, in a pub, James Stephens, the Fenian. He listens to Stephens praising violence and freedom, and attacking the preachers of resignation, and his conversion is described in a singular and important passage:

> Donnel forgot everything as he listened to the envenomed passion of this man. . . . He had always disliked the priests, now he could hate them . . . a seed of interest in his people and his country . . . burst through him like a well.

The "desperate character," now turned Fenian, joins in the rising of 1867, and is betrayed to the police by a girl. Released from prison after a long term of penal servitude, he marries the girl who betrayed him and settles down as a small shopkeeper, to bring up a family while still continuing his conspiracies. From

The Parnellism of Seán O'Faoláin 89

then on, the interest gradually shifts away from Leo to his family. His daughter Biddy grows up and marries a policeman, Johnny Hussey, a pious and promotion-minded young man, who spies on his father-in-law. The home-life of the Husseys is described at great length from the point of view of their son, Denis, who now takes the central position in the novel. Denis Hussey, who is contemporary with the author and probably represents him – Mr. O'Faoláin's father, too, was a member of the Royal Irish Constabulary – grows up in an atmosphere in which piety is almost synonymous with loyalty to the Crown. Like his grandfather before him, he has his religious difficulties but his are of a different order, questions which are not answered, essays slashed by indignant semi-literate teaching Brothers. He hates his father and interests himself tentatively in the doings of the "physical-force" men but is rebuffed as "a spy and the son of a spy." Finally, however, the news of 1916 summons him to make the decisive step; after a violent scene he breaks with his father and goes to the house of his grandfather, the old rebel, Leo Donnel.

As a story of family life, a "saga" in the Galsworthian sense, *A Nest of Simple Folk* suffers from a great hiatus by reason of the author's failure to interest himself in the personality of any member of the middle generation; this leaves a long stretch of time, from Leo's release about 1880 to Denis's childhood in the early 1900's, to be filled with the uncentred activities of dim and subordinate characters. As the story of the fate of an individual it fails for a similar reason; towards the end Leo Donnel, although physically active, declines from the status of protagonist into that of phenomenon, a vague enigma or a potential symbol. In fact his creator is tired of him and wants to get on to Denis. This gap in interest, enough to kill the attention of most readers, spoils the novel from any point of view. And yet *A Nest of Simple Folk* is a memorable work; memorable as an instance of the power and passion of memory. The last part of the book, encrusted with long, loving descriptions of things seen in youth, is evidence both of a superhumanly efficient retina and of a fanatical will to recapture lost time with details noted by the eye. In the earlier parts, where memory cannot directly help, one is conscious more of hearing than of sight; the effort is to "explain" what the boy Denis is to be and see, by penetrating the dark of history guided by the remembered voices of the elders. And out of this dark, expounding and explaining it, there partially emerges the apparently liberating figure of the ancient Fenian. His "explanation" is the explosion of 1916, which sets Denis free from his family.

Bird Alone is, in a sense, less deeply sunk in the past than *A Nest of Simple Folk*. Its narrator, Corney, an old man telling the story of his childhood and youth, was born in the 1870's, a quarter of a century or so after Leo Donnel and before Mr. O'Faoláin. But behind Corney, and dominating the early part of his story, is again the figure of his Fenian grandfather, old Philip Crane. Old Philip, perhaps because he is described as seen by his grandson and not merely reconstructed, is far more vivid and convincing than Leo Donnel. Reading aloud the "great play of Faust, by George W. M. Reynolds, M.D.," or "galloping out the country in wagonettes, decorating the graves of the Fenian dead," he carries young Corney with him, both physically and spiritually. And with him Corney soon learns lessons of many-shaped rebellion, against Church and State and family. One such lesson is provided by the burial of Arthur Tinsley, a Fenian friend of old Crane whom the old man refuses to have registered by the cemetery authorities as a Catholic. The corpse is brought from the cemetery to the local Rabbi and from him to the dissecting room until it is finally rescued from "the Grander's" hands and given Christian burial. This is a scene in which Mr. O'Faoláin's flair for comedy shows itself at its peculiar best; it is also an important scene, for it is one of the most clear-cut statements of that conflict between "Irishness" and Catholicism which so encompasses his mind. It is worth while therefore to quote a rather lengthy passage, describing old Philip's encounter with the caretaker of the cemetery:

> The man drew out a sail of a handkerchief and blew his nose.
> "Write down R.C.," he ordered like a Pope.
> "No!" said my grander and he flung down the pen in a fury. "The church never said yiss, aye or no to Arthur Tinsley. But

you know and I know and everybody knows that no Fenian could get absolution in confession or the sacrament from the altar unless he retracted his oath to live and die for his country. And . . ."

"Mister Crane . . ."

"And . . ."

"Excuse me one moment, mister . . ."

"AND if Arthur Tinsley was asked here and now whether he would retract that oath . . ."

"There's nobody asking him . . ."

". . . whether, to obtain burial in this bloody cemetery, he would bow the knee to the church, and the first question they'd put to him would be, Do you admit that oath was a sin? – What would he say? What would he say?"

The man walked away to the door.

"What would he say?" roared my grander. "He'd say 'I wo' NOT!' And what would *they* say?" he bellowed with a great sweep of his hand through the air. "They'd say, 'Then we'll have nothing to do with yeh and yeh can go to hell!' "

Looking back on his life Corney realizes several things about his "grander"; not alone his "hardness and cruelty," and the fact that he was an old lecher – "weak in the carnalities" – but his parasitism towards the young. As narrator, Corney grows obscure if not confused in his analysis of this last quality. At one point he says that he sees "how the old man was for years dragging me before my time, secret and timid that I was, into the world." A little later he says that it was his grander who sent him to the Brothers' school – "if it was a place where the innocence of me was forced and pampered, he wanted it pampered only because he could feed on it."

The old man soon finds an ally in his work of corruption or education. Corney's aunt, Virginia, returns to Cork from London. She appears to her simple relatives to be a fashionable lady; she is in fact a prostitute. She charms all her relatives: young Corney is "swept off his feet." "She was most pious and went to the altar frequently," and this so pleased the boy "that the surge of emotion, almost an incipient vomit, used to make me hide my face in my palms to see her come up the aisle." However, poor Virginia does not long remain a source of edification. A special party is given by Corney's mother in her honour and a contention arises, in the course of which her real occupation is revealed. It is the period – the spring of 1890 – when Parnell's relations with Mrs. O'Shea are beginning to be generally known in Ireland, and the subject comes up at the party. A Protestant solicitor, a Tory, teases his pious nationalist friends with innuendoes about their leader; grander and a friend respond hotly; a Canon disapproves; Virginia gets carried away with Parnellite emotion: "She kicked the whirl of frill with her heel and with a lifted glass she cried, 'He's a gentleman. London is a gay place. Gentleman . . .' " And the Canon says ponderously: "Such. Women. Cannot. Be. Defended." The quarrel grows hotter and hotter until the final catastrophe when Virginia calls one of her opponents a name and he replies with scorn: "I know one of your names ... one of your many names."

This scene and the disgrace of Virginia merge in a business squabble, in which Virginia does something to save the financial part of the family's reputation. Grander kisses her hand. The adolescent Corney walks bemused through the night streets of Cork, thinking: "Life is like that. Here am I and there is my da"– an example of dreary rectitude – "and then there is my grandfather – something that nobody at all expects."

Meanwhile, in the shadow of such unexpected things the decisive actions of Corney's own life are being prepared. He courts a girl, Elsie Sherlock, whose piety and innocence are stressed – she "clutches her rosary beads for protection" as she walks with him. The relation between her and Corney, whose own piety dies away in the "bitterness" over Parnell, is passionate and quarrelsome and slow in changing. Eventually in London, in the house of her brother the priest, he seduces her. In the dawn the houses stare at him "as, at the end of a long trial, a judge might stare at a murderer." And his grandfather is the first to find out his secret. "Two comrades in distress," he says.

Things move to their conclusion. Grandfather dies in the odour of sanctity. Elsie, distracted with the sense of sin, is pregnant. "It *was* a sin, Corney," she says, as he goes to fetch a priest for

The Parnellism of Seán O'Faoláin

her. "All the time, for both of us, it *was* a sin." She throws herself into the sea, and Corney, who drags her out again, has time only to say an Act of Contrition with her, before the priest comes to find her already dead.

Corney remains, a "Bird Alone," shunned by his fellows. Evidently he is drawn to the Church, but he is not held. On Spy Wednesday during Tenebrae he joins the worshippers and in the crowd, "I could feel all my solitariness oozing away and a craving in me, powerful as a lust, to yield up everything.... But I could not. For, and the revelation drew me erect as a spear, it was not that I did not believe in men but that I could not believe in what men believed.... I went out."

The most obvious feature that *A Nest of Simple Folk* and *Bird Alone* have in common is atavism. In both novels the significant figures are an old man and a boy; in each the old man is a being of power, an accumulation of rage and lust, an ex-Fenian and an ex-fornicator; and in each the boy, under the old man's influence, becomes an outlaw in the world of his parents. The old man is the vital centre, and seems to drag the temporal centre of the story back into the past along with him; the youth receives from him the radiations of history and begins to turn into something like him. So in *Bird Alone*, Corney, the narrator, in his own lonely old age an outcast from his tribe, enters easily now into the tormented mind of the "ageing wifeless man" who dominated his youth. Just as the middle generations are virtually "skipped" in both novels, the middle years of life are also "skipped" in *Bird Alone*; Corney is a youth listening to an old man, and then, quite suddenly, he is an old man himself. What happens in between is not a gradual process but a fracture: the youth has broken with the environment and beliefs of his youth and with the middle-aged people who represent them. Nothing remains real except the old man and the forces that through him went to cause the break.

What these rebellious forces are is best understood in terms of what they overthrow; a system of poverty, submission, abstinence, and resignation. The centre is the father – the policeman in *A Nest of Simple Folk* or the builder Crone in *Bird Alone* –

who is not in himself really frightening or oppressive but who passes on to his large family the lessons of subordination he has painfully learned himself. He tries to bring up his children in the ways of righteousness, beats them, teaches them respect for their pastors and masters, and checks all manifestations of the sin of pride – as for the sin of lust, it knows better than to manifest itself in his presence. He is a worried and unimposing martinet, with no endearing qualities to make his methods and doctrines less unpalatable. But behind him, insignificant and insecure as he is, is something enormous and seemingly impregnable: the Catholic Church. The policeman and the builder, extremely pious men assisted by pious and submissive wives, are giving their children a sound Catholic education. The whole great weight of the Church is behind them and they appear less as individuals than as the points at which that weight presses down on the youth, Corney or Denis. In the family, the nightly Rosary and, through the land, as far as sound can carry, the music of the church bells remind the mutinous adolescent that in revolting against his family he will be alone against a people, fighting a flagless war against a unanimous acceptance.

He finds, however, a natural ally in his grandfather and a flag in the traditions which his grandfather represents. The Irish rebels of the nineteenth century, so regularly condemned by the hierarchy, were inevitable heroes for the spirited son of a pious and "loyal" family. Prometheus and Faust were remote and tenuous symbols, but the Fenian dead, to punish whom, in that treasured episcopal phrase, "hell was not hot enough nor eternity long enough," lived in the people's mind. In their names, revolt, which otherwise was doomed to futile isolation, found a way into the open, a fissure in the wall of acceptance. And even mightier than theirs was the name of Parnell, whose struggle not only against Church and State but directly against the power of sexual prohibition made him the essential hero of rebellious youth.[1] The sort

[1] Mr. O'Faoláin has quoted Professor J. V. Kelleher of Harvard who said that he stressed to his Irish History students the importance of such leaders as O'Connell, the Fenians, and Collins. But where Irish heroes were concerned, "the class were Parnellites to a man." – (*Sunday Indpendent*, 22 February 1948.)

of conversation that Joyce remembered in *A Portrait of the Artist* and of which Mr. O'Faoláin captures the echoes in *Bird Alone*, the skirmishings of grown-ups about Parnell and purity and the priests, must have been wildly exciting to hundreds of young minds. In young Corney's case, as no doubt in many others, such scenes helped, along with his grandfather's example, to establish a firm connection between the separate ideas of national, spiritual, and sexual emancipation. As one name will be needed for this triple association we shall call it "parnellism" (as distinct from political "Parnellism"). A good example of the inclusive nature of "parnellism" appears in a subordinate episode in *Bird Alone*. Corney, owing to the recklessness of one of his friends, is brought up in court on a political charge and has to exonerate himself by proving the truth, that he was "in the woods at midnight with Elsie Sherlock." Elsie's father, telling her that she has "disgraced her brother in Maynooth," forbids her to speak to Corney again, and, for the time, she obeys. Corney hates her weak submission, "the way she lets her family crucify her," and broods on it until "my contempt spread to so many people that I felt what had happened to me was an image of the far worse that had happened to ... the Fenians, to the Land Leaguers, to Parnell."

Here "parnellism" is passive, an extension of self-pity, but it can be dynamic. *A Nest of Simple Folk* is planned to show the apotheosis of "parnellism" in a moment of historical decision. The 1916 rebellion frees Denis from his family and at the same time justifies the life of old Leo Donnel. The young rebel and the old, and their private rebellions, are merged in the national insurrection (in which their creator took part, at a later stage). They thus break out of their loneliness and recover through patriotism the unity with the people which they are unable to keep in religion. For them, and for almost all Mr. O'Faoláin's central characters, this unity, perhaps because it is so difficult to achieve, is profoundly important, a condition of spiritual life, almost a religion in itself.

The dynamic element is also strong in Mr. O'Faoláin's early short stories. The first collection, *Midsummer Night Madness*, published about the same time as *A Nest of Simple Folk*, is in one sense a sequel to it since most of the stories concern the Black-and-Tan War and the Civil War. Because these stories stress the brutality rather than the chivalry of the "Troubles," and because some of them are fairly outspoken about sex, they have been generally regarded as disillusioned and cynical or, by sympathizers, as coldly objective. Such views do not penetrate the surface, the impassivity of manner, which thinly covers an excitement that is almost exultation. The title-story, "Midsummer Night Madness," with its lecherous landlord, its equally lecherous brigand of an I.R.A. man, its scent of "lilac and dog-roses," and its burning house, is typical in its romantic nostalgia for the good old days of youth and anarchy. "The Small Lady," the story that presumably caused the Irish Censorship Board to ban the book, is a more extreme piece of romanticism. The hero of this tale, another Denis (or more probably Denis again), is a member of an I.R.A. group that captures an erotic female spy, Mrs. Sydney Browne, and brings her, pending trial, to Mount Melleray, where the Trappists are sympathetic to the cause. That night in the monastery Mrs. Browne seduces Denis. Afterwards, before she is shot, he gets to confession, to his great relief, and while she is writing her last farewells he, although he feels "a prig," is hoping that he will not be late for the Communion. In this exuberant and preposterous tale we may, if we remain calm, detect quite clearly the elements of "parnellism" in a most aggressive combination. The "national" and "sexual" elements need no stressing but, at first sight, the element of religious revolt seems to be lacking. Denis's behaviour is rather weak, but his faith is exemplary. In fact, however, the faith serves to emphasize the act of revolt: the sacrilege of the seduction in the monastery, with all around the silent cells of flagellants, and "the sign and adoration of the Ender of Life." The act and its sibilant setting are more important than the sketchy "repentance" afterwards, which (in so far as it is real at all and not merely a satirical-shocking intervention by the author) can be no more than a pause before departure, in the mood of Tyutchev's stanza on Faith:

She has not crossed the threshold on her way
She has not gone for good and closed the door

But yet the hour has struck. Kneel down and pray,
For you will pray no more.

For poor Corney, hero of a more mature work, the threshold has been crossed, and that without the romance of either insurrection or sacrilege. His dabblings in politics are doomed to ineffectiveness; his revolt remains essentially a private one and so his rejection of the faith debars him forever from the unity for which he longs. He is left with no other consolation than that of stoical pride: "Not one single thing would I change except that once, for a week, I was untrue to my sins."

The sad separateness of *Bird Alone* is also the predominant feeling in *A Purse of Coppers*, the book of stories published in the following year, but it shrinks into something more petty than Corney's stoicism. The protagonists of such stories as "The Old Master," "My Son Austin," and "A Born Genius" are all in their different ways artist-rebels and all are utterly defeated by the provincial life of Ireland. "Kitty the Wren," the girl who had once got into trouble and who is condemned to spend the rest of her life in a solitary house in a remote glen alone with her idiot brother, is the symbolic figure of the book. The old priest who has condemned her ("The poor girl will never enter this village again and 'tis better that way") is now completely master of the situation, for the romantic days of the rebellion are over, and the spiritual rebels, deprived of unity and direction, are being "mopped up" singly; even when two of them come together, as in the story, "A Meeting," they do not recognize each other any longer in the general flatness of things. The Church is all-pervasive – out of fourteen stories in the book only one lacks a clerical character – and the spiritual descendants of Leo Donnel are bogged in frustration, alternately resigned and irritable. The despair of *A Purse of Coppers* is unrelieved by any grandeur and the nearest approach to hope is contained in an unanswered question asked by the priest narrator in the first story, "A Broken World": "What image of life that would fire and fuse us all, what music bursting like the spring, what trumpet, what engendering love . . .?"

That Mr. O'Faoláin has not answered this question is not surprising, since history has not helped him. What is perhaps surprising is that he has continued to search history for an answer, digging deeper into the "racial mind" to find again the rebellious unity that Leo Donnel sought. His important biographies, *King of the Beggars* (1938) and *The Great O'Neill* (1942), develop and illuminate his half-mystical ideas of the nation. In *King of the Beggars*, his life of Daniel O'Connell, he speaks of "that most powerful of all emotional pistons known to man, a blazing love of place and a fond memory for the lost generations of his tribe, the ineradicable *pietas* of all submerged peoples"; and again and again he mentions "the mind of the race ... the racial genius ... the native instinct for life." In *The Great O'Neill* he is even more explicit: "What we venerate surely in these [Gaelic] customs is their intimations, as yet only half-realized, of a sensible philosophy of life which those who practise them have no other way of expressing. Sometimes this expression takes on the form of a religion as with the Arabs. ... But in all cases the racial bent must ultimately come ... to the surface of the mind." And in a heated controversial editorial he gave a name to this doctrine when he spoke of "Delphic Nationalism ... that wild and fine spirit which suffuses the very air of this country" (*The Bell*, November 1941). All this is plain enough: the ideas of Leo Donnel, as he listens to James Stephens, but expressed in the language of German romanticism. Yet this line of thought, or feeling, cannot go far without being deflected by a fundamental contradiction – the impossibility of making a race-religion about a "race" that already has a quite different religion of its own as moulder of its "racial" character. Mr. O'Faoláin violently resented an opponent's saying, "At the present day the sole traditional Irish public institution is the Church," but he admitted the underlying truth of this when he wrote in *King of the Beggars*: "So the people [at the beginning of the eighteenth century] set out on their long journey with but one possession, a not inconsiderable inheritance – their religion." The two biographies spin in a most fascinating manner around this central contradiction; their two heroes, O'Connell and O'Neill, are intuitively depicted in various shades of ambiguity, believing and not believing. They are "oblique," "labyrinthine," "winding," "tortuous," "serpentine," "involute"; their minds are compared to the many-layered onion, or yielding elastic, or to "a humming conch of *arrière-pensées.*" Between the known marks, often themselves contradictory, of their lives the biographer stretches his conjectural web, with its warp of "Delphic Nationalism" and woof of "reservations." A sort of historical introspection is at work and its results, although impressive, bear the mark of heavy mental stress. The simple momentum of the early stories and the first two novels is gone.

Come Back to Erin (1940), the third and latest of Mr. O'Faoláin's novels, is so lacking in momentum and in any centralizing element that it is difficult to give a coherent account of it. It differs from the other novels in being situated entirely in "the present" and being free from grandfathers. But the pressure that Denis and Corney felt, the pressure of the Church through the family, is there again, impalpable and inescapable like the pressure of the atmosphere. It does not suffice to unify action, but hinders the divergent wills of a number of unequally interesting human beings, the members of the Hogan-Hannafey family. This family consists of an old mad mother and her grown-up family. The mother is understood to be mad because of her second husband's infidelities; the children, all but one, are celibate for various reasons. Leonard is a priest, Clara a nun, Natalie and Eolie have mother to look after, Michael must earn for the family, and Frankie, in this aftermath of the Civil War, is "on the run" for Ireland. Only one brother, St. John, is married, and it is he who supplies the element of change in what seems a hopelessly static situation. The book opens on a familiar note and with a familiar character: rain and church bells and the frustrated small-town clerk (Michael) sidling into church with a copy of Maupassant. Then in a condensed, almost burlesqued, form we have the familiar situation of temptation by an old man – in this case not a Fenian but an aged brothel-tout. But Michael is there for background rather than as a central character; the two real protagonists are Frankie and St. John, to whom the interest now shifts. St. John is back in Ireland on a visit from America, where he has prospered in business. He has rather more than the average sentimentality of the emigrant and is drinking too much, because he is unhappily married. Frankie, the tracked I.R.A. man, living on his nerves, and beginning to lose faith in his cause, is smuggled out of the country to America with St. John's help. In America he learns from his brother, Leonard, the priest, the nature of St. John's troubles. St. John had "turned his back on Ireland" and had been civilly married to an American Episcopalian. Now he wants nothing but to become one with Ireland again, but religion and his marriage are in the way. Leonard condemns him, not so much for his religious defection as for his national apostasy; he had given no thought to Ireland, had not sent a penny home, et cetera. Frankie pities him as a man "caught in a net" – "he could not have Ireland until he had paid her the last penny of her price" – and goes on, amid a welter of minor events and descriptions, to seduce his wife, an unconvincing character named Bee. St. John becomes more and more frantically involved in nationalism and theology and eventually drowns himself. Frankie loses interest in Bee and also in the national struggle, returns home, and becomes a Warble-fly Inspector. We are left in apathetic doubt whether he will marry his Irish sweetheart, the consumptive Josephine, and what the other members of the family will do with their small legacies from St. John.

Through the gaseous flickering irresolution of *Come Back to Erin* there emerges the same cleft rock of contradiction that contorts the structure of the biographies. However much he wants to, poor St. John cannot "be Irish" without "being Catholic," and as he cannot be Catholic he kills himself, thus making himself as sure of hell as anyone can be. For Frankie on the other hand, and perhaps for some of the other characters, a sort of limbo is reserved. He is, of course, Irish in the parnellistic mode, aggressive, anticlerical, and "collectivist." He does not practise his religion but apparently continues, in some special way, to be Catholic. "I suppose I'm what you'd call a bad Catholic," he tells Leonard cryptically, "but never mind – I'm all right." What being "all right" means the priest does not ascertain, but we know from *King of the Beggars* that it is "the normal condition of most (educated) Irishmen" to believe in Catholicism, with such reservations as to make it a different religion from that of the "simple" and "artless." Such was Frankie's case apparently and the forswearing of revolution and Bee makes him more "all right" than before. The position of Warble-fly Inspector, perhaps conferred on him by his creator in a moment of understandable petulance, puts him into a realistic relation to the people. The parnellistic way out is no longer valid for either of the brothers. It is a side road that, after a brief historical detour, eventually leads back to the main enclosure, where "being Irish" and "being Catholic" are the same.

It is, however, possible to loiter in a side road without letting it lead you anywhere at all. *Teresa* (1947), Mr. O'Faoláin's last book of stories, reflects very much the same world as *A Purse of Coppers* did ten years before. The clergy are still dominant, artists are still frustrated. The "fusing image" longed for in "A Broken World" has clearly not been found. It still is being sought, however, perhaps less hopefully, but in the same places. The longest story in the book, "The Silence of the Valley," concerns the death of an old cobbler in the Gaeltacht, and the revelation to a group of visitors that this story-telling cobbler and his wife represented not merely the old Gaelic world but a primitive source of virtue, the natural state of innocence before the Fall of man. This cobbler – the earthiness of whose stories we know to have brought on him the castigations of the clergy – is a necessary hero in the mythology of "Delphic Nationalism." He is in fact the incarnation of the "true" Ireland: an Ireland before the Fall and therefore before Christianity, an Ireland which is its own religion and does not contradict.

This idea of the "true" Ireland has ceased to be an inspiring myth and has become a source of confusion and irritation. When Mr. O'Faoláin was still writing out of the experience of his youth romantic Ireland was not dead. It was natural for him, whose own youth had coincided and mingled with his country's successful revolt, to fuse subjective and objective, identifying his own inner experience with the Irish revolution. This identification, extending back into the penumbra which had helped to produce it, established itself as a general association. Nationalism was the communion of youth; freedom was a word of one indivisible meaning; the Irish-speaking districts of West Cork were a pagan Arcadia. Within a limited historical field, a period ending in the early 1930's – during which a powerful revolutionary tradition ran not only against the Crown, but against the Church also – this association was coherent and a source of power. But revolution is little more permanent than youth. The Ireland in which Mr. O'Faoláin now lives and writes is, as everyone knows, the least romantic and the least revolutionary of countries. It is one in which Church and State exist in harmony, as inexpugnable bastions of the family. Here the parents of Corney or Denis could live secure, for there is no fissure at all in the wall of acceptance. Parnell's place has been taken by a line of pious and blameless patriots and rebellion has become a praiseworthy but concluded activity. Ireland is now a middle-aged country. Youth can take it or leave it; and often leaves it.

Mr. O'Faoláin will neither take it nor leave it. He sees, of course, and bitterly resents, Ireland's staid paternalism, symbolized for him principally by the literary Censorship Board which has banned three of his books (*Midsummer Night Madness*, *Bird Alone*, and *A Purse of Coppers*). In scores of articles and letters he has denounced this institution and the spirit behind it, the spirit of Corney's father and of the teaching Brother who slashed young Denis's essay. His stories, with their great and increasing emphasis on the frustrations and stagnations of Irish life, show his oppression by that spirit and his knowledge of its power. But in combating it, which he has done more fearlessly than any other writer living continuously in Ireland, he has relied emotionally on something that has lost its meaning in the new environment – the old anticlerical nationalism. The clear-cut attitude of Mr. Frank O'Connor, who can laugh both at the people and at what they believe, is not for him, since he believes in the people. Corney's feat of believing in the people without sharing their beliefs is one that cannot be maintained for long, and *Come Back to Erin* is evidence of a sense that an Irish nationalist must, if only indirectly, be a religious man. Thus, starting as irreligion, or at least as anticlericalism, the patriotic emotion leads back to religion again. This flight involves a difficult mental revolution. It is hardly surprising that *Come Back to Erin* is a confused novel, or that, as Professor Kelleher has observed, it "disperses rather than ends." To end it, it would have been necessary to describe a full circle, for which the time is not yet.

Mr. O'Faoláin is not regarded in Ireland as a Catholic writer. You will not find his name in Father Stephen Brown's bibliography, *Novels and Tales by Catholic Writers* (1940), nor will you find any of his books in the Catholic Central Library in Dublin. Abroad, however, he is a Catholic; his books figure in the American *Guide to Catholic Literature* (though not always with favourable comment), and one of them, *King of the Beggars*, was actually a choice of the Catholic Book Club of America. The difference of opinion is not surprising. Mr O'Faoláin is a complex writer, and in any case it has long been a matter of doubt whether any novelist (or poet or dramatist) can be properly described as being in his creative function "Catholic." If we apply the strict test of edification, and insist, like M. Maritain, that the Catholic novelist should abstract himself from the sinfulness of his characters, and contemplate it, without collusion, from the "altitude," then Mr O'Faoláin fails, like every other writer worthy of the name. On the pragmatic test of simple comparison the result is not so immediately clear. M. Mauriac, now regarded as the very archetype of the Catholic novelist, held, at the time when he earned his reputation as a novelist, somewhat similar dispositions to Mr. O'Faoláin. Like the Irish writer, the Frenchman had a powerful sense of piety towards his ancestors, allied with a tenacious love of his native place. In both cases this love and piety did not exclude a spirit of youthful revolt and even hate and expressed itself not at all in panegyrics, but in very careful and unflattering re-creations of scenes and people rooted in the past and in the given place, Bordeaux or Cork. Both writers were born Catholics and both became sources of scandal, being attacked as pornographers, traitors to their religion. To both, in the complicated pattern of their loves and hates, the Catholic Church was a challenging central symbol. But – and here is the main difference between the two attitudes – in Mauriac's case the challenge is accepted. In his novels Bordeaux or the Lande is a setting, partly symbolical or collusive, for human action which has the universality of sin. If his characters revolt it is against God through the family; if they are oppressed or debauched it is by their own sins or the general sinfulness of man; even if they have a secret anti-Christian religion it is a universal one, like pantheism or sun-worship. They do not, usually, revolt against the Gironde; they are never frustrated by "France" or even by "provincial life"; they do not make a cult out of memories of La Vendée or of the death of Mme Roland. The piety of place is properly subordinated; man stands in a direct relation to the universal, affirming or denying God.

Mr. O'Faoláin, by comparison, is parochial. He neither affirms nor denies anything of universal importance, but thrusts into the foreground a sort of Heath Robinson historical apparatus, driven by "the most powerful emotional piston known to man," and manufacturing a substitute religion for local consumption. This glorified parish-pump is not the "nationalism" of Dostoevsky or Yeats or even Stefan George, which was in each case the vehicle for a general idea, apocalyptic or Messianic. Mr. O'Faoláin does not believe in "Holy Ireland," or in an aristocracy or in "the descent into the ancient Blood." The archaic nationalism which shows itself in his novels and stories is free from all taint of generality. His stories are illuminating about Ireland; an anthropological entertainment to the curious foreigner, an annoyance and a stimulus to the native. To Ireland the stimulus is of great value; in a time of sleepy simulation Mr. O'Faoláin's irascible and dissenting temperament has struggled, not without success, to preserve some honest intellectual life among his people. What he may have lost himself in that struggle we cannot know.

We know that once, in *Bird Alone*, he managed to move from particulars to the universal and to write a novel of real importance. Corney is ripped away from everything he had been bound to: from his home, from the sentimental religion of his boyhood and the patriotism of his youth, from Elsie, from his native city. In the end he is a naked man, helpless, confronted with the God of his father. If at that point he had made an act of faith, *Bird Alone* would have been hailed everywhere, even in Ireland

The Parnellism of Seán O'Faoláin 105

(outside Cork), as a great Catholic novel, for the whole book would have seemed to move to this end. The fact that he said "No" seems to me to put the book on a much higher plane than that of edification: the level of truth. The old man would not assent because he did not believe; and his creator was not willing to make him believe in order to please the readers of the novel. The reality of the character emerges in the stubborn rejection. *Bird Alone* is about human fate, which is harder than fiction.

It is probable that in a future novel Mr. O'Faoláin will scrap the obsolete machinery that has confused and restricted so much of his writing. One cannot prophesy what will happen then. He might write an empty, meaningless novel about America, like the dreariest stretch of *Come Back to Erin*. He might develop the refusal further and abjure Ireland and religion together. But whatever he actually does, he will, by dropping the idolatries of "parnellism," have a chance to turn his energies towards something of more than local significance.[1] It is exceedingly difficult to be a Catholic writer in a Catholic country: the pressure of a community varies inversely with its size; ingrowing nationalism destroys a writer's scope. Mr. O'Faoláin has been a living example of the truth and interrelation of these three propositions. He does not have to refute them all together in order to recover his direction as a writer. He may have to fly to the ends of the earth.

[1] In *A Summer in Italy* (1949), a travel book which appeared after this essay was written, Mr. O'Faoláin tells of his recent conversion to Roman, as distinguished by him from Irish Catholicism. "To myself I said: 'I have left a nation and joined an empire.' " This would seem to be a farewell to "parnellism"; it will be interesting to see the consequences when they are expressed in terms of creative work.

V
EVELYN WAUGH

Mr. Waugh was born in 1904 and was converted to Catholicism in 1930. Novels: *Decline and Fall* (1928), *Vile Bodies* (1930), *Black Mischief* (1932), *A Handful of Dust* (1934), *Scoop* (1938), *Put Out More Flags* (1942), *Brideshead Revisited* (1945), *Scott-King's Modern Europe* (1946), *The Loved One* (1948), and a historical tract-novel, *Helena* (1950). Biographies: *Rossetti* (1928), *Edmund Campion* (1935). Travel books: *Labels* (1930), *Remote People* (1932), *Ninety-two Days* (1934), *Waugh in Abyssinia* (1936), and *Robbery under Law; the Mexican Object Lesson* (1939). Other publications: *Mr. Loveday's Little Outing and Other Sad Stories* (1936), *Work Suspended* (1943). The last (limited edition 500 copies) is two chapters of an unfinished novel.

THE PIETIES OF EVELYN WAUGH

MR. EVELYN WAUGH'S seventh and most ambitious novel, *Brideshead Revisited*, was fortunate in earning the approval both of the reading public and of the theologians. In England, *The Tablet* saw in it "a great apologetic work in the larger and more humane sense," and in the United States, where it quickly sold over half a million copies, the critics of the leading Catholic journals concurred in this judgment. One, however, Father H. C. Gardiner in *America*, complained with justice that all the non-Catholic reviewers – including those who made it a Book of the Month Club selection – had missed the religious point of the book. It seems probable, therefore, that most of Mr. Waugh's readers, in America at any rate, did not know that they were reading a great apologetic work, and that, if they paid any attention to the Catholicism of *Brideshead Revisited* at all, they valued it as part of the general baronial decorations around a tale of love and high life.

In this, of course, they were wrong, but their mistake was not entirely due to "secularist" stupidity and indifference. *Brideshead Revisited* is, in its author's words, "an attempt to trace the divine purpose in a pagan world"; men and women try to escape from the love of God, to find human happiness, but God destroys their human hopes and brings them back with "a twitch upon the thread." This is the central theme, austere and theological, but obscured (for those whose approach to religion is different from Mr. Waugh's) by bulky memorials of devotion to other gods. These alien pieties, some of them hardly compatible with strict Catholicism, were perhaps for Mr. Waugh the forerunners of a more articulated faith – as, in *Brideshead Revisited*, Sebastian Flyte's affection for a teddy-bear was the forerunner of a vocation. They appear in varying degrees and shapes in all his work and mingle with Catholicism in a highly personal system of belief and devotion, well worth analysis.

The main emotional constituent of Mr. Waugh's religion – using the term in a wide sense – is a deep English romanticism. His earliest work, *Rossetti*, betrayed a pre-Raphaelite affinity; and his first "serious" novel, *A Handful of Dust*, deals with the injury inflicted by modern flippancy and shallowness on a romantic mind. The hero, Tony Last, lives in a great ramshackle country house of nineteenth-century Gothic which he dearly loves, and which his wife's friends sneer at; his wife betrays him, and when he realizes the extent of her treachery, his disillusionment shows us in a blinding flash his imaginative world: "A whole Gothic world had come to grief ... there was now no armour glittering through the forest glades, no embroidered feet on the green sward; the cream and dappled unicorns had fled. ..."

We should, of course, be wary of too easily attributing similar fantasies to the author – although he takes his hero's side so bitterly as to mar what is in many ways his best novel – but it is significant that Captain Ryder, the hero of *Brideshead Revisited*, lives in the same sort of climate. "Hooper," he says, referring to a member of the lower classes, "was no romantic. He had not as a child ridden with Rupert's horse or sat among the camp-fires at Xanthus. ... Hooper had wept often, but never for Henry's speech on St. Crispin's day, nor for the epitaph at Thermopylae. The history they taught him had had few battles in it. ..." And Captain Ryder hoped to find "that low door in the wall ... which opened on an enclosed and enchanted garden, which was somewhere, not overlooked by any window, in the heart of that grey city." This persistence and intensity of youthful romanticism are remarkable; so also is the fierce conviction that the romantic dream is directly menaced by some element in modernity. Tony Last's Gothic forest is withered by the cynicism of smart and up-to-date people in London; Captain Ryder's enchanted garden is crushed by the mechanized Hooper.

Closely allied with this romanticism is a nostalgia for the period of early youth. Tony Last is an adult, but his bedroom "formed a gallery representative of every phase of his adolescence – the

The Pieties of Evelyn Waugh

framed picture of a dreadnought (a coloured supplement from *Chums*), all guns spouting flame and smoke; a photographic group of his private school; a cabinet called 'the Museum' filled with the fruits of a dozen desultory hobbies." The only card game he can play is "animal snap," a bout of which is made to occupy him during an evening of agony and suspense. Captain Ryder, during part of his undergraduate life with the beautiful and charming Sebastian Flyte, felt that he was "given a brief spell of what I had never known, a happy childhood, and though its toys were silk shirts and liqueurs and cigars, and its naughtiness high in the catalogue of grave sins, there was something of nursery freshness about us that fell little short of the joy of innocence." And amid all this he is conscious of "homesickness for nursery morality." Sebastian himself is described as being "in love with his own childhood." He carries with him everywhere a teddy-bear called Aloysius, which he occasionally threatens to spank. Mr. Waugh's preoccupation with youth even permeates his more or less cynical comic novels (*Decline and Fall*, *Vile Bodies*, et cetera). There is no display of emotion in these, nor much analysis of states of mind, but sophisticated young people play "Happy Families" (*Black Mischief*) and a Communist journalist concentrates on working a toy train (*Scoop*). More important is the schoolboy delight in cruelty which marks the earlier books especially, and gives an almost hysterical tempo to their farce. One of the funniest scenes in *Decline and Fall* deals with the brutal murder of an inoffensive old prison chaplain. The convicts, in chapel, take advantage of the hymn-singing to pass on the news:

> *Old Prendy went to see a chap*
> *What said he'd seen a ghost*
> *Well he was dippy and he'd got*
> *A mallet and a saw.*
>
> *Who let the madman have the things?*
> *The Governor; who d'you think?*
> *He asked to be a carpenter,*
> *He sawed off Prendy's head.*

. . .

*Time like an ever-rolling stream
Bears all its sons away
Poor Prendy 'ollered fit to kill
For nearly 'alf an hour.*

Vile Bodies is rich in unregarded death: a drunken young woman kills herself by swinging out of a chandelier; a titled gossip writer puts his head in the gas oven; a Bright Young Thing expires after a lively party in the room in the nursing home where she is recovering after a car accident. The comedy of *Black Mischief* is ingeniously designed to lead up to a gruesome piece of cannibalism ("You're a grand girl, Prudence, and I'd like to eat you." "So you shall, my sweet, anything you want." And, as a result of later accidents, he does).

"In laughter," according to Bergson, "we always find an unavowed intention to humiliate and consequently to correct, our neighbour." One of the secrets of Mr. Waugh's comic genius is his keen interest in humiliation. Basil Seal, the adventurer-hero ("insolent, sulky, and curiously childish") of *Black Mischief* and *Put Out More Flags*, "rejoiced always," we are told, "in the spectacle of women at a disadvantage." Mr. Waugh is a great exploiter of human disadvantages, and his unscrupulous adolescent cruelty in this is the common quality of his two most obvious characteristics; his humour and his snobbery. Two of his comic novels, *Black Mischief* and *Scoop*, are based largely on a sly appeal to the white man's sense of racial superiority; much of the best fun in *Decline and Fall* comes from the exploitation of the manners of Captain Grimes, who, although he claimed to be a public-school man, was not really a gentleman and did not often have a bath; in *Put Out More Flags* the purest comedy lies in lurid descriptions of the appearance and behaviour of three proletarian evacuee children. Examples of his deft use of the snob-joke could be multiplied almost indefinitely. It can be said indeed that if he were not a snob, if he were not the type of man who refers frequently to "the lower orders" (as he does in *Labels*) and objects to the presence of natives in first-class railway carriages (as he does in *Waugh in Abyssinia*), he could not have written such

The Pieties of Evelyn Waugh 113

funny books. This is an unpleasant fact; it means that the countless liberal, progressive people who have laughed over these books unconsciously share these prejudices. Mr. Edmund Wilson, in *The New Yorker*, condemned the snobbery of *Brideshead Revisited*, but he had swallowed with delight the snobbery implicit in the earlier novels, from *Decline and Fall* to *Scoop*. Snobbery was quite acceptable as an attitude: the critic objected only when it was formulated as a doctrine.

It is true that in his later books Mr. Waugh's snobbery has taken on a different emphasis. As he becomes more serious, his veneration for the upper classes becomes more marked than his contempt for his social inferiors. This almost mystical veneration, entirely free from any taint of morality, may be discerned in a slightly burlesque form in his early books. Paul Pennyfeather, the drab hero of *Decline and Fall*, was cast into prison through the fault of the woman he loved, Mrs. Beste-Chetwynde, the rich, beautiful, and aristocratic white-slave trader. He forgave her, however, because he believed "that there was in fact, and should be, one law for her and another for himself, and that the naïve little exertions of nineteenth-century Radicals were essentially base and trivial and misdirected." *Decline and Fall* was, of course, published before Mr. Waugh's conversion to Catholicism, which took place in 1930; no doubt he would not now express his thought in the same way. But his almost idolatrous reverence for birth and wealth has not been destroyed by the Catholic faith; on the contrary *Brideshead Revisited* breathes from beginning to end a loving patience with mortal sin among the aristocracy and an un-Christian petulance towards the minor foibles of the middle class.

As might be expected, Mr. Waugh's political outlook is the expression of his social prejudices. In the introduction to his book on Mexico, *Robbery under Law*, he has set out his political creed in general terms: "I believe that man is by nature an exile and will never be self-sufficient or complete upon this earth ... men naturally arrange themselves into a system of classes ... war and conquest are inevitable." From these pessimistic premises he has drawn important practical conclusions: the propriety of strikebreaking, the justice of Mussolini's conquest of Abyssinia. As the title of his Mexican work indicates, his quarrel with the Mexican government concerned not so much their acquiescence in the persecution of the Church, as their encroachment on British oil interests. Taking Abyssinia from its Emperor is "inevitable" but taking Mexican oil from British investors is plain robbery. So phrased, the argument appears dishonest, but Mr. Waugh's sincerity is beyond all doubt. Indeed his conservatism is so intensely emotional that he is a sort of Jacobite by anticipation. In his imagination the class he loves is already oppressed; the King has taken to the hills. Already in *Decline and Fall* Lady Circumference and her friends were "feeling the wind a bit"; in *Vile Bodies*, the Bright Young People gad around gallantly, touched by the fever of impending doom, to be blasted in the final prophetic chapter by war and inflation. In *Black Mischief*, Basil's friends are impoverished by the Depression and in the later works the shadow deepens (brightened by the brief rally of the "Churchillian renaissance," 1940–41[1]) into the midnight of *Brideshead Revisited*. "These men," reflects Captain Ryder, contemplating the fate of some relatives of Lady Marchmain's, "must die to make a world for Hooper; they were the aborigines, vermin by right of law, to be shot off at leisure so that things might be safe for the travelling salesman with his polygonal pince-nez, his fat wet handshake, his grinning dentures." The Prison Governor in *Decline and Fall*, whose ideas on occupational therapy had such unfortunate consequences for the Chaplain, is, in Mr. Waugh's eyes, the typical reformer. He turns the full battery of his satirical power against "progressive" thinkers and workers, for he sees them as working to hand over power to a slavering mob of criminals, communists, and commercial travellers.

An interesting sidelight on all this is shed by the autobiography of his father, Arthur Waugh (*One Man's Road*, 1931). Mr. Waugh senior, a well-to-do publisher, recounts that Evelyn, as a little boy, "arranged theatricals in the nursery" and "marshalled a

[1] This is the period reflected in *Put Out More Flags*. A review of that novel in *Partisan Review* (Summer 1943) gave an interesting survey of Mr. Waugh's political development, but exaggerated its symptomatic importance for England.

The Pieties of Evelyn Waugh 115

'pistol troop' for the defence of England against Germans and Jews."[1] He edited a magazine about this troop, and his fond father was able to have it bound for him "in full morocco." *One Man's Road* also contains a photograph of the house in Hampstead in which Evelyn was reared, with the legend printed beneath: "No doubt it was never anything more than an ordinary suburban villa. But it was a great deal more to me."

The Gothic dream, nostalgia for childhood, snobbery, neo-Jacobitism – this whole complex of longings, fears, and prejudices, "wistful, half-romantic, half-aesthetic," to use a phrase of Mr. Waugh's – must be taken into account in approaching the question of Mr. Waugh's Catholicism. In Catholic countries Catholicism is not invariably associated with big houses, or the fate of an aristocracy. The Bordeaux of M. Mauriac and the Cork of Mr. Frank O'Connor are not Gothic cities or objects of wistfulness. But the Catholicism of Mr. Waugh, and of certain other writers, is hardly separable from a personal romanticism and a class loyalty. Is Lord Marchmain's soul more valuable than Hooper's? To say in so many words that it was would be heresy, but *Brideshead Revisited* almost seems to imply that the wretched Hooper had no soul at all, certainly nothing to compare with the genuine old landed article. And *Brideshead Revisited* is the most Catholic of Mr. Waugh's novels. His religion, even before his conversion, abounded in consolation for the rich. That obliging and ubiquitous priest, Father Rothschild, S.J. (of *Vile Bodies*), refuses to censure the goings on of the Bright Young People: "... it seems to me that they are all possessed with an almost fatal hunger for permanence. I think all these divorces show that. People aren't content just to muddle along nowadays.... And this word 'bogus' they all use...." The paradoxes of the wealthy Jesuit are not perhaps intended to be taken very seriously, but the same sort of spiritual consolation, this time with no perceptible trace of irony, may be derived from *Brideshead Revisited*. Lady Marchmain confesses that once she thought it wrong "to have so many beautiful things when others had nothing," but she

[1] He also "placarded Boscastle harbour with home-made labels championing 'Votes for Women.' " This is less easy to reconcile with his later activities.

overcame these scruples, saying: "The poor have always been the favourites of God and his saints, but I believe that it is one of the special achievements of Grace to sanctify the whole of life, riches included." In Mr. Waugh's theology, the love of money is not only not the root of all evil, it is a preliminary form of the love of God.

After the publication of *Brideshead Revisited* in America, a certain Mr. McClose, of Alexandria (Va.), wrote a postcard to Mr. Waugh, saying: "Your *Brideshead Revisited* is a strange way to show that Catholicism is an answer to anything. Seems more like the kiss of Death to me." Mr. Waugh in an article in *Life* (8 April 1946) dismissed this criticism with a sneer about halitosis. And yet it is much more to the point than are *The Tablet's* eulogies. The deathbed conversion of Lord Marchmain is the decisive crisis of the book; the death of an upper class and the death of all earthly hope are two of its principal themes. The lovers are forced apart by a sense of sin; the house is deserted; the family scattered; the only child that is born is dead. Mr. Waugh's political forebodings and the form of his private myths (of which a sense of exile is the main constituent) make his Catholicism something that is, in earthly affairs, dark and defeatist, alien to the bright aggressive Catholicism of the New World, as well as to the workaday faith of the old Catholic countries. Out of all the tragedy, and justifying it, one good is seen emerging – the conversion of the narrator. In Brideshead chapel he has seen "a beaten copper lamp of deplorable design relit before the beaten doors of a tabernacle," and he rejoices; but when he leaves the chapel, he leaves it empty of worshippers.

This rearguard Catholicism is not indeed "an answer to anything," nor is it intended to be, any more than Tony Last's Gothic city or Proust's rediscovered time is an answer to anything. The funeral is strictly private, and salvation also. There was once an Irish priest who refused to pray for the conversion of England, and Mr. Waugh, I fear, might refuse to pray for the conversion of Hooper.

And just as snobbery and adolescent cruelty gave edge and tension to his early work, so now the intense romantic and exclusive piety of his maturer years gives him strength and eloquence.

The Pieties of Evelyn Waugh

The clear focusing of remembered detail, the loving reconstructions of youth, and the great extension of metaphor in *Brideshead Revisited* all recall Proust more than any living writer, and the texture of Mr. Waugh's writing is both finer and stronger than is usual in Proust.[1] Mr. Waugh has evidently read some Proust – indeed in *A Handful of Dust* he twice pays him the tribute of mis-quotation – and there are passages in *Brideshead Revisited*, notably the opening of Book Two, that seem to paraphrase parts of *Remembrance of Things Past*. "My theme is memory," says Mr. Waugh, "that winged host that soared about me one grey morning of war-time. These memories which are my life – for we possess nothing certainly except the past – were always with me. Like the pigeons of St. Mark's, they were everywhere, under my feet singly, in pairs." He continues in this strain for much longer than I can quote, and we recall Proust, whose theme was the same, whose metaphors equally exuberant, and who developed his theme from a recollection of feeling, under his feet, two uneven paving-stones in the baptistry of St. Mark's.

The resemblance is neither accidental nor merely superficial and it has nothing to do with plagiarism. The outward lives of the two men are very different – one can hardly imagine Proust in the Commandos – but their mental worlds are, up to a point, surprisingly similar. Proust was tenacious of childhood, with a feverishly romantic mind capable of turning a common seaside town into an enchanted city. This romantic sensitivity to names, and perhaps also his social position (he belonged, like Mr. Waugh, to the upper middle class), led him to a veneration for the aristocracy. For him the name of the Duchess of Guermantes could evoke the Patriarchs and Judges on the windows of the cathedral of Laon, as well as the ancient forest in which Childebert went hunting, and it was in pursuit of these things that he entered the salons of the Faubourg St. Germain. There he acquired a sense of social distinction as marked as Mr. Waugh's, and much more delicate. So far the resemblance is striking, but there it ends. Proust never raised a political or religious superstructure

[1] This is not to imply that *Brideshead Revisited*, as a totality, comes within measurable distance of Proust's achievement in *Remembrance of Things Past*.

on these foundations. Once he remembers wondering, in a fashionable restaurant, "whether the glass aquarium would always continue to protect the banquet of the marvellous beasts," but he does not make an issue out of it. He shows Parisian society decaying and breaking up under the pressure of the war, but he writes as a spectator, even as a connoisseur, not as a partisan. More than this, his mind is able at last to disentangle the Duchess of Guermantes from Childebert's forest, and to regard fashionable snobberies as not different in kind from disputes on precedence among greengrocers' wives. Mr. Waugh has not yet taken this decisive step. And Proust's religious experience, if we may call it so, is confined to the discrepancies of mortal life in time. He never took Mr. Waugh's decisive step, from romanticism to the acceptance of dogma.

The difference between the two men may in part be explained by their historical setting. Proust lived and wrote at a time when the upper classes were menaced, but not severely damaged. They had suffered an infusion from the classes below, but their money was still safe enough. It was easy for Proust – especially as his health was bad – to feel that "society" would last his time. As he had no children and did not believe in immortality, he did not have to worry about what happened after that. He could therefore cultivate an easy and speculative detachment. In our time, however, the upper classes, even in England, are not merely menaced; they have been gravely damaged. They feel not merely frustrated or irritated but actually oppressed by the high level of modern taxation and they see their equals levelled all over Europe. Proustian detachment and sense of nuance tend to perish in this atmosphere, and the wistful romantic easily develops, as Mr. Waugh has done, into embattled Jacobite.

It would, however, be a simplification to insist too much on the direct influence of economic history. Even if the two men had been born contemporaries, their evolution would have differed widely because of the great difference in the manners of their education. The efforts of Proust's parents to "harden" him were neither consistent nor successful, and no one else seems to have made the attempt at all. This easy upbringing did not produce an ideal citizen or soldier, but it did ensure a continuity of emotional life, with, in this case, a certain lucidity and calm. The young Waugh, on the contrary, was subjected to the discipline of an English public school, and a religious one at that. Captain Ryder speaks sadly of "the hard bachelordom of English adolescence, the premature dignity and authority of the school system." Mr. Waugh endured these things and emerged an English gentleman, with slight symptoms of hysteria. Cream and dappled unicorns clearly have no place at a public school, and an inner life that includes such creatures will feel itself menaced. If it does not die, it will take on a new intensity, becoming a fixed intolerant mythology. Such is Mr. Waugh's private religion, on which he has superimposed Catholicism, much as newly converted pagans are said to superimpose a Christian nomenclature on their ancient cults of trees and thunder.

The hero of *Scott-King's Modern Europe*, the first of the satires which Mr. Waugh has published since *Brideshead Revisited*, "found a peculiar relish in contemplating the victories of barbarism", and so, undoubtedly, does his creator. Both *Scott-King* and its successor, *The Loved One*, contemplate, not without relish, aspects of victorious barbarism, the first in Europe, the second in America. The relish in both cases is satirical: the bitter delight of the aristocrat who finds the rabble living down to his worst expectations.

The European satire is much the less successful of the two. It is set in a *lieu vague*, Neutralia, which might be Spain without the clergy or Yugoslavia without the Communist party. The idea behind this is presumably that of the uniformity of modern totalitarianism, the two-aspects-of-the-same-bestial-visage theory of Miss Odette Keun. Unfortunately the visages of Communism and Francoism, bestial though they be, are quite separate and sharply distinct, so that a satire assuming the identity of the two degenerates easily into querulous confusion. The troubles of Scott-King, a middle-aged classics teacher who accepts an invitation to take part in cultural celebrations in Neutralia, are as many as those of Candide but neither so terrible nor treated so lightly.

He becomes involved in the insolence and delays of air travel; the grandeurs and miseries of totalitarian entertainment; obstruction by a Second Secretary at the British Embassy, who wears pencils in his breastpocket and behaves like "a clerk in the food-office"; finally the black underground, and return via illegal immigrant ship. After undergoing these scourges of modernity he goes back to teach the classics, refusing to take up any more practical subject, on the ground that "it would be very wicked indeed to do anything to fit a boy for the modern world." This tale has its amusing moments, but it fails; indignation is diffused over miscellaneous objects, some of them more worthy of the attention of the club bore than of the satirist; the style itself, still touched by the elegiac afflatus of *Brideshead*, is blown about at times between the pompous and the mock-heroic: "To even the Comic Muse, the gadabout, the adventurous one of those heavenly sisters, to whom so little that is human comes amiss, who can mix in almost any company and find a welcome at almost every door – even to her there are forbidden places."

The Loved One, which immediately followed *Scott-King*, throws such prudery to the winds and invades forbidden places – the mortuary and the cemetery – in a spirit of atrocious levity. This time the satire is precisely aimed – through the great burial place of Southern California, Forest Lawn Memorial Park – at the materialist civilization of America. When he visited Hollywood, Mr. Waugh was powerfully impressed by Forest Lawn. In what is possibly the only article ever to have appeared both in *Life* and in *The Tablet*, he gave a factual account of that incredible necropolis, with its zones (Slumberland, Inspiration, Hope, Babyland), its concealed radios giving out popular songs, its mausoleum, columbarium, and non-sectarian churches, and its slumber-rooms, decorated in satin, where the newly dead, in new suits and with elaborately painted faces, await burial. He showed, with quotations and illustrations, how Forest Lawn substitutes for the old morbid conceptions of death its own sunny eschatology which guarantees eternal bliss for all clients (Negroes and Chinese excluded) and inspires 300 smiling acres studded with curvilinear statuary. Not content, however, with mere description, he set

The Pieties of Evelyn Waugh 121

himself to capture "the Spirit of Forest Lawn" – a deity often invoked by the proprietors of the cemetery – in a short novel entirely devoted to funereal affairs. Dennis Barlow, the hero of *The Loved One*, is an unsuccessful young film writer who gets a job in a pets' cemetery, "The Happier Hunting Ground," and falls in love with a mortuary cosmetician, Aimée Thanatogenos, who works in "Whispering Glades" (Forest Lawn). In his wooing of Aimée, Dennis becomes the rival of the senior mortician of Whispering Glades, a Mr. Joyboy. This gentleman, who regards the profession of embalming as a high and solemn vocation, conducts his courtship in terms of his work. His is the science of adjusting the expression of corpses, with the aid of little pieces of cardboard and according to such categories as "serene and philosophical," "radiant childhood," "judicial and determined," and, as a lover, he turns his skill to good account on the dead that go to the cosmetic room:

> Of recent weeks the expressions that greeted Aimée from the trolley had waxed from serenity to jubilance. Other girls had to work on faces that were stern or resigned or plumb vacant; there was always a nice bright smile for Aimée.

Love among the slabs and kidney bowls moves its predestined course to a grotesque catastrophe. Aimée, torn by the contradictions of the mortician's code, kills herself and her body is disposed of, to avoid scandal, in the incinerator at the pets' cemetery. Dennis makes an entry in the register of that institution, so that in accordance with a custom whereby the owners of deceased pets are annually consoled, "tomorrow and on every anniversary as long as The Happier Hunting Ground existed a postcard would go to Mr. Joyboy: '*Your little Aimée is wagging her tail in heaven tonight, thinking of you.*' "

And Dennis leaves sunny California to return to his "ancient and comfortless shore."

In its calculated outrageousness *The Loved One* is one of the most effective stories Mr. Waugh has ever written. Sober and economical in language, neat and coherent in structure, it makes every blow tell, both on the reader's nerves and on the civilization it condemns. A lesser artist might have found Forest Lawn pathetic, worthy of no more than a passing and fastidious remark – such as Mr. Aldous Huxley's refined treatment of it in *After Many a Summer*. Mr. Waugh's is neither compassionate nor refined. The central jest of *The Loved One* is cruel, the story itself is cruel and abounds in cruel embellishments, variations, and subordinate episodes, from the scene near the beginning dealing with the humiliation, suicide, and embalming of an elderly film writer to the final humiliation, suicide, and incineration of the hero's fiancée. Beneath the unemotional language and casual timing which give the twist of wit to these horrible events there is a perceptible undercurrent of sheer delight. It is this delight – Mr. Waugh himself speaks of "over-excitement with the scene" – that makes the pages of *The Loved One*, in contrast with *Scott-King*, so electrically alive.

Delight in what? There is no simple answer to this. It is partly the professional satisfaction of the satirist in range of a colossal target, partly a reactionary rejoicing in the imbecilities of modernity. At a rather deeper level it is that delight in cruelty for its own sake which has always been a mark of Mr. Waugh's best work; the incineration of Aimée Thanatogenos is a brutal variant on the scene in *Black Mischief* where Basil Seal eats his fiancée. More important than these sources of excitement, though mingling with them, is a complex feeling that might crudely be described as a natural affinity with lunatics. The hero falls in love with Aimée because of the "rich glint of lunacy" in her eyes. He almost falls in love with Forest Lawn for the same reasons: "Whispering Glades held him in thrall.... In a zone of insecurity in the mind where none but the artist dare trespass, the tribes were mustering. Dennis the frontierman could read the signs."

The tribes ... the frontier.... We are brought back to the picture of that interior nostalgic castle holding out against the barbarians. These sharp divisions and dramatic pictures belong to a youthful imagination which Mr. Waugh has jealously and vividly retained, and which is the true key to his work. Inwardly the sensitive adolescent with his Gothic dream, to be guarded from his brutal companions; outwardly the rowdy schoolboy,

The Pieties of Evelyn Waugh 123

organizer of cruel pranks, picturesque adventurer. The first of these personalities is dominant in *A Handful of Dust* and *Brideshead Revisited*: it inspires also, less happily, *Helena*, a shapeless and sentimental piece of historical fiction about the piety of a British lady in the age of Constantine, epoch of the conversion of the upper class. The second, the personality of Basil Seal, rules over all the earlier novels and now reappears in *The Loved One*. In so grotesque a setting and in the safety of satire, the great Catholic writer, who also happens to be a beleaguered Jacobite, can let his natural irresponsibility have free rein. The result is a foray disciplined in its tactics but anarchic in its aim; the sack not merely of Forest Lawn, but of adult dignity.

So fantastic a mind is hardly qualified to make great contributions to Christian thought, or to render balanced judgment on the political issues of the day. It is, however, pre-eminently well equipped for artistic creation. An indomitably childish imagination, which refuses equally the sway of modernity and of middle age, is Mr. Waugh's incalculable force.

VI
CHARLES PÉGUY

Charles Péguy (1873–1914) wrote a number of long religious poems between his conversion in 1908 and his death in action in 1914. The first three of these, *Le Mystère de la charité de Jeanne d'Arc* (1910), *Le Porche du mystére de la deuxième vertu* (1911), and *Le Mystère des Saints Innocents* (1912), are loosely linked. *La Tapisserie de Sainte Geneviève* (1913), *La Tapisserie de Notre Dame* (1913), and *Eve* (1913) are independent, although the Joan of Arc theme runs through the first and third. His tripartite tragedy, *Jeanne d'Arc* (1897), although largely in prose, is usually classed with his poetry and is included in the complete edition of his poetical works (*Bibliothèque de la Pléiade*, 1948). His other prose works, not considered here, consist of many enormous tracts and polemics. There are several full-length studies of him, including a sympathetic and scrupulous one by his contemporary, Romain Rolland (*Péguy*, 1944).

THE TEMPLE OF MEMORY: PÉGUY

*Les jours sont des Sporades et la nuit est la pleine mer
Où naviguait saint Paul.*
PÉGUY, *Le Porche du mystère de la
deuxième vertu.*

As children we instinctively apprehend darkness not as an absence of light but as a positive element like air or water, only more far-reaching, dangerous, and unknown. Above the crowded lamp-lit streets the night is without end in space, just as to one whom a nightmare jolts out of sleep the dark hours seem stronger than time. Sleep itself, the conquest of the mind by night, gives us in dreams the kinds of freedom which we later use to fill out the names of eternity and infinity. A sound or a light moving on the edge of the part of darkness of which we are conscious – a head lamp or the distant shunting of a train – takes on an urgent significance that just eludes us. Then, when we are first at night upon the seashore or on a height within sound of the seas, we catch the glimpse again: and again, with delight, as if approaching in:

*Magic casements opening on the foam
Of perilous seas in faëry lands forlorn.*

From that border of the dark, marked with such signs, most men retreat all their lives until they find it again at last on the far side. A few only, poets or adventurers, spend their lives along the border, following it through many different territories and still always through landscape of the same character, between childhood and night. That nocturnal world with its terror and its aggression, its beauty and mystery and cruelty and its profound unreason, has also been the object of planned research by explorers based securely on the daylight world. Among these, in whom the rational faculty was dominant, was Freud, and we might also, not without temerity, class Joyce among them. Only a buffoon would affect to dismiss, or to have exhausted, the results of such explorations as these. Yet the territory is not yet so fully mapped or its resources so thoroughly known that we can afford to neglect or to sum up too schematically the accounts of those irrational, violent, and prejudiced people who live there. Of these accounts one of the most interesting and voluminous is contained in the poetry of Charles Péguy.

The difference between those writers who explore the unconscious and those who, like Péguy, live in it is revealed to some extent by different means of using words. The explorers use words as a means of approach and communication, each word (whether of scientific nomenclature or of telescoped association) lying as close as possible to a supposed meaning. They thus show their confidence in the human will and comprehension, the power of speech, and the rational faculties generally. Péguy, on the other hand, writes as if each individual word were so shifting and unreliable and in general of such little account that it had to be followed up by waves of other words to the same general effect.[1] The *mot juste*, he seems to say, is a will o' the wisp of pedants; truth is so far beyond words that one can only let the words follow it in a great mass as the tide follows the moon. At most one can point it out as one points out a star to a child, with repetitions, gestures, shiftings of ground, exclamations, and random references to well-known landmarks; or one can induce a state of mind accessible to truth by hypnotic repetition as in a lullaby or a litany. When rhyme is used, it must be used to exhaustion; not alone must all conceivable words ending in a given syllable be pressed, like monsters in a cathedral, into reiterating the same truth, but if the rhymed conjunction of any two words is found especially affecting, it may be repeated almost indefinitely. Thus, in *Eve*, his last work, there is, as part of a vast litany, which is in itself only a small part of that extraordinary poem, a series of forty-nine quatrains each of which begins:

Il allait hériter des listes cadastrales

[1] The comparison is not between a supposed "prosaic" use of words and a supposed "poetic" use. Poets are probably more likely than anyone else to use words in an exacting and "exploratory" fashion.

and the final rhyme in each is *cathédrales*. Throughout this poem quatrains differing often by no more than a single word, and that of no special significance, quatrains that any normal writer would have regarded as alternative, succeed each other at fantastic and often intolerable length. Reading some of the sequences, one might imagine that the poet was trying to recapture a grace obtained fortuitously. Such an idea suggests itself immediately when in the unfinished poem called *Suite d'Eve*, in a sequence on the change in the world after the birth of Christ, the following stanza occurs:

> *Dans le même printemps c'est une autre hirondelle*
> *Sur les mêmes chevaux d'autres chevaliers.*
> *Dans les mêmes bateaux d'autres bacheliers.*
> *Dans le même tourment une amour plus fidèle.*

and is immediately followed by forty-eight stanzas on the same plan, containing such variations as,

> *Sur les mêmes chameaux un autre chemelier*

and

> *Et dans la même Auvergne un autre Puy de Dôme.*

But there is really nothing to show that Péguy was conscious of any unusual degree of felicity in the stanza quoted – it is not the first of the sequence – and it is much more probable that the long catalogue, with its mixture of the lyric and the grotesque, is there for its own sake, because the poet wished to insist, to hold the attention fixed on the one subject. The theme – the fact of the change, not its nature or effects – was far too great to be dealt with by a few words, however beautiful, so he holds to it by prolonged enumeration around the incessantly repeated words "the same" – "another." Where the thing, apprehended or pursued, is outside time or dominates it, the poem endeavours to transcend time or at least to ignore it. It is in the earlier poems, however, that this technique is most obviously effective. So in *Le Mystère de la charité de Jeanne d'Arc* the nun Mme Gervaise, reciting to Joan the story of the life of Jesus, proceeds by catalogue and repetition, but with tact:

> *Il était généralement aimé.*
> *Tout le monde l'aimait bien.*
> *Jusqu'au jour où il avait commencé sa mission.*
> *Les camarades, les amis, les compagnons, les autorités,*
> *Les citoyens,*
> *Les père et mère*
> *Trouvaient cela très bien.*
> *Jusqu'au jour où il avait commencé sa mission.*
> *Les camarades trouvaient qu'il était un bon camarade.*
> *Les amis un bon ami.*
> *Les compagnons un bon compagnon.*
> *Pas fier.*
> *Les citoyens trouvaient qu'il était un bon citoyen.*
> *Les égaux un bon égal.*
> *Jusqu'au jour où il avait commencé sa mission.*

The enumeration, simple, colloquial, almost gay, with its sense of pleasant, humdrum, everyday life, is increasingly overshadowed by the cumulative and supernatural message of the repeated line. But when Mme Gervaise, striving to convince Joan of the completeness of Divine justice and to reconcile in her mind the idea of damnation with that of infinite mercy, is at the climax in her story, which is the cry of Jesus on the cross, the repetition is weighty and prolonged in sound, marking the prolongation of the cry itself:

> *Clameur qui sonne encore en toute humanité;*
> *Clameur dont chancela l'Eglise militante;*
> *Où la souffrante aussi connut son propre effroi;*
> *Par qui la triomphante éprouva son triomphe;*
> *Clameur qui sonne au cœur de toute humanité;*
> *Clameur qui sonne au cœur de toute chrétienté;*
> *O clameur culminante, éternelle et valable.*

Repetition and enumeration are common oratorical devices, and Péguy does indeed employ them in his polemical prose works just as much as in his verse. In parts of his vast diatribes the reader's only guiding thread is in a single sentence, repeated at

The Temple of Memory: Péguy   131

intervals of a page or so, just as lines like "La colère des imbéciles remplit le monde" return in *Les Grands Cimetières sous la lune* of Bernanos, Péguy's spiritual heir. Yet it is impossible to dismiss Péguy as no more than a rhetorician. The rhetorician, like the scientist, uses words as tools, consciously and confidently, differing from the scientist only in that he aims to communicate not knowledge but a single emotion, which he does not necessarily feel himself. Péguy has certainly his merely rhetorical moments, but at his best he is preoccupied with a vision and allows the words suggested by the vision to express it as best they can. His emotions are not simple and in so far as he aims at communicating anything, it is not his emotions or even his vision but the capacity of sharing a view of life which is related to them in a complex fashion. We shall try to explore that relationship by following up to the point of intersection the lines of the main ideas that connect and characterize his poetry.

2.

The first idea, which is the point of departure and in a sense also the pulse of the whole work, is the idea of suffering. The first *Jeanne d'Arc*, written before Péguy's conversion, begins and ends in pain, both natural and supernatural. In the opening scene Joan speaks to her friend Hauviette of two hungry children, orphans of the war, whom she had fed and who had gone off again "on the hungry road." From contemplation of the suffering caused by the war she is led not only to desire her own death – "O que vienne au plus tôt, mon Dieu, ma mort humaine" – but to offer her own soul for the salvation of the damned:

O s'il faut pour sauver de la flamme éternelle
Les corps des morts damnés s'affolant de souffrance,
Abandonner mon corps à la flamme éternelle,
Mon Dieu, donnez mon corps à la flamme éternelle.

Her adviser, the nun Mme Gervaise, tells her that this is a blasphemous excess but that she can and should suffer as much as possible for others here on earth: "nous devons tâcher de toutes nos forces humaines à souffrir du mieux que nous pouvons et jusqu'à la souffrance extrême sans nous tuer jamais, tout ce que nous pouvons de la souffrance humaine." Nonetheless Joan still stands undecided between the contemplation of temporal suffering, with the possibility of action, and the paralysing idea of eternal suffering: "quand je pense qu'à présent que je vous parle toutes mes paroles vous trouvent occupé à damner des âmes, pardonnez-moi, mon Dieu, si je dis un blasphème; quand je pense à cela, je ne peux plus prier." Only when God grants her a sign, answering her long-repeated prayer by the news that the English have raised the siege of Mont-Saint-Michel, does she accept and take the road of history. In the next section of the tragedy, *Les Batailles*, we are made aware that her progress is a progress in awareness of suffering and in suffering itself. From the foul insults directed at her by the English in the hour of her glory, through the ignorant brutality of her own soldiers and the Satanic cruelty of a companion-in-arms (Gilles de Rais, the prototype of Bluebeard), she moves to the treachery of her master and her own defeat and capture. In the third part, *Rouen*, we are spared nothing, not even the conversation of the mechanics employed for the torture, not even a last sermon preached to fill Joan with the fear of hell. She who was shown in the beginning as almost in despair at the mere thought of the existence of hell must now face not only the probability of hell for herself but also the responsibility for having damned others:

> *Faut-il que je m'en aille aux batailles damnées,*
> *Avec mes soldats morts, morts et damnés par moi,*
> *Faut-il que je m'en aille aux batailles d'en bas?*

The idea of damnation, the perpetuation of human suffering, which at the beginning and end of *Jeanne d'Arc* forms a perspective of the Hundred Years War extending into eternity, was for the youthful and compassionate Péguy the great obstacle to belief. "There must," he wrote this time in one of his prose tracts, "be some horrible complicity at the back of the Christian mind, some hideous desire to connive at disease and death."[1] Did he,

[1] Quoted in Rolland's *Péguy*. A character quoted in the same tract advances another reason for not believing in Christianity – "that it is not true."

The Temple of Memory: Péguy 133

when he finally entered the Church, become persuaded that these words were altogether untrue? Or did he continue to believe in a complicity with suffering while finding this complicity no longer horrible but perhaps even beautiful? Was the idea of hell, at first a barrier, finally the gateway by which Péguy entered the Church? All we can say definitely is that to the end he remained a poet of suffering and that it was in suffering he felt most joined to the Church, as if his communion were more with the souls in purgatory than with the Church militant on earth. Few poets, even Christian poets, can have laid such stress on pain or have accepted it with such ardour, as of free choice. He not only felt that man on earth was by nature inevitably unhappy but he discerned in himself a natural vocation to suffering. When in the *Prière de confidence*, which he made at the time of his pilgrimage to Chartres (1913), he speaks of his great temptation, it is in these words that he explains his resistance and his renunciation:

> *Et non point par vertu car nous n'en avons guère,*
> *Et non point par devoir car nous ne l'aimons pas,*
> *Mais comme un charpentier s'arme de son compas,*
> *Par besoin de nous mettre au centre de misère,*
>
> *Et pour bien nous placer dans l'axe de détresse,*
> *Et par ce besoin sourd d'être plus malheureux,*
> *Et d'aller au plus dur et de souffrir plus creux,*
> *Et de prendre le mal dans sa pleine justesse.*

3.

We know that this "implacable need to be more unhappy" did not lead Péguy into despair or into a form of stoicism, but on the contrary brought him into a religion of hope – and that it was hope rather than faith or charity which he most celebrated in the Christian religion. The need to suffer and the need to hope together formed the basis of his Catholicism. And, as the way of conversion for each individual is different, so both his "suffering" and his "hope" were somewhat different from what Christians normally understand by these ideas. The orthodox believe in mortification of the flesh, not for its own sake but as a way to true happiness; the attitude of Péguy, who loved unhappiness for its own sake, was no doubt not heretical (for heresy is not a matter of the emotions), but it is peculiar, and perhaps more likely to be regarded as a peculiar sin than as a peculiar form of sanctity.[1] The lineaments under which he envisages the virtue of "hope" seem at first less peculiar and personal, but they are, as we shall see, intimately connected with his conception of suffering.

The starting point of hope for Péguy is the point of greatest suffering and despair: the cry of Christ on the cross, "My God, my God, why hast thou forsaken me?" In both the first *Jeanne d'Arc* and the later *Le Mystère de la charité de Jeanne d'Arc*, the nun Mme Gervaise refers to these words in her attempt to lift Joan from her state of despair concerning the damned. Christ's sufferings, she explains, did not avail to save the damned, and it was his despair – Péguy uses the word – at this which made him cry out on the cross:

> *C'est que le Fils de Dieu savait que la souffrance*
> *Du fils de l'homme est vaine à sauver les damnés,*
> *Et s'affolant plus qu'eux de la désespérance,*
> *Jésus mourant pleura sur les abandonnés.*

Because of the suffering, knowledge, and despair of Christ Himself over the damned, it is vain for Christians to trouble themselves with this question: why try to save better than the Saviour? It is enough to follow, to listen, to imitate, and to accept the mystery.

The argument is not easy to accept and in the pre-conversion *Jeanne d'Arc*, Joan can hardly be said to accept it. She knows well, she says, that Mme Gervaise is right, that God is right, and that her complaint is evil. Yet "when I think of the damned my soul revolts," and it is not until she receives her sign, the raising of the siege of Mont-Saint-Michel, that she accepts. Thus, a uni-

---

[1] This raises another question, in itself peculiar, which I am not casuist enough to resolve: if this morbid disposition of Péguy's was sinful in itself, and if it nevertheless led him to accept Christianity, was the form of his acceptance necessarily heretical, being warped from its origin? Like many other questions which suggest themselves on the study of a Catholic writer, this goes far beyond the competence of the literary critic.

The Temple of Memory: Péguy 135

versal problem, that of reconciling the existence and punishment of evil with the idea of an omnipotent and merciful God, receives a purely historical and accidental "solution" which is satisfactory enough for dramatic purposes but otherwise irrelevant. The problem is in fact shelved, to be taken up again in *Le Mystère de la charité* and its sequel poems, *Le Porche du mystère de la deuxième vertu* and *Le Mystère des Saints Innocents*, this time to be given a generally valid answer. *Le Mystère de la charité* ends with no "sign" but with Joan still unconvinced. Then there is the direction: "Madame Gervaise had left. But she comes back before there is time to lower the curtain." She comes back to deliver the great sermon on hope which is entitled *Le Porche du mystère* and which is the beginning of the answer of the Catholic Péguy to the problem of evil:

La foi que j'aime le mieux, dit Dieu, c'est l'espérance.

Neither Joan nor Mme Gervaise is heard any longer, but only God speaking through the mouth of Mme Gervaise about the virtue of hope, its function in human life, and its allies. Hope, which is the sap of the tree, which gives life to the whole system,

Elle seule conduira les Vertus et les Mondes.

is compared, first and throughout, to a child and to childhood. She is a little girl, skipping along in the grave procession of Corpus Christi, tugging at a cord of the canopy. She is also the immortal essence of childhood and of birth itself:

Cette naissance
Perpétuelle.
Cette enfance
Perpétuelle.

This essential virtue communicates itself to adults through children. The woodcutter can stand the icy wind when he thinks of his children and what he hopes for them. The sickness of the poet's children leads him to confide them to the care of the Blessed Virgin, who is herself "all hope," and thus brings him to hope himself. God Himself knows hope through the sins and repentances of His children, as is expressed in the parables of the lost lamb and the prodigal son, parables that both reveal the hope of God and keep alive the hope of His children – in a point of pain:

> *Point de douleur, point de détresse, point d'espérance.*
> *Point douloureux, point d'inquiétude.*
> *Point de meurtrissure au cœur de l'homme.*

When all the other virtues have abandoned the sinner, hope alone remains, for it is a disguised virtue and seems to be no more than a fatuous belief that "something will turn up." This belief thrives on persistent disproof; the rain of misfortune, of the innumerable "bad days," is turned by a perpetual miracle into the living spring of hope which irrigates the fields of France in an especially abundant manner. The most effective agent in this transformation is sleep. God praises sleep and night, the reserve of hope and of being itself:

> *C'est la nuit qui est continue. C'est la nuit qui est le tissu*
> *Du temps, la réserve d'être.* ....
>
> *C'est le jour qui rompt et le jour n'ouvre là-dessus*
> *Que par de pauvres jours*
> *De souffrance. C'est le jour qui crève et les jours sont comme des*
> *îles dans la mer.*
> *Comme des îles interrompues qui interrompent la mer.*
> *Mais la mer est continue et ce sont les îles qui ont tort.* ....
> *O nuit, ma plus belle invention, ma création auguste entre toutes.*
> *Ma plus belle créature. Créature de la plus grande Espérance.*
> *Qui donnes le plus de matière à l'Espérance.*
> *Qui es l'instrument, qui es la matière même, et la résidence de*
> *l'Espérance.*

And the poem ends with the gratitude of God to night for having covered the descent from the cross and the burial of Christ.

The sequel, *Le Mystère des Saints Innocents*, which is a continuation of the monologue, takes up the same themes again, beginning with the promise of hope and of night, and of the two efforts of confidence that go with these – prayer and sleep. God does not love "the man who does not sleep," who is identified with the intellectually active:

The Temple of Memory: Péguy 137

Que sa tête surtout ne marche plus. Elle ne marche que trop, sa tête.
Et il croit que c'est du travail que sa tête marche comme ça.
Et ses pensées, non, pour ce qu'il appelle ses pensées.

Those whom he loves are the uncomplicated and virile, like those of old France, whether saints like Saint Louis or sinners like Joinville. Saint Louis would rather catch leprosy than commit a mortal sin and Joinville would rather commit thirty mortal sins than catch leprosy, but both are free men who can say what they think. It is to obtain this gratuitousness, this capacity for love, that God gave man free will and with it all the capacity for sin and suffering. Leprosy and mortal sin are necessary, for without them the charity of Saint Louis and the other virtues of man, which are necessary to the perfection of the glory of God, could not come into being. It is not for man to preoccupy himself with these problems, but to work and pray, and sleep and hope:

Que donc celui qui est né pour dormir, dorme.

And again, as a similitude of hope, the story of a lost child is told; the story of Joseph, which in the Old Testament, is, by a strange duality, both a first telling of the parable of the prodigal son and a figure of the life of Christ:

Il fallait que cela fût joué, dit Dieu. Et deux fois plutôt qu'une.
Car il y a dans l'enfant, car il y a dans l'enfance une grâce unique.

There follows once more the praise of childhood, but this time it takes a new direction, the direction of death. The words *Sinite parvulos venire ad me*, repeated in the Office of the Dead for the Burial of a Child, lead on to the Mystery of the Holy Innocents, which gives the poem its title. The 144,000 children massacred by Herod sing *quasi canticum novum* (in the words of Saint John) before the throne of God and this new hymn is the hymn of childhood:

> *C'est un cantique* nouveau *poir marquer*
> *Cette éternelle nouveauté qu'il y a dans l'enfance.*
> *Et qui est le grand secret de ma grâce.*

And the poem ends with the picture of the murdered children in Paradise playing hoops with their wreaths of martyrdom.

4.

Truth, which is of God, is not accessible to the operation of human "reasoning", which is mere folly. It can be reached only by a process of semiconscious acceptance, called "hope," which occurs when the rational intellect is in some way eclipsed. The salutary eclipse may occur in mere undevelopment, as is the case with children and with childlike people, such as medieval barons; or it may occur by sympathy with external darkness, as in sleep, or, as is common, by suffering, which distracts the intellect from its presumption. Universally it must occur in death, with images of which both the poems discussed end. Those are most happy who pass direct to death out of the semiconsciousness of childhood; the rest must use suffering and sleep as best they can, until both converge at last in death.

This is a reduction to rational language of the ideas and image-sequences that animate *Le Porche du Mystère* and *Le Mystère des Saints Innocents*. It omits nothing that is essential to the rational understanding of Péguy's "theory" of hope, but it necessarily omits all the poetry and the rhetoric, the non-logical order and the humanity of the poems themselves; it is therefore something closely related to Péguy's thought but different from it as a hydrographic chart is different from the ocean itself with its tides and currents and changing lights. The rational chart immediately suggests, and indeed seems to impose, an interpretation that does not, I think, occur to an unbiased reader of the poetry itself. That interpretation is, of course, a psychoanalytical one: "hope" is a desire to return to the womb, the experienced state of darkness and unreason. Sleep is a partial return to this state, but the waking self realizes that the original bliss, lost in the pain of birth, can be attained again only through the pain of death. "Hope" is therefore also a cult of suffering and a death-wish. It presents itself in a theological disguise in order to protect itself from the discipline of the conscious mind; it also tries by the prestige of

The Temple of Memory: Péguy 139

theological symbols to weaken and dispel the authority of consciousness.

Such an interpretation is a great deal more than plausible; it is convincing so far as it goes, for it can relate itself at every step, through an undistorted analysis, to the poetry. There would be no need in Péguy's case for the convinced disciple of Freud or Rank to strain meanings or plunge into pedantry; the rational meaning of the text itself makes his arguments for him. He could no doubt state his case much more subtly than I have done and elaborate it with triumphant references to Péguy's symbolism. None of the constantly recurring water metaphors – symbols of birth in Freud's system – would escape him and he would find even more satisfactory meaning in Péguy's other poems of the same time – the twin sonnets "L'Epave" and "L'Urne" – and the somewhat longer poem *Les Sept contre Thèbes* on the fratricidal strife of the two sons of Oedipus. The very nature of Péguy's style – the extraordinary reluctance to budge from any position, the theme-lines recurring like a recurring pain – would serve the argument of the Freudian critic. Nor, certainly, would he lack the confidence to relate all this to certain known events in Péguy's life – his strong affection for his mother, the failure of his marriage, and even his early death in action.

It is sufficient at this stage, before going on to discuss Péguy's remaining major poem, *Eve*, to note the great strength of the Freudian case as based on the logical analysis of the two poems, and to note also that the case could be augmented to some extent by detailed examination of Péguy's imagery. The analysis, however, is here the more formidable contributor to the Freudian argument, and that argument is, in a corresponding degree, related to the poetry by an indirect attachment. What may be lost or omitted by reason of that indirectness is best discussed at a later stage, in relation to Péguy's poetry as a whole.

5.

Eve is Péguy's last complete poem, his longest, and his most ambitious, taking in, in its nineteen hundred rhymed quatrains, not only a great sweep of human history but also all the main articles of belief – the Fall, the Incarnation, the Redemption, the Resurrection, and the Last Judgment. The speaker is Jesus himself, the Son of Man addressing the mother of mankind:

> – *O mère ensevelie hors du premier jardin,*
> *Vous n'avez plus connu ce climat de la grâce,*
> *Et la vasque et la source et la haute terrasse,*
> *Et le premier soleil le premier matin.*

He speaks to her, in the first stanzas, of the lost Paradise and the beauties of a creation "at once chaste and carnal." "Vous n'avez plus connu," the opening words of a long series of stanzas, emphasize the loss and convey the sense of a once-shared secret. Here the attention is still concentrated on the world before the Fall, but gradually and by a curious and characteristic process it turns towards the state of fallen man. Into the majestic procession of the things "you knew no longer" is slipped a bleakly abstract "all you know now" –

> *Vous n'avez plus connu qu'un sévère destin.*

The older theme continues dominant for several stanzas; then there is a sequence in which the two themes alternate, then one on the fallen world alone, which leads to the picture of suffering Eve herself. Here and throughout this poem, Péguy does something which, so far as I can learn, no other poet ever did, probably because no poet less long-winded than Péguy would think of attempting it. That is the use of masses of words in a manner comparable to the use of masses of sounds in a symphony, with themes overlapping, accumulating, and entering into increasingly complex relations. This is not to say that *Eve* is, in its whole structure and organization, a complete word-symphony. It is, as we shall see, very far from being a harmonious whole, and form was never Péguy's chief preoccupation. The "musical" form in which his ideas present themselves, recur, and combine is not so much a planned structure as a subversion of the "logical" order of narration in favour of simultaneity and direct emotional apprehension. The result is sometimes wearisome and heavy with in-

The Temple of Memory: Péguy 141

verted pedantry, but it can be fresh and strange, as it is here at the beginning of *Eve*, where the two opening themes, contrasted but unrelieved, mingle and turn slowly in a sort of pool into which fall like a rock the sudden tender words of Jesus:

> *Et je vous aime tant mère de notre mère.*

It is now not primarily the Fall that concerns us, but fallen Eve as the archetype of woman. The stanzas describing "things now known" and "things no longer known" continue to reappear, but the new theme or rather two new and alternating themes, of woman suffering and woman managing, are now dominant and are served by the older ones. Jesus speaks with love and compassion of Eve in her suffering, with her back bent under the rage of heaven, and her heart "full of terror on the threshold of new days." She is the "first servant" and "the mother of Our Lady." But she is also, and here he speaks of her with irony, the mistress of the house and holder of the keys. He reminds her of her great primal error in housekeeping:

> *Je vous vois aujourd'hui fidèle et scrupuleuse,*
> *Attentive et sévère et sage désormais.*
> *Mais quand on avait tout, ô grande audacieuse.*
> *Quand on avait toujours on ne comptait jamais.*

Woman, in this aspect, is the fundamental rationalist; she attends to her household accounts and when spiritual things come to her attention, she tries to tidy them away. She would tidy away God Himself if He came to her house, but she forgot – and this is the theme of a long sequence – to tidy away the cross and the crown of thorns, and the tears of the crucified Christ:

> *Que n'avez vous alors, ô mon âme, ô ma mère,*
> *Essuyé les deux pleurs jaillis des mêmes yeux.*

Yet this sinful, evasive, forgetful, and managing woman is the mother of man and knows man's inmost temptations – the meaning of a certain "accent of the choir" – as well as his suffering and her own. She knows what it is to bury children, and especially, what it is to fear for them, to wait dumbly while they are in danger:

Et votre front cerné d'un stupide bandeau.
Et l'immobilité de la nuit et des ombres.
Et les vagues croulant en énormes décombres.
Et vos enfants partis sur un frêle radeau.

Her housekeeping is in part a futile service – picking up the stones that were thrown at the martyrs – but it is also, as here, a vigil of suffering. It is her doom to wait and watch and know and still to be helpless on the steps of history. If she is self-important in small tasks, it is because she is not allowed to forget the things that are beyond the power of housekeeping. In a strange and almost vengeful manner Jesus reminds her that she, in the person of the holy women, "tidied up" his body after the crucifixion but that there will be a last "tidying up" which will not be woman's work. Will she, he asks, in a long lyrical question, be able to light the way for her children when they rise from their tombs on the last day and, led by their priests, pass through their silent villages to Judgment, as once to midnight Mass?

Quand l'homme relevé de la plus vieille tombe
Écartera la ronce et les fleurs du hallier,
Quand il remontera le vétuste escalier
Où le pied du silence à chaque pas retombe:

Quand l'homme reviendra dans son premier village
Chercher son ancien corps parmi ses compagnons
Dans ce modeste enclos où nous accompagnons
Les morts de la paroisse et ceux du voisinage...

. . .

Quand ils iront en bande et les curés en tête,
Quand ils contempleront le dernier tribunal,
Quand ils chemineront tout le long du canal,
Comme ils allaient en bande aux jours de grande fête,

Quand ils s'avanceront dans l'éternelle nuit,
Quand ils auront passé devant le four banal,
Et le moulin à vent et le pré communal,
Comme ils allaient en bande aux messes de minuit.

The Temple of Memory: Péguy 143

The incredible thing is deliberately contrasted with the ordinary humdrum scene in which it is to happen, so that Eve may be reminded that the house she tries to keep cannot be kept. Yet no sooner has Jesus established her helplessness than he turns to emphasize her importance. She is great in her passivity and in her instinctive knowledge "that God's being replenishes itself eternally in its profound night." She knows that man exaggerates everything except his inward fear and, unlike "our great scientists who make jam," she knows the power of indefinable forces, of poetry and the sea:

> *Et nos tours de vertu et nos efforcements*
> *Ne sont devant les bords du plus ancien cantique*
> *Pas plus que les lambris de vos appartements*
> *Ne sont devant les bordes de la mer atlantique.*

In her suffering she transmits this knowledge, this instinct, and this sense of loss to her children:

> *Vous avez tant versé sur vos pauvres enfants*
> *Le long ressouvenir des morceaux de la grâce.*

She whom the wings of death brushed as she passed along the Dead Sea is the queen of disgrace and at the same time the mother and the memory of humanity:

> *Vous seule vous savez, ô temple de mémoire,*
> *Comment on inventa d'entrer dans cette honte.*

About this point a remarkable double change begins to come over the poem. Its original subject, Eve, recedes and in a short time disappears altogether, while Jesus, the supposed speaker, becomes the subject. These changes are not prepared or announced in any way nor are they carried out altogether consistently. We are made aware suddenly by a casual use of the first person that the speaker is identifying himself with modern men and with sinners, but a little further on we find that Jesus himself is speaking of his passion and crucifixion. There is a stretch of nearly two hundred stanzas in which it is difficult to make out who is the speaker and what is the subject. Eve has ceased to be of interest, for Péguy has nothing new to say about her, but she is still present and the poem still addresses her, whether on behalf of Jesus or of humanity, as "mother." It is at this transitional and chaotic moment, when the old structure has ceased to hold and the new one has not yet appeared, that there comes, altogether surprisingly, the famous and prophetic cry, the beatitude of the soldiers:

> *Heureux ceux qui sont morts pour la terre charnelle,*
> *Mais pourvu que ce fût dans une juste guerre.*
> *Heureux ceux qui sont morts pour quatre coins de terre*
> *Heureux ceux qui sont morts d'une mort solennelle.*
>
> *Heureux ceux qui sont morts dans les grandes batailles,*
> *Couchés dessus le sol à la face de Dieu.*
> *Heureux ceux qui sont morts sur un dernier haut lieu,*
> *Parmi tout l'appareil des grandes funérailles.*
>
> *Heureux ceux qui sont morts pour des cités charnelles.*
> *Car elles sont le corps de la cité de Dieu.*
> *Heureux ceux qui sont morts pour leur âtre et leur feu,*
> *Et les pauvres honneurs des maisons paternelles.*
>
> *Car elles sont l'image et la commencement*
> *Et le corps et l'essai de la maison de Dieu.*
> *Heureux ceux qui sont morts dans cet embrassement,*
> *Dans l'étreinte d'honneur et le terrestre aveu.*

These lines, the best known of all that Péguy wrote, have been regarded as irrelevant to their context, a mere intrusion into the poet's mind of the external events that were then, in 1913, preparing the First World War. Such a simple interpretation is almost as unjust to Péguy as an over-subtle one would be – as it would be, for example, to ascribe to him the intellectual engineering of a James Joyce, and discern in this passage an intention to point a historical moral by the sudden incursion of a warlike theme at a transitional stage in the poem's development. Nothing, we can be sure, was farther from Péguy's mind than such dialectics, yet his mind had its own patterns and its own system; not a master plan

The Temple of Memory: Péguy 145

but a coherence of ideas about a powerful emotional persistence. The idea here, far from being irrelevant, is a key one: the interdependence and intermingling of carnal and spiritual things. From the blessing on those who died for carnal cities the poem moves steadily into its central subject, which is not Eve, although it springs from Eve. Jesus – for he is speaking again, for the last time – asks the Father to consider that these fallen men who died for earth were made of earth, and asks him to put a handful of earth in the scale of mercy. He asks this for the blood which he himself shed for men and which was their own blood, and for the tree of grace which is rooted in the ground:

> *Car le surnaturel est lui-même charnel*
> *Et l'arbre de la grâce est raciné profond*
> *Et plonge dans le sol et cherche jusqu'au fond*
> *Et l'arbre de la race est lui-même éternel.*

The poem, twining in itself its various themes, conveys with various images the intertwining of the natural and supernatural until at last it comes to the supreme image and the central mystery:

> *Et Jésus est le fruit d'un ventre maternel.*

In this one line the poem itself comes to fruition. Its subject is and has been, we now know, the greatest a Christian poet can take, the Incarnation. Jesus is the fruit of a mother's womb. The whole first part concerned a mother, the rest will concern Jesus. This line and those that are near it, at the physical centre of the poem, represent the actual birth itself. Thus stated, the scheme appears logical and the balance orthodox. But schematic statements, logic, balance, orthodoxy are little help in dealing with such a poet as Péguy. The mother round whom the first half of the poem moves is not the Blessed Virgin, of whom Péguy had written so movingly in *Le Porche du mystère*, but fallen Eve. The birth of Christ is reached by no temporal sequence but through a defence of the sons of Eve who fall in battle and whose blood is like Christ's blood. There is nothing here to represent the Immaculate Conception and what it means in Catholic theology: the isolation not merely of Christ but of his mother from what is sinful in carnality. By the order of his poem and by his heavy emphasis on the carnal, Péguy is conveying, though not logically stating, that Christ is a son of Eve in a sense which the Church denies. This idea contains so much of Péguy that it is better to defer its examination to a later stage. It is enough to note here that Péguy himself must have felt that he was open to attack from the orthodox, for, in the series of stanzas that swell on the physical presence of the infant, he finds it necessary to emphasize that eternal life is not "a dry contracted business":

> *Le réseau qui tremblait sous la lèvre lactée*
> *Battait comme les nœuds d'une souple dentelle.*
> *Car la vie éternelle et la sacramentelle*
> *N'est point une entreprise aride et contractée.*

This human child, the beating of whose veins is "like a net in the deep sea" and whose eyes are "deeper than the ocean," sleeps in his manger watched by the ox and the ass. To these creatures Péguy devotes some forty stanzas of tender ridicule – these two big bisons, these notaries, these zebus, these ambassadors, these chamberlains, these hairy muzzles, these conservatives, these economists, and so on with a perplexing but endearing gusto. Their dumb presence is compared with the absence and ingratitude of man:

> *Et ces deux donateurs et ces adorateurs*
> *Gardaient ce fils de Dieu que nous avons perdu.*

The child sleeps – the words run through the next long sequence, and the rest of the poem is as if spoken during the child's sleep, in a sort of pause between the old world and the new. Asleep in this vessel of the manger, the Church to be, he is about to begin the tremendous voyage:

> *Car il allait lancer sur l'énorme océan*
> *L'impérissable nef, ce fragile berceau.*

But at the same time that he is to undertake so new a thing, he is to inherit what is very old, the whole complex and intractable ancient world. Here the pause spreads outward from the sleeping

The Temple of Memory: Péguy 147

child, and the Roman Empire stands still for a moment to be catalogued: the City and the provinces; the trireme and the Latin sea, bitter Zion and a ridiculous thunderbolt, the Western world and the hair of seaweed and of drowned men, the abysses and the promontories, basilicas and huts, and the catalogues themselves, catalogues of woods and saints and kings, of the dead, of loyalties and misery. To this inheritance are added all of history, all the past actions and thoughts of men, which had prepared the world for this sleeping child:

> *Les éléphants d'Afrique avaient marché pour lui*
> *Du fin fond des déserts jusqu'aux portes de Rome.*
> *Et pour lui les soleils d'Israël avaient lui,*
> *Du haut du Sinaï jusqu'au fin fond de l'homme.*

All the heroes, Hannibal and Caesar, Hercules and Theseus, Darius and Alexander, were his, and his also were the thinkers and their thoughts, or, as Péguy says, their dreams:

> *Les rêves de Platon avaient marché pour lui*
> *Du cachot de Socrate aux prisons de Sicile.*
> *Les soleils idéaux pour lui seul avaient lui,*
> *Et pour lui seul chanté le gigantesque Eschyle.*

The Child will have to remake this world, "as an old woman sews up the pieces of torn trousers," but comparatively little is heard of the remaking. Among the long continuing echoes of the heritage we hear, at the turn of a stanza, of vice being turned into sin, and Latin into liturgy, and that is almost all.[1] Then unexpectedly, from this lull, the poem rises with a burst of passion into its third and last phase, in much the same way as it moved from Eve to the nativity through the cry:

> *Heureux ceux qui sont morts pour la terre charnelle.*

This time the movement is less sudden and the passion more cumulative. The new theme is, as it seems, stumbled on in the catalogue of the heritage and not at first recognized:

[1] The change is dwelt on, though not developed, in the unfinished *Suite d'Eve*.

> *Il allait hériter de nos maîtres avides,*
> *De ceux qui nous font dire: Une science est à nous.*

Knowing Péguy's hatred for intellectuals and the works of the intellect, we are a little surprised at the mild way in which the stanza ends:

> *Seigneur nous n'avons rien que nos cartables vides*
> *Et l'abdication de nos roides genoux.*

This mood of Christian meekness, continuing the tranquil "heritage" passage, lasts for three stanzas. Then he catches sight of the Sorbonne again and is off with a snort:

> *Ce n'est pas de mémoire et de certificat*
> *Que nous aurons besoin dans le commun désastre.*

Here follows what is, even for Péguy, a prodigiously prolonged piece of invective: more than four hundred and fifty stanzas on the spiritual uselessness and general bankruptcy of educators and the educated. The abuse is monotonous and dogged, each stanza built on the same pattern and repeating the same message: it is not these people who can save us. "These people" are by turns defined, symbolized, and mocked: geographers, archaeologists, philologists, history professors – the most vilified class of all – bibliographical rats, pedagogues and mystagogues, pens and boxes of notes, weights under glass covers, chemists' bottles, cashiers, haberdashers, hangmen's lackeys – this last a reference to authorities on jurisprudence – sorcerers, urchins, chiefs of protocol, distinguished woodlice, influential centipedes, translators, acrobats, gasmen. We see the damp skin of their pale shaven faces, their obscene lips, their arms full of glossaries, and their paternal grimace. These masters of disdain are the warders of our prison; they are also the clumsy "divers in mittens" who cannot reach us under the wave:

> *Et ce ne sera pas ces plongeurs en mitaines*
> *Qui viendront nous chercher sous la vague profonde.*

Half-criminals, half-colonels, they cannot complete the crime or take the fortress. Passion and reason alike are false in them:

The Temple of Memory: Péguy

> *Et ce ne sera pas ces faux passionnels*
> *Qui sauront emporter le cœur de la maison.*
> *Et ce ne sera pas ces faux rationnels*
> *Qui sauront emporter le cœur de la raison.*

This invective is wildly disproportionate in length – for it takes up nearly a quarter of the whole long poem – but it is much more relevant than it appears. It corresponds in the closing part of the poem to the passage in the first part where Jesus rebukes Eve in her aspect of housekeeper and reminds her that there will be a last tidying-up which will not be carried out by her. The first passage stressed the natural poverty and inferiority of the calculating brain. Reason was rebuked in its first and fundamental application: the housekeeping accounts. The second passage attacks more presumptuous and triumphant applications of reason and is correspondingly more vehement. At the same time it carries a greater charge of emotion, for it comes after the description of the nativity and recalls that these flourishing impostors were part of the heritage of Christ. It develops overtly and violently what has hitherto been the more or less concealed motive of the poem: the conflict between reason and, not faith, but something more carnal and less rational, a sort of spiritual instinct. Grotesque as the attack sounds, it is furiously sincere, and it is accompanied by an undertone of passionate prayer. The professors, the Renans, and the Lavisses are actually contrasted with Christ himself:

> *Une autre, une autre lèvre un peu plus catholique*
> *Mettra sur nos deux yeux notre baiser de paix.*
> *Une main moins aveugle et plus apostolique*
> *Saura nous retrouver sous les hêtres épais.*

At intervals the barrage falls silent for a moment, while the true healers, Christ, the Blessed Virgin, and, strangely, Saint Peter (not usually a favourite of Péguy), come to give the kiss of peace among the myrtles or the olive trees. These passages are the most vibrant with emotion that Péguy ever wrote and among the very few in all his work that touch upon a personal torment and a personal renunciation:

> *Un autre effacera de nos livres de peine*
> *La trace de la ronce et de la fleur de mai.*
> *Un autre effacera de l'écorce de chêne*
> *La trace du seul nom que nous ayons aimé.*

From which he turns again, with fury heightened by other emotions, upon the history professors. This alternation continues until, at last, the professors are dismissed, and "the others," alone, in the persons of two saints of France make the concluding set of stanzas. Saint Joan and Saint Geneviève will end the poem that began with Eve. These two saints are contrasted first and last in their deaths: Saint Geneviève who died among her adoring flock and Saint Joan who died amid execration. Péguy handles the contrast with unusual restraint, leaving for long the death of Joan to the imagination:

> *L'une est morte au milieu des pâles citoyens,*
> *Pieusement couchée en un lit de parade.*
> *Soigneusement dressée en une haute estrade*
> *L'autre est morte au milieu des pâles citoyens.*

The aged Saint Geneviève died among a simple and uncorrupted people, but Saint Joan was put to death by the intellectuals of the Church:

> *Au milieu des docteurs, des savants, et des traîtres.*

The old Saint has, in heaven, whatever age God wills, but the young Saint's age is absolute and independent of God's will:

> *Mais l'autre dans le ciel ne peut avoir qu'un âge.*
> *Et quand Dieu le voudrait il n'y pourrait rien faire.*
> *Et quand Dieu le voudrait il n'est pas son affaire.*
> *Elle est montée au ciel dès son apprentissage.*

The young Saint is the Saint of France, and according to Péguy, God Himself does not know whether the love of one's country really must come after the love of God. The old Saint died in January in the snow in the city of Paris, for which history was preparing such a glorious destiny, but the other died in May:

The Temple of Memory: Péguy 151

Et l'autre est morte ainsi d'une mort solennelle.
Elle n'avait passé ses humbles dix-neuf ans
Que de quatre ou cinq mois et sa cendre chernelle
  Fut dispersée aux vents.

Thus the whole poem ends with the same theme and even the same rhyme as in the prophetic and apparently irrelevant interjection:

Heureux ceux qui sont morts pour la terre charnelle.

6.

In the case of *Eve* as in the case of *Le Porche du mystère*, the summary suggests and sustains a psychoanalytical interpretation. From the opening passage addressed to the mother buried outside the first garden to the final evocations of martyrdom – the invariable ending of all Péguy's major poems – the scheme of the poem with its alternation and interrelation of birth and death, conveys the same ideas as we have noted before: the return to the womb, the death-wish. It is not necessary to insist on what the summary itself reveals: the duality of the attitude to Eve; the way in which the poet assumes an august mask in order to address the mother, and unconsciously drops it when it has served its purpose; the symbolism of the eerily homely passage which describes the body rising from its grave and returning into its village and its house; the cult of suffering carnality; the static description of the nativity and of its social matrix; and the violent covering barrage against the conscious mind. The analysis, like an X-ray, shows significant shadows. It reveals, though not without ambiguity, what are certainly important elements in the poet's mind. Yet, noting this much, we do not need, I think, to dispel the ambiguity or to erect our intepretation into a hazardously logical structure. The work gives us glimpses of a mind; it is better not to pretend that they are more than glimpses. In any case what is important to us is not so much the exact nature of a psychological pattern, whose salient features we can discern, as the relation of that pattern to the universal. Not every Oedipus is a king and riddle-guesser. We are justified in saying: Péguy wanted to return to the womb, Péguy wanted to die. But we must ask, what then?

The question is, in a sense, answered immediately: the *what* confronts us – the poems themselves as a totality and the main overt subject of the poems, the great all-covering dome, which all other subjects and ideas serve to support or ornament, Péguy's idea of the Catholic Church. That idea is of something not abstract but embodied, historical, hereditary, and emotional. Péguy seldom speaks of Christianity (*christianisme*) but almost always of Christendom (*chrétienté*). The difference between the two ideas, corresponding to a certain difference between Péguy's position and orthodoxy, is well shown in a dialogue in the first *Jeanne d'Arc*. Thomas de Courcelles, the famous Doctor of the Sorbonne who was the most *intellectually* eminent of all Joan's judges, gives her the definition of the Church:

THOMAS: The Church is the communion of the faithful who follow the true religion instituted by Our Lord Jesus Christ under the authority of their legitimate pastors.
JOAN: I don't understand everything that you say, Master.
THOMAS: I don't think you could get a better explanation, Joan.
JOAN: Then the Church, as you call it, is Christendom?
THOMAS: No, Joan: the two words don't mean quite the same thing.
JOAN: Then I don't understand.

This dialogue was written before Péguy's conversion, but there is no evidence anywhere in his work to show that he ever made any real distinction between the Church militant and Christendom, or attached any great importance to the authority of legitimate pastors. His famous and sometimes mistranslated saying, "The sinner is at the very heart of Christendom," gives the true orientation of his system. The most important personal elements of Christendom are ordinary laymen (sinners) and the saints, and in Christendom spiritual loyalty and historical loyalties are inextricably mingled. God Himself, as we have seen, does not know whether patriotism should really be put below charity. Saint Joan, round whom the greater part of Péguy's work revolves, has the double character of saint and patriot and, as such, a doubly sacred vessel of faith and history, she was destroyed by the intellectuals

The Temple of Memory: Péguy 153

of the Sorbonne who were also the Doctors of the Church. Catholicism for Péguy is the religion which the women of France have handed down, in carnal cities for which it is good to die. He accepts it not as an antique curiosity or a reliquary of symbols, but as something that is true, yet he accepts other beliefs not less fervently. His dark and atavistic mind, contemptuous of any merely rational difficulties, assimilates and fuses into poetry all the great traditional beliefs of his ancestors. Dreyfusard, nationalist, and Catholic, he felt the blood of kings and saints and revolutionaries to be one blood, one common passion. The Christian religion is the highest expression of this common passion which forms the essence of historic France and is the only element within which Péguy could live. One cannot imagine Péguy interesting himself in the work of English converts or subscribing to the African mission. What he believed in was the religion of his own people, the religion which once had covered them all, and to which, at least in a submerged part of themselves, they all still belonged. In fact its being submerged, its state of being apparently recessive and no longer acceptable to the rationalizers, made it easier for him to make his own personal adaptation, identifying Christianity with the truth of the instincts and the secret ancestral alliances of the mind. Carnal and spiritual enter a closer relation than the orthodox allow; the soul and what the post-Freudian world calls "the unconscious" are one. Christ is the son of Eve.

If all this, so stated, sounds more Germanic than French, it is only partly because the Germans are more inclined than others to try to describe in prose the things that poetry communicates. It seems Germanic because it uncovers a stratum long laid bare in Germany and cropping out in remote places like Ireland, but usually deeply hidden in countries with relatively comfortable histories. Comfort and intellectuality, suffering and the ancestral Gods have historically gone in pairs. In a poet such as Péguy personal suffering and withdrawal join and express collective movements of the same character. A country, already once defeated, bracing itself for the second imminent shock, found in him a choral poet expressing, on different levels, the sweetness of death, the weariness of suffering, the will to fight and also that which called to be fought for, the inward essence and the spiritual frontiers of France. In a deeper and more abiding sense he expressed the great latent community of emotion which exists in a nation or a Church, or nation and Church together, and which can so easily blow aside the reason of the most rational peoples. That community, that mass of hereditary feeling, normally for the individual a distant sound, was in 1914 about to become a roaring, storm-tossed sea. It was Péguy's peculiar vocation to catch and turn to words the sound of that sea in its apparent peace and as it grew to anger. Like Victor Hugo, whom he venerated and whose oceanic speech he made his own, he became a "sonorous echo" of history, but the sound he echoed came from a deeper level, more muffled and more ominous. Once, his somnambulism was capable of instigating murder, when he called for the blood of Jean Jaurès, whose crazy assassin was to clear the way for war. Always he heard and made others hear: "Ancestral voices prophesying war."

Yet the temple on the dark seashore was not a mere barbaric temple of war. It was a temple of memory, both of a man's birth and death and of the long history of Western Christendom. In that sacred place of power and poetry one cannot tell where the personal joins the collective; one only knows that it does join it and that no "explanation" which is purely personal or purely collective can hold. The history that was present so intensely in the romantic Péguy certainly moved also, and not merely by external compulsion, those who died with him on the Marne. We may guess that his case was not the only one in which history took the form of a kind of poetry, touching the sunken faith, the fringe of darkness, and the sea.

VII
PAUL CLAUDEL

Paul Claudel was born in 1868 and was converted from agnosticism to Catholicism on Christmas Day, 1886, in Notre Dame. The following is a list of his principal works. Dates of composition, where given, are in italics following the date of publication.

Plays: *Tête d'or* (1890 – *1889*: second version 1901 – *1894-5*)
La Ville (1893 – *1890*: second version 1901 – *1897*)
La Jeune Fille Violaine (1914 – *1892*: second version 1901 – *1899–1900*)
L'Échange (1901 – *1893–4*)
Le Repos du septième jour (1901 – *1895–6*)
Partage de Midi (1906)
L'Annonce faite à Marie (1912)
Protée (1914)
L'Otage (1911)
Le Pain dur (1918 – *1913–14*)
Le Père humilié (1920 – *1916*) – these last three forming a trilogy, and
Le Soulier de satin (1930 – *1919–24*)

Poems: *Vers d'exil* (1912 – *1895*), *Cinq Grandes Odes* (1910 – *1900–1908*), *Corona Benignitatis Anni Dei* (1915 – *1906–13*), *Cantate à trois voix* (1913 – *1911*), *Feuilles de saints* (1925)

Essays *Connaissance de l'Est* (1900)
etc.: *Connaissance du temps* (1904)
Traité de la co-naissance au monde et de soi-même (1907)
L'Oiseau noir dans le soleil levant (1929)
Conversations dans le Loir et Cher (1935)

and a number of Biblical studies, translations, and fables.

THE RHINEGOLD OF PAUL CLAUDEL

*L'Or ou connaissance intérieure que chaque chose possède d'elle même
Enfoui au sein de l'élément, jalousement sous le Rhin gardé par la Nixe
et le Nibelung.*

CLAUDEL, *Les Muses*.

PAUL CLAUDEL, throughout his creative career of about forty years, constantly employed two dominant images: gold and water. Such a durability of imagery may be ascribed to an obsession, or to a deliberate system of symbolism, or to both: a system derived from an obsession. In Claudel's case at least we can have no doubt that a system exists, for it is in part explained. Yet the imagery is so much more subtle and multifarious than the explained system, and its associations so strangely ramified, that exploration is required. The overt content of Claudel's work – which is exceptionally explicit – has been often and indefatigably paraphrased; but the latent content and the esoteric structure of the symbols have received little attention.

M. Jacques Madaule[1] has referred to the *métaphysique de l'eau* scattered through Claudel's work and has quoted Claudel's reference to his *dramaturgie de l'or* (in *L'Echange*), but it has not been his task to develop these ideas. An approach to the meanings of Claudel's poetry through his use of certain dominant images may therefore be warranted.

I. GOLD

Simon Agnel, the golden-haired hero of Claudel's first play, *Tête d'or*, is a rebel against a loveless, hopeless, and irresolute

[1] M. Jacques Madaule's *Le Génie de Paul Claudel* (1933) and *Le Drame de Paul Claudel* (1935) provide careful summaries of the content of all the principal works. Individual works have also received the tribute of exhaustive paraphrase – see, for example, Dr. Kathleen O'Flaherty's book *Paul Claudel and the Tidings Brought to Mary* (1948).

society. He has led the army to victory against an external enemy, and he returns to murder his legitimate sovereign, the aged and futile Emperor. Focusing on himself the devotion of his troops, he carries unceasing war to the edge of the world and finds his last victory, and death, in the Caucasus. The qualities that lead him to this destiny and mark him off from the old world are symbolized in his long golden hair. His oath of action and resolution is sworn by his hair:

> *Par ces cheveux*
>   Il secoue et déploie ses cheveux.
> *Splendides, imprégnés par l'Aurore, toison*
>   *trempée dans le sang de la Mer,*
> *Voile d'or que je soulève avec mes mains!*
> *J'oserai . . .*

and it is the gold in him which his adoring lieutenant, Cassius, then salutes:

> *O Espérance d'or! très-chère violence arrivée à la*
>   *fin de notre journée lugubre!*
> *Comme le soleil fait paraître plus douce sa potion,*
> *Quand il inonde les vieux toits après des siècles de suie.*
> *Laisse-moi te toucher! O notre très splendide automne, guide-nous!*

Gold here is kinship with the sun and this kinship is stressed more than once in *Tête d'or*. Simon, whose hair is dawn and autumn, hails the sun as his father and dies in the "incorruptible gold" of sunset. Dying he calls on the sun as the object of his desire:

> *O soleil! Toi mon*
> *Seul amour! ô gouffre et feu! ô sang, sang! ô*
> *Porte! Or, or! Colère sacrée!*

But the hero of *Tête d'or* is not alone in his devotion to symbolic gold. The "heroine," the Princess, who is joy and grace and also, intermittently, a real woman, offers to the demoralized courtiers "gold in exchange for blackberries" – eternal love instead of earthly love. So also the dying Cébès, the young beloved disciple of Tête d'or, offers gold to his surviving master:

The Rhinegold of Paul Claudel

Je ne peux tromper dans le marché, je ne puis donner
Que moi! mon cher, pas autre chose
Que la vérité qu'il faut que tu aimes!
Et comme la lumière d'hiver, je te la montrerai
tout entière comme son or!

Gold, then, appears as the characteristic of the highest moments in the play: the transfiguration of the Princess; the death of the disciple; and the death – it is almost an Assumption – of the hero.[1] Gold, in the sequence of passages I have quoted, means by deliberate symbolism in turn the following concepts:

Will
Hope-violence
Likeness to the Sun
Love-rage
Truth-self.

Before attempting to analyse the relations of these concepts we may add to them the other contributions Claudel has made in the rest of his work towards a deliberate "theory of gold." *Tête d'or* remains the work in which he has made the most emphatic use of the symbol, and comes nearest to evolving a theory. Yet the image continues to permeate all his work, and its meaning is fairly often illumined by explicit reference. Leaving aside the permeative use for the moment and collecting only the more explicit symbolic references we have the following:

Mais les enfants de Dieu ... exhalaient ce chant d'or: Il existe!
(*La Ville*)

Car de même que le Soleil enveloppe tout le monde de ses rayons,
C'est ainsi que l'or splendide et subtil m'est nécessaire pour
Cette jouissance universelle, pareille à une considération de l'esprit,
Au dessus de quoi je suis constitué entre les hommes.

(A capitalist speaks here.)   (*La Ville*)

[1] An article entitled "Symbolism in Claudel's *Tête d'or*," by a religious in *Commonweal* some years ago, had the following remark on the Princess's death: "Thus she of the golden heart meets death beside him of the golden head." Apart from this comment the seeker after symbols had nothing to say about Claudel's use of gold. Unfortunately much "Catholic criticism" in English-speaking countries is little more than a sort of sublimated table tennis.

*Comme l'or est le signe de la marchandise, la marchandise aussi
est un signe,
Du besoin qui l'appelle, de l'effort qui la crée
Et ce que tu nommes échange, je la nomme communion.*

(The woman speaks to the capitalist.)

L'or est tout; il n'est valeur que de l'or.

(By this is meant gold as a medium of exchange – a millionaire
speaking against bimetallism.)
(*L'Echange*)

Le temps vient en or que tout y soit transmué.
(*Connaissance de l'Est*)

*L'émanation du profond 'a', l'énergie de l'or obscur
Que la cervelle par toutes ses racines va puiser jusqu'au fond des
intestines comme de la graisse . . .
L'Or ou connaissance intérieure que chaque chose possède d'elle-
même
Enfoui au sein de l'élément, jalousement sous le Rhin gardé par
la Muse et le Nibelung.*
(*Les Muses*)

FAUSTA: *Tout ce qui était de la nuit est devenu comme de l'or . . .
Ce qui était comme de l'or devient comme de la neige!*

BEATA: *Ce qu'il y a comme de l'or est la chère de l'âme et du
corps.*
(*Cantate à trois voix*)

Je te donne rendez-vous sur un lac d'or.
(*Le Soulier de satin* –
the reference is to music)

*La paix d'un cœur instruit de Dieu . . . chaude et pro-
fonde comme de l'or!*
(*Feuilles de saints*)

La Sagesse . . . a été pour lui plus que l'or. . . .
(*Feuilles de saints*)

*Scruteurs de toutes les archives à cause de ce secret qui
peut-être y est enfermé.
L'or sous le Rhin, le talisman tout à l'heure qui va te
donner la possession de l'univers.*

The Rhinegold of Paul Claudel 161

La formule qui permet d'avoir à soi ce qui est à Dieu et qui est tombée du Ciel avec Lucifer!

(Addressed to the defeated Germans in 1918)
(*Feuilles de saints*)

Adding, then, these concepts to those already found in *Tête d'or*, we get the following list of meanings or associations for the magic element:

Will	Exchange-communion
Hope-violence	Value
Likeness to the Sun	Transmutation of time
Love-rage	Blood-thought (>self-truth)
Self-truth	Transmutation of mortality
	Music
Knowledge of God	Peace of God
Exchange-power	Wisdom
Talismanic power	

"Meanings" thus dehydrated and detached from their context are incomplete and must be admitted to be so. But their incompleteness is of a different kind from the incompleteness of an individual work, and may complement and illumine the work. Schematic presentation can, I think, be a valuable approach provided it is recognized as just one line and not the key to the whole. Making this reservation, let us pursue the line without undue timidity as far as it seems to take us.[1]

Gold, is first, a symbol for several different attributes of divinity. The largest group among the concepts listed is the "divine" group – Truth, Knowledge of God, Peace of God, Wisdom; we may add Likeness to the Sun. These are definite and unequivocal Godimages; a divine aspect can be seen in several of the other concepts. Can we then say, inclusively, that gold is Claudel's symbol, or one of his symbols, for divinity? To do so without qualification would plunge us into difficulties. The golden hero of *Tête d'or* is after all a murderer and a war-lord and his bloody qualities

---

[1] "On n'analyse pas Claudel," says M. Madaule (*Le Génie de Paul Claudel*). A critic has no business to be so modest. Jacob might as well have said, "one doesn't wrestle with angels."

are carefully linked to his goldenness: "O golden Hope! O most dear Violence!" The "golden" qualities of rage and pure Will, as revealed in *Tête d'or*, are not reflections of divinity, at least in any direct sense, but products of anarchy. And even long after *Tête d'or*, it is hard to see divinity in the "gold" of visceral thought: "the gold which the brain through all its roots sucks up from the entrails like fat"; or in the exchange mechanism through which the capitalist in like manner sucks up wealth. Furthermore, the "gold under the Rhine" which the Germans are always seeking is the diabolic talisman for the diversion of divine things to the selfish ends of the creature. The relation of gold to divinity is obviously not an equivalence. The symbol of gold relates to desires and ambitions of fallen man as well as to attributes of the Creator.

But there is, between the "carnal" and the "spiritual", a frontier region, to which a number of the images belong. This is the region where time is being transmuted; the region where gold, the food of body and soul, is itself in process of turning from darkness into snow; the region of music and of the sort of exchange that is a communion. This is the region of flux where other more obscure images become partly intelligible, the "fugitive gold" of flowers which becomes honey, the spray which will turn to gold if the mystery is respected, and the soul's own "golden sound" which serves as the ears of God. This last image is perhaps more central than any, for it is set at the most intense moment of Claudel's most passionate play. Ysé, the heroine of *Partage de Midi*, waiting to die with her lover Mésa, exclaims in a long spiritual-sensual rhapsody:

Et donne-moi seulement l'accord que . . .
Jaillisse et m'entende avec mon propre son d'or pour oreilles
Commencer, affluer comme un chant pur et comme une voix véritable
  à ta voix ton éternelle Ysé mieux que le cuivre et la peau d'âne!

In its setting of sex and death, at the junction of the two borders of mortality, this spiritual exaltation is at the same time an orgasmic cry. The "golden sound" – like the "fulminating flame" in Mésa's reply – is a sun-image, and the sun, high over the mirror-

The Rhinegold of Paul Claudel

ing sea, is itself, throughout the play, an image of passion and, finally, of the transfiguration of passion ("the victorious Spirit in the transfiguration of Noon"). One is irresistibly reminded of the collusions and sleight of hand of the earlier Mauriac; of works like *Le Fleuve de feu* and *Le Désert de l'amour*, in which the sun provides a theological symbol and at the same time a climate of sexual passion. Claudel is far more intellectual and more rigorously devout a writer than Mauriac was, and yet the comparison is not altogether inept. For Mauriac as for Claudel (both in *Le Soulier de satin* and in *Partage de Midi*), sexual passion, doomed to frustration in terms of mortality, is a way towards divine love. Thus there is nothing incongruous except to the literally minded or verbally rheumatic, in the sun-gold being at one time carnal and at another spiritual. Nothing incongruous but something dazzling and shifting, the treacherous surface of poetic theology; for no one – not even the poet – can know exactly at any given moment whence the gold is mined or from where the sun is shining. I mean by this no reproach to the poet and no challenge to his Catholicism; only a warning to seekers of the Single Meaning and against writers who would turn complex poetry into simple and edifying prose.[1]

Another dimension is given to this complexity by the associations of words. No English-speaker can ever know what *or* means to a Frenchman but he can be sure that it never means the same as "gold." The English monosyllables that rhyme with "gold" are extremely weak in emotive force: "bold" and "scold" when linked may induce from juvenile recollections a faint sense of guilt and retribution; "old" and "cold" are mournful words, and so is "mould," but the emotional charge in any of these is hardly a powerful one; the rest of the bunch, "fold" (or "foaled"), "hold" (n. or v.), "polled," "rolled," "sold," "told," are emotionally insignificant. The shortage of nouns is remarkable. On the other hand, the *or* group is extraordinarily strong. The words are grave and basic, many of them nouns. One can form arbitrary but meaningful patterns with them: *tort* and *corps* convey together the idea of original sin, and therefore of mortality; *bord*, *port*, and *sort* (v.

[1] E.g. Dr. Kathleen O'Flaherty, op. cit. *passim*.

and n.), joining in the conception of a predestined departure, point the way, through *dort*, to the key-word of the series, *mort*. No general validity is claimed for this arrangement, but there is no denying the predominance of the idea of death; the terrible force of the word itself makes it dominate and permeate any setting; *corps* and *dort* reinforce its meaning and help to impose it on the gong-like sound of *or*.[1] Other associations arise from the colour, power, and desirability of gold: but its *sound* in French has, above all, the meaning of death.

Claudel is, we know, by no means indifferent to the shadow-meaning of the pun. He has expressed his admiration for the pun-linking pivot language (*kenyôgu*) of the Japanese *Noh* plays, and he often, as we shall see, allows his thought to be guided by the sound, rather than the registered meaning, of words. In the case of the *or* group Claudel does not, as far as I know, pun directly on the sounds, and ordinary rhymes (being as it were a mandatory form of association) are of little significance, although, of course, *or . . . dort*, *port d'or*, *or . . . corps*, *or . . . mort*, et cetera, are to be found scattered through his works. Curiously the shadow-meaning of *or* is most clearly to be seen in disjunction from the word itself and in connection with its co-symbol, the sun (gold and the sun are used interchangeably through all Claudel's work). It takes the form of the pun *soleil . . . sommeil*, which occurs first in an unrhymed context in *Tête d'or*, reappears in *Vers d'exil*, and emerges in more complex form in the rather precious prose of *Connaissance de l'Est*: "Soleil des Songes consomme le sommeil." There the "sun of dreams" is, of course, the moon, the symbolic link between the idea of the sun and its sound-shadow, sleep. This *soleil . . . sommeil* reflection, obviously important for Claudel, exactly parallels the *or . . . dort* rhyme, which is itself emotionally only a form of the death-gold association. Not only the moon but sunset also figures forth this association, in several works, notably in *Tête d'or* and *L'Echange*, the gold of

---

[1] There are, of course, several other rhymes in *or*, including monosyllables, like *hors*, *lors*, *fort*, and the ridiculous *sport*. My contention is that, at the poetic level of emotional use of words, the seven monosyllables given in the text are the active ones; the others more or less neutral.

The Rhinegold of Paul Claudel 165

sunset is the preliminary to death. "Cet or," as he says elsewhere, "ne fait pas vainement appel à nos ténèbres...." And the whole plot of *L'Echange* – that *dramaturgie de l'or* – turns on the transferability of gold and death: the husband who accepts gold in exchange for his wife is really, without knowing it, accepting death.

Claudel has been called a decadent symbolist, and that view could be plausibly supported from the evidence collected in this essay. It could be argued that his "gold" represents nothing real in terms of thought but is a mere pseudo-symbol, or emotional nimbus cast round any vast concept: God, or death, or sex. This "gilt-wrapping theory" – as we might briefly call it – has some truth in it but, before we decide how much, it may be worth while to attempt a dictionary definition (conceived as a contribution to a hypothetical Claudel glossary) of Claudelian gold:

GOLD (OR): An element characterized by its *colour*; a medium of *exchange*. Associated by its colour with the *sun*, and especially with sunset; less often with dawn and noon, the moon, harvests, bees, roses, oranges, honey. Derives from its solar aspect and from direct association with *flame* and *blood* a connotation of male *passion*, *violence*, and *intensity*. Derives from its monetary function the sense of absolute *value* and also of *meaningful flux*, movement which is at the same time *communion*. Derives from its *sound*, reinforced by the associations of sunset, the sub-connotation, partly concealed, of *death*. Derives from all these senses and from their coalescence, added to the idea of *alchemy*, a *supernatural meaning*, which could be roughly stated as the atmosphere of the frontiers of the divine.[1] This supernatural meaning in turn affects and elevates the natural meanings.

Through this definition we see the symbol as a means of fusing theory and feeling: something which it would be inadequate but not altogether wrong to describe as an emotionally propelled philosophical vehicle. Although Claudel, particularly in his earliest

[1] Compare the description of a cloud-sunset in *Cantate à trois voix:* "La petite ville / Repose dans une fumée divine et dans une atmosphère d'or." Or the imaginary marine *Noh* play in *L'Oiseau noir*: "Un dieu apparaît dans le brouillard mêlé de morceaux d'or." Or the Assumption sunset at the end of *Tête d'or*.

work, does sometimes use gold for purposes of mere emotional touching-up or decoration, it is clear, even from so summary a "definition" as I have given, that gold is used for far more than mere wrapping purposes, and that it is a true symbol, related in definite ways to complex ideas. It does actually function as a kind of currency, abstractly representing value, making possible the exchange of different psychic "commodities," providing a common measure for divergent feelings, and even an "international" standard between feelings and theories. And as money makes social life more efficiently productive and also more specialized, complex, and hard to understand, the use of multi-valued poetic symbols has precisely the corresponding effects in such poetry as Claudel's; the "increased efficiency" lies in the use of a language that is more adequate to experience, since it is less simplified than ordinary speech.

But the full meaning of the symbol does not emerge except in its relation to other symbols. In the present case, the Rhinegold can only be reached by diving.

2. WATER

*J'ai attaché mon cœur et mon esprit sur l'eau vive et vivifiante;
L'eau subtile et liquide, circulante, ambiante, médiatrice, source première et veine commune.*

CLAUDEL, *La Jeune Fille Violaine.*

Gold is an element more frequently discussed than encountered; water on the other hand is everywhere there is life. Water is the first environment of consciousness, the prime element of dreams and poetry. It courses through all literature from Homer to *Finnegans Wake*. Yet some areas are more inundated than others, and rarely can a poet have been more water-logged than Paul Claudel. Not merely does water fascinate him as an object of contemplation, but it floods his metaphors and ways of speech. A girl will "soak herself in midnight"; a twilit garden is "like a poem submerged in thought"; the future is "a country reflected in the water"; the sinner fleeing from God is "a diving otter"; he returns to grace "like a corpse to the surface at the sound of a gun"; the poet "soaks up and ingurgitates light like a fish hears through his gills"; in church he feels "like Jeremiah in the cistern, under deep water"; an Emperor is "drenched in darkness"; learned men are like "fish in twilight water"; the dawn is night becoming "diaphanous as water ... or a receding flood"; the night is "so calm that it seems salt"; all great movements of men are invariably compared to movements of the sea.

The list is not exhaustive and, seeing the universality of this image in poetry, it would be foolish to attempt to make it so. The water-metaphors of Claudel, of which these are a characteristic selection, reflect the invasion of his speech by a preoccupation with humidity, not unique but unusual in degree of intensity, which prevails in all his work, at many levels. This preoccupation is perhaps most obvious in a very elaborate and self-conscious book of essays, *Connaissance de l'Est* (1900). On almost every page of that book, water spurts or trickles or drips, is observed, felt, heard, imagined: the very titles of many essays reveal their humidity, and even where water is not physically present, the air and light themselves are felt to be liquid. The poet's existence seems to pass in the liquidity of the womb: he is under a waterfall, or, writing in the rain, he feels "like an insect in a bubble," or, in a storm at sea, he feels "lost in the interior of death"; the framework is appropriate – his house, as he describes it, is "a case of wood attached to the vault of a great porch cut out of the mountain." The essay "Rêves" in the same collection tells of seven dreams, six of which are similarly humid: two are concerned with rowing a boat through the air; one with being pulled up through the air by a hook; one with being carried away by floodwater; one with walking through the air; and one with leaving handmarks during sleep in places that could only be reached by flying or floating. The general impression is of living in a medium of density comparable to that of water. There is matter here to which I shall return; for the present it is enough to note the fact of liquidity as a principal mode of the poet's imagination.

This liquidity is not, however, an object of desire merely, but also of speculation. There is a Claudelian theory of liquidity, fairly elaborate in itself, and far more explicitly stated than his "gold theory." The first and fullest statement of this theory is given by a character in *La Jeune Fille Violaine*, Pierre de Craon, an engineer, known as "the Master of Water." The living lifegiving water, which in blood or sap or milk, responds to the invitation of the sun, fills the whole body of nature, for the same function of mediation and construction. Its innumerable and many-formed circulation corresponds to (or is the visible and external form of) the common principle of all human souls, in virtue of which they communicate with each other and with God. There is a spiritual moisture which responds to the invitation of grace as the sap of the tree responds to the sun; or which, in another sense, flows to us from God as necessarily as mother's milk to the infant; and this liquid, although it takes a different form in each of us, is essentially the same, and eternally circulating:

> *De même que l'eau, que ce soit la mer ou mêlée à une*
> *chair d'homme ou de raisin,*
> *Ne change point de nature et ne cesse point d'obéir*
> *au Soleil,*
> *De même toutes les âmes humaines, chacune libre et*
> *différente, tirent*
> *D'un principe commun dont elles se servent pour être*
> *ce qu'elles sont,*
> *Leur jus intérieur.*
> *Nous ne sortons point de nourrice.*

The thirst of man, spiritually unweaned, is insatiable and can only apply itself to what is inexhaustible. And to this, rather than to Violaine, Pierre addresses himself:

> *...j'ai soif*
> *Et ma bouche cherche une autre réponse que*
> *celle des lèvres de la fiancée, non point*
> *celle d'un époux*
>
> *Mais de l'enfant sur le sein avec une passion*
> *d'homme, toute fraîche et jaillissante.*

Thus far the explanation of Pierre de Craon. It may be permissible to make on it, at this stage, one gloss. What is that by means of which men communicate with God and with each other, that which is desired (milk) and desiring (the sap of the tree) at the same time? Surely it is love, and love is the essential meaning of this "water", which is also a circulating thirst.

To this statement of Pierre de Craon's, Claudel has added little, in the domain of theory; his additions have taken the form of different distributions of emphasis. In *Connaissance de l'Est* he writes: "All water is desirable to us and certainly more than the blue and virginal sea, the river-water calls to that which in us is between body and soul, the water of humanity, charged with virtue and with spirit, the dark and burning blood." And we are reminded elsewhere of the male significance of rivers, the bull-like torrent of the Rhone which rushes roaring to the sea. Thus it is made unmistakably clear that the love which is symbolized by water includes a part of sexual passion. Here as elsewhere Claudel's symbolism is not a mere system of equivalents for spiritual things but is a means of relating the spiritual and the carnal. So in *L'Esprit et l'eau* (1906), although he still writes within the same system as that described by Pierre de Craon, the poet's emphasis seems to fall on the human rather than on the divine. There is "a liquid link" between God and his creatures, but nonetheless water is something different from, and contrasted with, spirit:

Mon Dieu vous voyez que je ne suis pas seulement esprit,
  mais eau! ayez pitié de ces eaux en moi qui meurent
  de soif!

Et l'esprit est désirant mais l'eau est la chose désirée.

And then a passage remarkable for its fusion of the spititual and the carnal:

  ... J'ai connu cette femme. J'ai connu
la mort de la femme.
J'ai possédé l'interdiction, J'ai connu cette source
  de soif.
J'ai voulu l'âme, la savoir, cette eau qui ne
  connaît point la mort!
J'ai tenu entre mes bras l'astre humain!

Although water is not spirit, yet the soul is "that water which knows not death"; possession is a source of thirst for this water of the soul. The waters are human souls and also the love these souls have for each other, a love which is expressed through the body.

Water is love: that is an equivalence from which Claudel never departs, but it can have many meanings as love can have many objects. These meanings are by no means exhausted by the "theoretical" statements we have examined. The idea of the sea, for example, reveals associations not overtly present in the theory, which are worth considering.

The sea, omnipresent in Claudel's work, has several meanings. It is, first of all, a female principle. "Rendre une lumière comme la mer femelle," says a character in *La Ville*, and the producers of the Comédie Française, when they portray the sea in *Le Soulier de satin* by undulating grey-draped women, are faithfully interpreting the poet's idea. The sea is, of course, a woman in most languages, from obvious physical associations, but in French these associations are enormously strengthened by a verbal association: the words for "mother" and the "sea" are the same in sound. Claudel, as we saw in the first part of this essay, is inclined to this sort of association; the poet who three times plays on the assonance of *soleil* . . . *sommeil* is not likely to miss the more essential pun of *mer* . . . *mère*. And indeed he has shown signs of regarding the two words as interchangeable. The hero of *Tête d'or*, swearing, by his long golden female hair, his great oath of will, speaks in the first version of the play the words I have mentioned in a different context:

> *Par ces cheveux*
> *Splendides, imprégnés par l'Aurore,*
> *toison trempée dans le sang de la Mer.*

In the second version of the play he says the same words, but the hair is now "trempée du sang de la Mère." The significance of the change is far from clear, but the readiness with which one idea can be converted into the other is notable. But a far more startling example of this phenomenon occurs in *L'Esprit et l'eau;*

The Rhinegold of Paul Claudel

C'est la mère, je dis, qu'il me faut!
Possédons la mer éternelle et salée,
la grande rose grise! Je lève un
   bras vers le paradis! Je m'avance
vers la mer aux entrailles de raisin.

The shock of this mystically incestuous dip comes from the fusion in the poet's mind of the two words with the one sound; clearly for him meaning adheres to sound with such force that it is impossible for two words with the same sound to keep their meanings entirely separate. The sea is therefore not merely female but maternal (and must remain so in some degree even where the association is not overt), but it is much more as well, and even in virtue of its sound. In French the sound of the sea is also bitter (*amer*), and since this sound corresponds to the saltness of the sea it has a double force. Tête d'Or exclaims that the sight of his dead disciple "contient plus d'amertume que la mer," and this is a bitterness both of love and of death. In another poem, *Sainte Thérèse*, the "holy prison" of a Carmelite nun in Indo-China revives the same idea:

Ah, non moins étrange que l'Asie, non moins profond,
  et non moins amer, et non moins désiré

Ce pays entre la mer et la mort où vous étiez déjà,
  ma sœur, et où vous m'appeliez.

In *La Ville* when the poet Cœuvre, addressing his bride, four times uses the word *amère*, the word has clearly far more force than *bitter* has for us:

O femme! ô compagnon féminin! amère amie!
O notre amère vie! ô amour comme l'orange amère,
Aussi suave à l'odeur, aussi étrange et amère au
  cœur et à la bouche!

The sea is heard, though not seen.

We can already perceive a group of words which for Claudel have a tendency to attract each other: *la mère, la mer, amer (amère), l'amour, la mort*. The attraction is not merely a phonetic one: there are psychological connections between the ideas that these words represent, but these connections are greatly reinforced, for such as Claudel at least, by the coincidence of sound.[1] But before attempting to reach any conclusion it will be necessary to say a little more about the most far-reaching associations of the group, those which revolve round *la mort*.

The idea of Night, universal symbol and precursor of death, mingles with the ideas of water and the sea. We have seen several examples of the metaphorical commingling of darkness and humidity, and many more could be added. But there are more explicit suggestions of identity:

> *Encoré! encore la mer qui revient me chercher comme une barque . . .*
>
> *Encore la nuit qui revient me rechercher Comme la mer . . .*
>
> (*La Muse qui est la grâce*)

But the night which is the sea (and here is both grace and inspiration) is elsewhere, as we should expect, a mother:

> *O Nuit, mère!*
> *Ecrase-moi ou bouche-moi les yeux avec*
> *de la terre!*
>
> *Mère pourquoi as-tu fendu la glaise de mes*
> *paupières! Mère je suis seul!*
>
> *Mère pourquoi me forces-tu à vivre?*

For Tête d'Or night is not only a mother, but death who refuses to come to him; and this is not the only place where the motherhood of death is asserted. "J'appartiens à la mort, il me faut

---

[1] Whether unconsciously perceived similarities in the ideas have helped to shape the sounds is a question that should be investigated by psycho-philologists, if there were any. In any case, whether or not ideas shaped the sounds, the sounds certainly help to relate ideas. Hence possibly some of the differences between the psychological attitudes of the Latin peoples and those of English-speakers.

The Rhinegold of Paul Claudel 173

retourner vers la Mère," says the Emperor in *Le Repos du septième jour*. The sea, likewise, is constantly compared or related not only to night but directly to death; the tide rises as the sun sets, prefiguring death; the dying revolutionary has his last dream within sound of the sea; the dead themselves are like a pity-seeking sea; in the remarkable "Ballade" (in *Feuilles de saints*), written at sea, the poet speaks of his longing to be drowned:

> *Rien que la mer à chaque côté de nous, rien que cela qui monte et qui descend!*
>
> *Assez de cette épine continuelle dans le cœur, assez de ces journées goutte à goutte!*
>
> *Rien que la mer éternelle pour toujours, et tout à la fois d'un seul coup! la mer et nous sommes dedans!*
>
> *Il n'y a que la première gorgée qui coûte.*

It is at this point in thought that the "instinctive" response to the sea rejoins the general theory of water. The sea, so longed for as a means of ending earthly misery, is also a prefiguration of what may be found beyond death. The lyrical raptures of Doña Sept-Epées in *Le Soulier de satin*, as she swims to join the crusade in response to the call of her mother's spirit, express this idea, but there is a more explicit statement of it in a poem, *La Route interrompue*,[1] which, for its central position in Claudel's thought, deserves to be quoted at some length:

> *Au lieu de ce texte à dechiffrer mot par mot, que l'on me donne la mer à boire!*
>
> *La volonté de Dieu, non plus pour un moment solide, et selon que tous ces plans et reliefs et découpures la divisent et l'interprètent,*
>
> *Mais telle quelle, à l'état humide, la présence à l'intérieur de tout, qui pousse, qui ausculte et qui pénètre*
>
> *Et maintenant là, à ma disposition, en cette chose bleu-noire apparue, les Eaux en un seul poids réunies,*

[1] In the collection *Feuilles de saints*, dated July 1923 – about the same time as the monologue of Sept-Epées must have been composed.

La grande fosse à mouvement et le membre essentiel de la Vie!
Plus besoin de ce mètre à chaque instant coupé que j'essaye de reprendre bout à bout,
Je tiens le centre, je suis là, un seul battement de ce cœur énorme ouvre tout!
Mon cœur à ce battement de la route énorme s'attend et s'accoutume peu à peu.
O Mer que je te désire! et mon âme, par tout ce qu'il y a en moi d'humide je touche à Dieu!

Final immersion is here as ardently desired as in the *Ballade*, but the emphasis now falls on spiritual life rather than physical death; there is of course no contradiction. It is notable, however, that the idea of the beginning of spiritual life is accompanied by an undertone of the beginning of physical life: the idea of the world being pregnant with the will of God – the interior presence in the humid state, thrusting. Thus the ideas of motherhood and of the sea are found again, in a different mode, conjoined.

We can now attempt, as we did with "gold," a multiple definition:

WATER (EAU):[1] A fluid and *circulating* element, common to rivers, the sea, milk, sap, blood, tears; an object of *desire* (thirst); used in the sacrament of *Baptism*; a *medium of imaginary existence*, comparable to actual air; associated with darkness and the conditions of the *womb*. From its presence in torrents and in blood derives the sense of *sexual passion*. Through the sea (and the word *la mer*) strengthens its association with *motherhood* and with *love*, and takes on also meanings of *bitterness* and *death*. From its circulation, its desirability (milk), its responsiveness (sap), its sacramental property, and probably also from clusters of its other attributes derives a supernatural meaning, variously stated, which can be defined as love in its pure form, spiritual or divine love.

[1] I have not dealt in the text with the sound of the word *eau* because I do not think it seriously affects the meanings. Nonetheless it may be worth remarking that the sound of *eau* is that of the exclamation "O!" which Claudel has described as a love-cry, imitating the cry of seabirds in a storm. He speaks elsewhere of a Japanese word, *ahity* – that quality which, in anything, is capable of making us exclaim "Ah!" Any interpretation based on this would be too far-fetched even for words.

The Rhinegold of Paul Claudel 175

With water, then, even more than with gold, we discern the working of a great system of theory and instinctive association, vertical and horizontal in operation. It is a system enabling the natural or carnal world to be seen as flooded with the spiritual and expressing the spiritual in carnal terms: a system of moving backwards and forwards across the frontier between body and soul; and yet also a system that is the expression of the poet's own inmost desires and even obsessions. The poet moves on the water from what is personal and particular to the superhuman and the universal; and back again.

But we have yet to see in what relation this system of water-symbolism stands to the symbolism of gold, and how the two systems, taken together, affect the consideration of Claudel's poetry.

3. WATER AND GOLD

> *O le pauvre amoureux des pays chimériques!*
> *Faut-il le mettre aux fers, le jeter à la mer*
> *Ce matelot ivrogne inventeur d'Amériques*
> *Dont le mirage rend le gouffre plus amer?*
>
> BAUDELAIRE.

The ideas symbolized by gold (or the sun) and by water (or the sea) are far from being completely exclusive or opposed. Both "gold" and "water" circulate and both are desirable, and these qualities form in each case the essence of the symbolic system. Both are related by the poet to blood, to sexual passion, and to death. Both finally have a supernatural significance, being identified in some degree with the divine. These coincidences of meaning are important and we shall have to return to them. But the divergences are no less important.

The principal difference is, more obviously, of light, and, more fundamentally, of sex. Gold, belonging to the sun, is invariably associated with light and predominantly associated with maleness. Its connotations of energy and violence are male, personified in the sun-hero, Tête d'Or, and it is, in *Partage de Midi*, a principal symbol of male passion.[1] Water on the other hand belongs to darkness and is overwhelmingly female. The two elements are Ormuzd and Ahriman, Yin and Yang, man-light and woman-dark. The opposition, or alliance, of these principles forms the counterpoint of a very great part of Claudel's poetry.

Yet this opposition, or alliance, is not at all an equal one: the water-dark-woman group is predominant, or rather continually present, a great stream of under-meaning; while the gold-light-man group is something intermittent, a frequent flicker and a rare flash. The "theory of water," as we have seen, is far more fully developed than the "theory of gold," and water moves in a closer and more consistent relation to God than does gold. But that is not all: the associates of water, darkness and femaleness, have also a powerful religious significance, deep roots that sustain the complex system. Mother Night is also the home of the faith:

Salut, grande Nuit de la Foi, infallible Cité astronomique!
C'est la Nuit et non pas le brouillard qui est la patrie d'un Catholique.

(*Corona Benignitatis Anni Dei*)

The darkness that reveals the stars could be a merely mechanical figure, but it is clearly much more for Claudel. So, too, subjective darkness, blindness, has more than the trite significance of extra-sensory perception; its meaning is in the two blind women, Violaine (*La Jeune Fille Violaine*), who miraculously restores sight to another, and, more profoundly, Pensée de Coufontaine (*Le Père humilié*), who is loved because of her blindness and who "teaches night" to others. Darkness is holy – *minuit sacré* – whether interior or exterior, and one kind of darkness calls to the other; the "stored shadows" of churches "are needed to melt the envelope of our personal night." And this ecclesiastical darkness is both liquid and mortal – "sunk under deep water [at Notre Dame] you

[1] It is not invariably male as a line in *Vers d'exil* shows: "Femme, *or par terre*, feu au loin, détour et gouffre." Even Tête d'Or himself is not without ambiguity. His disciple, Cébès, addressed him as "Mère, mon frère," and he himself frequently speaks of being about to give birth. Absolute consistency cannot be found in symbolic language, but a general pattern can be seen.

The Rhinegold of Paul Claudel 177

will taste the very taste of death"; Claudel has proposed (for Chicago) an underground church with the altar rising out of a dark lake. The biological parallels hinted at in these passages are clearly and strongly expressed in the essay, "Le Développement de L'Eglise," where he describes the transformation of "the house" into the temple, as the roof is replaced by the dome: "The roof is purely the invention of man, who needs the complete enclosure of this hollow place – like the hollow of the tomb or of the womb – to which he returns for the refreshment of sleep or of nourishment. And now [in the Church] the hollow is filled out, big as with a living thing: the dome appears."

At this point the logical post-Freudian materialist can no longer be held back. Here is his text and he must preach on it. Let us hear him speak out now, for he has been muttering a long time:

"Surely the case of Claudel is less complex than you make it appear, is indeed abundantly plain. This obsessive preoccupation, this constant manipulation and exchange of images of water, darkness, and woman (which you have described at such unnecessary length and with such ridiculous circumlocution), is a very well-known and clinically recognized complex. The unhappy victim – for the intensity of the symptoms in the present case betrays a psychopathic condition rather than a 'normal' state of the unconscious – is the prisoner of an incessant desire to return to his prenatal establishment. In this condition, unable to bear without anodyne the tensions and demands of the extra-uterine world, he soothes his nerves by the distillation of a product, poetry, which gives him an illusory satisfaction in at least three ways. First, and most obviously, his obsession finds release along the extraordinary web of womb-images which, on your own showing, runs through all his work; as primitive man thinks to 'possess' an object by naming it, so the 'poet'-patient derives a similar 'benefit' from his imagery. Second, the very nature of poetry and dramatic fiction comforts such a person; since what he desires is unattainable in reality, reality must be forsaken for fantasy – and poetry, especially such poetry as Claudel's, is nothing more than fantasy, all the more dangerous because it is sufficiently organized to be communicable. Finally, the religious element in the poetry, closely linked to the basic images, and also to the idea of death, provides the poet's inner compulsion with an apparatus of rationalization and also with substitute goals: death, the structure of churches, heaven. It is impossible to say this more plainly than the poor man has said it himself, with the acute but intermittent clairvoyance so characteristic of his kind. We have seen the same thing in the case of that other religious poet, Charles Péguy, although you tried to evade the conclusion. Poetry, religion, and regressive fantasy are indissolubly conjoined misfortunes of humanity. Dr. Joystone, in *The Autarky of Earth*, is as formal on this point as he is convinced that the condition is not incurable. 'Spiritual' in Joystone's irrefragable judgment 'means animistic, and animistic means both ignorant and frightened. In this sense I am prepared to concede' – the touch is characteristic of Joystone's impish humour – 'that all art is spiritual. The ecstasies of art, like the consolations of religion, are satisfactions in fantasy for privations in reality: the economic privations of our ignorant working masses, the emotional privations of our frightened ruling class.' And he concludes, in the famous passage that has earned him the name of the most outspoken scientist of our time: 'Everything which we now call by this archaic name of *spiritual* – art, religion, and various glorifications of sexual inhibition, "chivalry" for example – is about to crumble away. It is a truism that the abolition of poverty has become technically possible but the corollaries of this proposition have not been grasped. When we abolish privation we shall also abolish privation-psychology or, as I prefer to say, privation-behaviour, or, better still, privation-play. The scientifically organized and regular distribution of food, fuel and sex will automatically dry up, within one generation, the sources of this privation-play which we now call *spiritual life*. To a new generation, completely carnal and completely rational, the idea of poetry will be as incomprehensible as the idea of typhus. They will be very happy.'[1] I know from your general approach, and

---

[1] The element of philistinism in this tirade is not, of course, derived from Freud, but from Anglo-Saxon schools: the logical positivists and the neo-behaviourists. Even they are not altogether consistent and, overawed by the panoply of culture, often fail to grasp that hostility to religion-in-general logically implies hostility to art-in-general.

The Rhinegold of Paul Claudel 179

your respectful attitude to this eloquent French somnambulist, that the courageous conclusions of Joystone will not be acceptable to you. But what I should like to know – and I imagine your more *spiritualized* readers will ask the same question – is why, if you do not accept our conclusions, you have gone to such pains to accumulate the evidence on which these conclusions, in so far as they concern Claudel, are based? Were you not, in fact, thinking along these very lines, and are you now shrinking from the logical conclusion?"

These questions deserve answers. The "evidence" of the quotations was gathered because of its abundance: one cannot read Claudel without, for example, noticing the fascination that water has for him, and what is important for the poet deserves the attention of the critic. The critic's attention, following the central imagery, must discern the patterns I have noted. These patterns are, to a very great extent, uterine: they do indeed reflect the "regressive" preoccupation on which the materialistic critic swoops with such a curious mixture of scientific rigour and implied moral condemnation. Where the materialist goes wrong is not in discernment of a set of facts, or even in his interpretation of the facts, but in his unscientific assumption that only one set of facts is relevant and only one interpretation, on one level, is possible. The critical mechanic, when he discovers a poet's obsession, will say that he has found "what makes him tick." The falsity of this idea can be demonstrated by experiment: do any two writers, similarly obsessed, "tick" in the same manner? Charles Péguy, for example, shows in his poetry obsessions almost identical in kind and in degree with those of Claudel: the same association of darkness, water, and woman, the pull of birth and death. Yet if, departing from this fact, we were to attempt a generalization on "uterine" poetry, we should find ourselves immediately in difficulties. The two poets are profoundly different in personality, in style, and in ways of thinking. Claudel has an impenetrable and impersonal exterior, an extreme vehemence of acceptation, and a natural tendency to intellectualism and philosophical abstraction; like a hermit-crab, he ensconces his vulnerable but flexible self within a great time-encrusted shell of dogma. The shell, in its totality, without detraction and without addition, becomes not merely his intellectual home but a great part of his personality, hardened, as it were, into the impersonality of the thing taught. It is impossible to imagine any *intellectual* collision between Claudel and the Church, because Claudel's intellect seems to be entirely conjoined to the Church and to function only in the medium of orthodoxy. That which drew him emotionally quickly drew also the entire and willing assent of his mind. His is an example of a religious conversion so complete as to assume the literal meaning of the word: his mind was literally converted into something new, a living and expressive part of the Church militant. The case of Péguy is almost the reverse of this. Where Claudel's personality tends to be absorbed in the Church, Péguy's personality actually threatens to engulf, for him, the Church in the form of a personal mythology. Tides of emotion, with their endless waves of repeated verses, sweep across the dykes established by the Doctors of the Church, dash away reason and philosophy, and leave in their place an undifferentiated and turbulent expanse: the Church identifiable with France, France identifiable with Saint Joan, Saint Joan identifiable with Péguy. Authority outside this inner system is accepted in name rather than in fact –

Et quand Dieu le voudrait ce n'est pas son affaire –

and the Church, when it decides something which is not in Péguy, is not "really" being the Church. In short Péguy is of the stuff of which the great heretics are made; the Church is in him. Claudel, as one who is in the Church, stands at the other side of a great and partly hidden gulf. The poetical results on the two sides are naturally different, and the orthodox side does not necessarily produce the most attractive fruits. Péguy's poetry *is* his religion, in a sense that Claudel's can never be, for Péguy's religion is part of his personality. Claudel's poetry is sometimes stiff and cerebral, abounding in asseverations which are issued through him: everything in Péguy comes from within, from deep and continuous springs of emotion.

These, then, are fundamental differences between men who have really nothing in common except that they are poets, that

The Rhinegold of Paul Claudel

they are religious, and that they have a similar obsession. "Quite enough," exclaims the materialist, "to support my thesis. This obsession, this privation, this maladjustment – for it is all three – produces poetry and religion, and the products can and should be done away with along with the causes. The differences that you spin out between two sorts of poetry and two sorts of religion do not interest me in the least, or interest me only in the same way as the differences which a microscope reveals as existing between two sorts of malignant tumor. All religion is bad, including heresy, and all poetry is bad, including blank verse. If one were sufficiently interested one could no doubt trace the relation between one sort of trauma and the rise of Arminianism and between another sort and the decline of the heroic couplet. But what really matters from the practical point of view is that all this misbehaviour is of the same kind and needs to be corrected in the same way."

To this one could reply that most obsessions remain without artistic or religious fruit other than a private and incommunicable myth. The mystery of how the anonymous and general dream becomes in certain beings differentiated and communicable in the form of art has never been explained. But if the materialist errs in exaggerating the importance of classifying obsessions, and tends to treat poetry as a disgraceful disease, Catholic critics too often tend to fall into even more futile daydreams. Most Catholic critics examining the work of Catholic writers can be relied on to ignore all meanings other than surface meaning. They will be edified or disedified; they will say that the later work reflects a spiritual advance; they will tell you the plots, and that is about all.[1] A critic of this kind will take any detour to avoid what he regards as the mire of "Freudianism"; even if on every page of his subject a signpost points to the same "Freudian" situation, he will bicycle past with hardly a wobble. For fifty years processions of "Catholic critics" have wound their way round Claudel, happily clanging

---

[1] Mr. Sheed, of Sheed and Ward, the Catholic publishers, once published a book consisting entirely of the "blurbs" for other books he had published. The only way in which that book differed from certain other works of "Catholic criticism" was that the chapters were shorter.

together like cymbals the words "great" and "Catholic," but saying nothing more specifically relevant than halleluiah. Their vague idolatry is inferior, as a substitute for criticism, to a cocksure materialistic "diagnosis," which would at least have to take account of *some* facts.

The truth is that there should be no opposition between the recognition of the existence of an obsessive situation in a writer's work, and the recognition of the work's spiritual value. On the contrary, it is necessary to recognize the obsession (if it exists) before arriving at any real understanding of anything in the writer's work, including its spiritual meanings. Claudel's poetry is not abstractly about God, but centres in his own pain and desire as a man. Through what is in him of the pain of light and life, the desire for death and the darkness of the womb, he communicates with what there is in others, less intense or less articulate, of the same feelings. His roots – to use a favourite metaphor of his – go down deep into things common to humanity, touch some essential all-underlying tufa. He comes to religion, like the Emperor who descended into the obscurity of hell to find his mother and a faith, by a dark entrance.

But – and here he differs from Péguy – the religion of his poetry has not only a dark side. There is as well as "water" also "gold," the system of imagery related to the sun. This gold is, on the emotional side, as we have seen, predominantly male; on the spiritual side as it approaches the divine it is predominantly intellectual, standing for "power," "knowledge," "wisdom," "truth," rather than for love. In this system the maleness probably derives from the idea of the sun, the opposition of light to "female" darkness, while the intellectual element derives from the idea of gold as the symbol of abstract value. This male and intellectual side to his poetry gives it a certain harshness, the unscrupulous ruthlessness, dealing with personal feelings and ideas, which conformity with a larger idea requires. The quality of ruthlessness – that quality allied at the same time to absolute value and to the "very dear Violence" of Tête d'Or – is manifest in many places but nowhere more conspicuously than in his most satisfactory dramatic work, *L'Otage*. In that play the aristocrat Sygne de Coufontaine breaks

The Rhinegold of Paul Claudel 183

faith with her ruined cousin, Georges (to whom she is betrothed), at the request of a priest; a repulsive revolutionary, Turelure, who was responsible for her parents' death by the guillotine, discovers the Pope (in hiding from his persecutor, Napoleon) in her house, and will denounce his presence unless he can have Sygne in marriage; at a priest's urging, and in a spirit of utter horror, she consents, abandoning her cousin to despair. We know, from the account of a contemporary,[1] of Péguy's disgust that the "morbidity" and "sacerdotal idolatry" of this play could be confused with religion. Humanly speaking, we may sympathize with Péguy. Claudel's is the spirit, if not the letter, of orthodoxy: the full acceptance of the primacy of the absolute over the merely temporal and relative. This is not human and it is not meant to be. Péguy's approach to religion is human and darkly emotional. Claudel's approach on the "golden" side is also intellectual and thereby tends towards the inhuman and the superhuman. It could be said that "water" (or "love") takes Claudel only as far as the religious emotion in its general sense and that "gold" ensures his passage to the rigorous abstractions of Catholicism, the "frontiers of the divine."

This, however, does not imply any mechanical division. Gold has, as we have seen, its shadow of death and femaleness; its differentiation from "water" is dynamic and partial, not static and total, and resmbles in this, significantly, the actual difference between the sexes. More than this, even at the moment of most perfect differentiation, the two elements rejoin each other in a kind of marriage: the "hymen de l'or et de la nuit," which is sunset (and sunset is also "l'heure où l'homme communique avec sa mère"). Sunset and the moon – "ce soleil qui est entre l'âme et le corps" – are the conditions of this marriage, which therefore takes place, like all human marriages, in the shadow of death. So in the great climactic Scene XIV of *Le Soulier de satin*, the mystic marriage between the ocean-separated lovers, Rodrigue and Prouhèze, is presided over by the moon. Here, combining, are all the principal elements of Claudel's poetry: the sea, woman, man, the sun, and darkness (associated in the moon). And nothing, at this central

[1] Daniel Halévy, *Péguy et les Cahiers de la Quinzaine*.

intersection of all the main lines of his poetry, could be more significant than that it is dominated by the cross of sacrifice. "Sœur," says the moon to Prouhèze, "pourquoi pleures-tu? N'est-ce point ta nuit nuptiale aujourd'hui? regarde le ciel et la terre illuminés! et où donc pensais-tu la passer avec Rodrigue autre part que sur la croix?"

The marriage on the cross is the juncture of the great lines of the poet's personality, through suffering, in Christianity.

This means that in Claudel the poet and the Catholic are indissolubly conjoined. He is as completely integrated a Catholic person as it is given to fallen man to be. The sincerity of his poetry may be known because of the dark depths from which it reverberates: it is not Christian in any safe or antiseptic way, but is often dangerously equivocal; its importance lies in its perfect continuity, from the least edifying elements in human personality through natural pieties to the heights of dogma.

"And what," our materialist would ask, "might the importance of *that* be? Except that if you once start talking nonsense you can talk yourself into believing anything. And even if you *read* enough nonsense, apparently, and know enough long words, you get to talking about mystical validity. I think that this is all mischief and misbehaviour, a more or less deliberate attempt to subvert reason, in the interests of either a frightened person or a frightened class. That is clear-cut. But what you think is not clear at all. Of what use do you imagine all this magic is anyway?"

This may best be answered by means of a comparison. There is probably no poem, in any language, of greater verbal brilliance than Valéry's *Le Cimetière marin* and no poem in which the religious sense is so conspicuously and glitteringly absent:

Tout va sous terre et rentre dans le jeu.

In the result, this perfect jewel of cultivated materialism is curiously null, an eternally abandoned pyramid of virtuosity. Its conclusion, with

Le vent se lève! . . . Il faut tenter de vivre!

gives, in a literal sense, the game away: all that elaborate and

The Rhinegold of Paul Claudel 185

impeccable felicity was no more than a game, of which the ivory pieces are put away when the serious business of "living" is resumed. The beauties of *Le Cimetière marin* have more in common with the goldsmith's art than they have with such a work as Baudelaire's *Crépuscule du soir* –

Recueille-toi, mon âme, en ce grave moment –

for in Baudelaire we know that poetry is not being used as a game or decoration but with profound seriousness, as incantation for admission to another dimension. That is to say that for the religious poet poetry is a kind of magic. This is "bad," from the materialist – and suspect from the orthodox – standpoint but it is undeniably true to the origin of poetry, in ritual, in magic, and in hymns, and true also to what all of us, whether consciously or unconsciously, expect from the highest kind of poetry. If we resent in *Le Cimetière marin* a kind of profanation or vacuity, it is because of this expectation, this magical conception on our part of the nature of poetry. We do not like to be told at the end of a story that "it was only a dream," for we know obscurely that this represents an arrogant and philistine intrusion of the rational mind. We apprehend that poetry, and stories, and dreams themselves, are not "only."

The strength of a truly Catholic poet, as a poet, is that he takes poetry, in its highest function, seriously. He can believe in its giving access to a supernatural world, because he believes in a supernatural world: more than that, he can fuse the great common symbols of his faith and his own private systems of symbols into a poetry that is at once personal and general, emotional and spiritual. This is the meaning of the "Rhinegold," which is both self-knowledge and a divine talisman sunk in the darkness of the waters of love. (The talismanic idea in its literal or "scientific" sense Claudel bestows upon the Germans; in its poetic sense it is his own.) Claudel speaks of "the Muse who is grace" – communication with God through poetry – and we feel that, while the expression may be strained, it refers to something real for him: a current connecting his passions with the idea of God. Such a conception excludes timidity and frivolity and allows the revelation of power.

And it is power, not grace or sympathy, which affects one in Claudel: the word as a raw and dangerous force, without suavity or indulgence. Neither of the two poles of the current of power should be forgotten, for it is not more futile to overlook the predominance in the poet's work of the idea of God than to fail to see that the other pole lies, as Yeats knew:

In the foul rag-and-bone shop of the heart.

VIII
LÉON BLOY

Léon Bloy (1846–1917) wrote, as well as the two novels *Le Désespéré* (1886) and *La Femme pauvre* (1897), several works of mystical exegesis, of which the most important are *Le Salut par les Juifs* (1892) and *L'Exégèse des lieux communs* (1902); a volume of short stories, *Histoires désobligeantes* (1894), and several volumes of polemical and critical articles, of which probably the best are contained in *Belluaires et porchers* (1905). Much of his best writing is contained in his diaries – published under the titles, *Le Mendiant ingrat, Mon Journal, Quatre Ans de captivité à Cochons-sur-Marne, L'Invendable, Le Vieux de la montagne, Le Pèlerin de l'absolu, Au Seuil de l'apocalypse*, and *La Porte des humbles*, which together cover the years 1892–1917 – and in his letters, notably the *Lettres aux Montchal* (1884–90) and the *Lettres à sa fiancée* (1889–90). The crucial events of Bloy's life up to 1882 are recounted in the third part of this essay. He was married in 1890, and had four children; two of them died, apparently of hunger.

THE PARADISE OF LÉON BLOY

> Aimer une religieuse sous la forme d'une actrice! ... et si c'était la même! – Il y a de quoi devenir fou! C'est un entraînement fatal où l'inconnu vous attire comme le feu follet fuyant sur les joncs d'une eau morte ...
>
> GÉRARD DE NERVAL, *Les Filles du feu*.

"GOD," said Léon Bloy, speaking of the Bible, "cannot talk about anything but Himself."

M. Sartre, if the remark were brought to his attention, would certainly point out that the same was true of Léon Bloy, and he would be right after a fashion. Bloy's two novels, *Le Désespéré* and *La Femme pauvre*, are certainly autobiographical, if the apotheosis of the author, combined with lengthy and scurrilous abuse of his rivals, may be so described; the great bulk of his other writings consists of letters, diaries, and pamphlets, revolving around the same themes: even his exegetical works cannot safely be assumed to lack a personal source and application. The whole body of the work – and it should be taken as one composite body – is the soliloquy of a historical misfit: "A contemporary of Tertullian," in Maritain's phrase, "strayed into the nineteenth century." The monstrous iterations and wildly contorted metaphors, the extravagance of verbal violence, the powerlessness to define character except in terms of white (self and temporary allies) and black (the world), all reveal a state of mind very close to the self-absorption of certain types of lunatic.

Yet the work, despite its omnipresent egotism and intermittent insanity, has its own peculiar extralogical system, and a power of implicating the reader, however complacent in his own sanity he may be, in a world whose incoherence seems in some way familiar. In that tufted fantastic forest, where appearances blend and reverse themselves with such ease, one cannot help picking up the scent of a quarry: that equivocal or "amphibological" game, Saint Hubert's stag or will-o'-the-wisp, which Bloy spent his life pursuing. He hunted on a horse that was lame in one wing: the critic must follow dubiously on foot, or swing himself perilously by the contagious poison ivy of metaphor above the swamp of pseudo-science. By any method a kill is unlikely, but the chase may not be without interest.

2.

The place to which Bloy's pursuit persistently tends is Paradise: "The lost Eden whose recovery is the aim of all human effort." The terrestrial Paradise, *Paradisum voluptatis*, constantly recurs in his work, in different, yet related, guises. Only once does he describe it in conventional terms, as "an Annunciation meadow full of dandelions and buttercups under very humble apple-trees, looking like confessors and kissing the earth with chalice-laden branches" (*Les XII Filles d'Edmond Grasset*). This is a caption and reads like one, but with it there goes a strange warning to the young lady in the picture who sits under the tree: if she follows one of the mystic rivers from this Paradise she will reach "her real home on the calcined shore of an Orinoco of blood lit by furious stars." No doubt there may have been several immediate reasons for thus bringing hell into heaven – dislike of the work for which he was being paid, dislike of the woman in the picture, or of some other woman – but one feels a deeper motive: an utter dissatisfaction, reflected in the clumsy wording of the first part of the caption, with the conventional Paradise, and an instinctive linking of the idea of Paradise with the idea of pain. This strange connection is made more explicitly elsewhere. His own childhood, he tells us in an autobiographical part of *Le Désespéré*, was spent in "coveting a Paradise of torture": in a letter to a friend he writes of knowing "the ecstasy of the Paradise of pain";[1] he notes in his diary that Paradise can be reconstituted only by all the sufferings of the Gentiles and the Jews;[2] the sufferings of Jesus were the Paradise of his Saints. Paradise is pain, or the counterpart of pain, or both: this unsolved equation was something fixed in his mind as these references, scattered over twenty-five years of his life, clearly show.

[1] *Lettres aux Montchal.*   [2] *L'Invendable.*

The Paradise of Léon Bloy

But Paradise is not only pain, it is death itself: not death as a transition, but the place of physical disintegration, the cemetery. "Paradise is the cemetery," he exclaims again and again in his diary. And in his most considerable work, that in which his idea of Paradise is most developed, *La Femme pauvre*, he elaborates this through a fable. A "formidable Pilgrim" seeks throughout the world for the lost Eden. This Pilgrim, who "sweated psalms through all his pores" and looked like "an old hymn of impatience," avoided the sun, and travelled along the bottom of rivers and the sea bed, seeking "the brazier of beatitude which the Deluge could not put out." After more than a hundred years "he stops for the first time and dies, in a lepers' cemetery in the middle of which is the Tree of Life and under it the Spirit of the Lord walking, like us, amid the tombs." One remembers that Bloy liked to speak of himself as not an artist, but a Pilgrim of the Holy Sepulchre.

Besides the images, or identities, of pain and death, there is only one other of equal, or greater, power. It is that of woman and, specifically, the female sexual organs. "The second chapter of Genesis with the description of the earthly Paradise," he wrote to his future wife in November 1889, "is, in my eyes, a symbolic figure of *Woman*." A month later he elaborated this idea in a very remarkable letter, which he himself regarded as of such importance that he reproduced it several years later with a few amendments in *La Femme pauvre*. It is worth quoting at some length in the form preserved in *Lettres à sa fiancée*. He is describing the central idea of a novel, *La Prostituée*, which he was never to write:

> For woman – a temporarily, *conditionally* inferior creature – there are only two ways: the most august maternity ["beatitude" in *La Femme pauvre*] or the title and quality of an instrument of pleasure, pure or impure love, holiness or prostitution. Between the two there is only the *respectable woman*, that is the female of the *bourgeois*, the absolute reprobate whom no holocaust can redeem. A saint can fall in the mud and a prostitute mount to the light, but the horrible brainless gutless ruminant they call a respectable woman, who once refused the hospitality of Bethlehem

to the Infant God, can never escape, either up or down, from her eternal non-existence. But all women have one point in common – the assured conviction of their dignity as dispensers of joy. *Causa nostrae laetitiae! Janua Coeli!* God alone knows in what ways these sacred formulae blend in the meditation of the purest women and what their mysterious physiology suggests to them.

As for me, believing only in absolute ideas, I shall ignore all known systems of psychology and go straight to the monstrous affirmation by which I believe it possible to explain everything: Every woman, *whether she knows it or not*, is persuaded that her sexual organs ["her body" in *La Femme pauvre*] are Paradise. *Plantaverat autem Dominus Deus Paradisum voluptatis a principio* (Genesis 11. 9). Therefore no prayer, no penance, no martyrdom has power enough to win that inestimable jewel and the weight of the nebulae in diamonds could not purchase it. Judge of what she gives when she gives herself, and measure her sacrilege when she sells herself. Assuredly this is all very ridiculous. But here is my quite unexpected conclusion ["taken from the Prophets" in *La Femme pauvre*]: Woman *is right* to believe all that and assert it so ridiculously. She is infinitely right since that part of her body was once the tabernacle of the living God and no one can set limits to the *solidarity* of that confounding mystery.

Pain, death, the womb, Paradise – the quadruple association requires, in itself, little commentary: we have seen the same constellation, somewhat obscured, in the work of Péguy and Claudel:[1] here it blazes in the sky. What is worth discussing is the idea of *solidarity* and the relation in which this group stands to Bloy's view of the universe and of history. But before we can approach his system of thought, or intuition, it will be necessary, in the case of so self-regarding a writer, to have some idea of his conception of himself. His life, that *roman vécu*, is no more separable from his work than his novels can be separated from the letters, articles, and pamphlets so liberally spatchcocked into them.

[1] A passage in *Le Désespéré* – "Sommeil du Paradis ... dans une crique lunaire" – brings Claudel forcibly to mind.

The Paradise of Léon Bloy 193

3.

The "horribly unhappy child" was born near Périgueux in 1846, the second of a family of seven brothers. His parents were both "systematically severe": the father harshly "free-thinking," the mother Catholic in the Spanish manner. The mother ceded her maternal rights over Léon to the Blessed Virgin, and offered up her own health in exchange for the protection of her son;[1] after her death he was to feel profoundly involved by this vow. "My mother who is a saint," he wrote to a priest in 1870, "educated me for suffering as one educates missionaries for martyrdom." In this respect he was an apt pupil. "The mere word 'misfortune,' " he wrote later to his fiancée, "carried me off in transports of enthusiasm." This is the childish "concupiscence of pain" of which he speaks in *Le Désespéré* and he described himself in the same novel as "one of those beings moulded for misfortune who look as if they had spent nine hundred years in their mother's womb."

Yet for a time, on the appearance of "the hog-headed lion of puberty," he turned his back on religion and his mother. "There was a period," he says, "– and that on the eve of the Commune – when the hatred of Jesus and his Church became the only idea in my mind, the only feeling in my heart." This period did not last long: he was converted, under the immediate influence of Barbey d'Aurevilly, in Paris in 1869, and a few years later – after the Franco-Prussian War, in which he fought bravely, and the suppression, which he approved, of the Commune – his faith already corresponded to the strange exaltation of his childhood. About 1875, a half-starving journalist in Paris, he deliberately vowed himself to suffering. "I asked God continually to send me extraordinary and enormous sufferings, exquisite torments so that I could expiate the sins of all those whom I loved, or would love, or should love, whoever they might be, including murderers and harlots. I think my prayer was answered."[2] The prayer, in which

---

[1] In this part information and quotations of letters, et cetera, are (unless otherwise indicated) drawn from Joseph Bollery, *Léon Bloy: Origines, jeunesse et formation*, 1947.
[2] Letter to Mme Adèle Montchal.

we can discern a *payment* for his mother's vow, was answered without much delay.

The year 1877, in which his mother and his father died, was the crucial one. In January of that year he is "positively haunted by hell" and spends nights walking round Paris "to escape immobility and sleep."[1] And about the same time: "Terror of everything ... I am not mad ... I am psychologically poisoned." In February 1877, at a period when all his correspondence reveals a state of mind very like the onset of a kind of insanity, he met Anne-Marie Roulé, "la première femme," according to Stanislas Fumet,[2] "avec qui Léon Bloy eut une liaison." Anne-Marie was a prostitute who had been a postulant: her life with Bloy[3] was in the beginning intermittently sensual and ecstatic – "prayers of ten to fifteen hours," he reported to Mme Hello – with the ecstasy rising up to the final disaster in 1882. Bloy's mental equilibrium did not benefit. "I feel myself radically stricken with impotence of the mind and will," he wrote to Ménard on 22 May, 1877. "I am going mad, mad, mad!" His father died on 24 May: he calculated that at the very hour of that death he was making love to Anne-Marie: he was therefore "a parricide" – the starting point of *Le Désespéré*. He was also "a holocaust" offered by his mother to be "entirely consumed by the fire of sacrifice."

In this extraordinary condition of mind and life, and in this same Annus Mirabilis of 1877, he met the priest, the Abbé Tardif de Moidrey, who gave him – and Anne-Marie – a form of exegesis which they carried to unheard-of lengths. The Abbé de Moidrey taught that every sentence in the Scriptures must be taken as referring to the Holy Trinity – that God, in Bloy's more pungent expression, "cannot talk about anything but Himself." He preached also the vision of La Salette, where in the year of Bloy's birth the Blessed Virgin had appeared to two shepherd children, with the words:

[1] Letter to Michel Ménard.
[2] *Mission de Léon Bloy* (1935). Fumet makes no comment on Bloy's mental condition at this time, and Bollery contents himself with quoting the letters.
[3] Recounted, with much transposition, in *Le Désespéré*.

The Paradise of Léon Bloy

"Si mon peuple ne veut pas se soumettre, je suis forcée de laisser aller le bras de mon Fils. Il est si lourd et si pesant que je ne puis pas le retenir. Depuis le temps que je souffre pour vous autres!"

In Bloy's mind the Moidrey exegesis rapidly extends itself: not only the Bible but human history and the events of his own life – seen as in a mysterious relation to the vision of La Salette – are symbolic, incalculably important parts of the autobiography of God. The "general system" that remained when all this had cooled we shall consider later: this is the moment of the melting of the rocks, when all his categories of thought were being re-formed at an intense emotional heat. The doom prophesied at La Salette is at hand and he and Anne-Marie are to play some signal part in it. The transposable symbols of their new-found exegesis allow vast scope for their ardour, which, deprived of physical outlet from about the end of 1878, became increasingly visionary.[1] It is the end of the world: Elijah will take down the Saviour from the cross to which he is still nailed and which is the Holy Ghost, the Church Suffering, the Immaculate Conception, the Glory of God, Love, *Misère*, and Fire and is prefigured by Cain, the Prodigal Son, Columbus, Joan of Arc, Napoleon, and Louis XVII.[2] The Holy Ghost, liberated in his turn by this double decrucifixion, will descend in his form of Fire and destroy the world. These events were to be announced by the liberation of Saint Joseph from his chains. In all this the parts of Bloy and Anne-Marie are now obscure and were probably unstable. Anne-Marie, he told his fiancée years afterwards, confided in him "an amazing secret which I can tell to no one – a crushing appalling burden, which has often flung me to the ground drunk with pain and sweating blood."[3] The secret concerned the cross; beyond that we know nothing certainly. Anne-Marie called him "her Saviour – her Joseph" – possibly figures of speech, but it was a setting in which figures of speech could not be trusted very far: they turned into

[1] This condition lasted for several years. The gentle Abbé de Moidrey, who could no doubt have restrained their *élan*, died in 1879, and his place was taken by the invalid writer, Ernest Hello, like Bloy an *énergumène*.
[2] Collected from references scattered through Bloy's writings. The list could be extended.
[3] *Le Désespéré*.

"figures" in the medieval sense or into gross identification. Bloy certainly believed all his life after this period that he *was* someone mysterious: he never ceases to hint that things are not in their right place, that he is not what he seems to be,[1] and that "no one knows his name."[2] If we take this with his theory that God, absent from human hearts and thoughts, must always be among men "in human form!"[3] we glimpse the possibility that he thought he himself might be God. This would give a clear sense to the words of "Véronique" [Anne-Marie] in *Le Désespéré*, addressing "Marchenoir" [Bloy]:

> "You don't know *who you are*, my dear, you seem to see nothing, guess nothing. This vocation for saving others, despite your own privations, this thirst for justice that devours you, the hatred which you inspire in everyone and which has made you an outlaw, does all that convey nothing to you – you who read the dreams of history and the figures of life?"

If this idea is correct it would give a startling extension to "the enormous anguish of the sleeper who need only move a finger to save others, but is paralysed by an inexplicable force."[4] The "crushing burden" and "sweat of blood" connected with his "secret" would also have a precise cause. Such an identification would not of course exclude, in Bloy's system of interchangeables, other possibilities. He may have been Saint Joseph – as "Véronique" hints – or Elijah, or some precursor of the Holy Ghost. Anne-Marie for her part *was* "Véronique": if Bloy *is* Saint Joseph, or God, she must "be" the Blessed Virgin – there would be, for Bloy, nothing exorbitant and no suggestion of sacrilege or blasphemy in such an idea. His figures are, indeed, often antithetical, as when he makes Lucifer a figure of both the Holy Ghost and the Blessed Virgin,[5] or distributes the seven deadly sins among the Three Divine Persons.[6] She is certainly, as we see later, the Church, and would therefore, by virtue of a recurring equation in the system,

[1] *Diaries*, passim.
[2] *La Femme pauvre*.
[3] *Le Fils de Louis XVI*.
[4] *L'Invendable*.
[5] *Le Salut par les Juifs*.
[6] *Le Mendiant ingrat*.

be the Cross.¹ We cannot wonder at Bloy's acute remark, on the reading of novels: "What excited me most was the uncertainty about the identity of persons.... Since Oedipus and Jocasta, no change."²

The end of this long bout of collective spiritual exaltation or hysteria came in 1882. Anne-Marie went mad. Denouncing Bloy as "a hangman" who had supplanted "her Joseph," she was removed to the Asylum of Sainte Anne; she never recovered.

"The Church is shut up in a hospital for madwomen," Bloy wrote afterwards, "for having married a beggar on a cross, who was called Jesus Christ."³

4.

Bloy was proud of his "Véronique," "as if of a fine book that he had written."⁴ She was really his only book. There is hardly anything of significance in his work that does not relate to this period and to the tortured Tree of Paradise that grew from the Abbé de Moidrey's exegetical seed in the torrid climate of "Marchenoir" and "Véronique." To the Paradise of Bloy's own pain and passion corresponded henceforth – since the stormy revelation of La Salette – the Paradise of the Immaculate Conception: "When the Apparition of Lourdes said 'I am the Immaculate Conception' it is as if she had said 'I am the earthly Paradise.' "⁵ "All [the elect]," he writes of La Salette," will rise together like an unceasing storm, the blessed tempest of the interminable End of Ends, an Assumption of cataracts of love, and such will be the Garden of Delight, the ineffable Paradise named in the Scriptures."⁶ The idea of the Immaculate Conception is central for him: the hinge of the firmament, the pivot of his whole system, the point where the world of his own emotions and experience touches infinity and illuminates for him heaven and human

¹ The Latin note in *Le Mendiant ingrat* with which many Catholics reproached Bloy is perhaps also relevant: "Membrum virile symbolice Crucis effigies ab antiquitate videtur. Christus moriens in patibulo emisit spiritum. Vir coitans et hoc modo cruciatus in muliere anhelans emittit semen."
² *L'Ame de Napoléon.*
³ *Le Désespéré.* The passage occurs long before the point in the novel where "Véronique" goes mad.
⁴ Ibid. ⁵ *L'Invendable.* ⁶ *Celle qui pleure.*

history. The Immaculate Conception is "the mystery of mysteries reserved for the End, it is the Song of Songs, it is the Passion, it is the Resurrection, it is the Ascension, it is Pentecost, it is the Ten Persecutions and the Ten Crusades, it is, in a sense, Napoleon, it is the universal Judgment."[1] All human suffering is the counterweight to this, and history has no other sense than "to pay for Mary." The same idea is expressed in another way about the earthly Paradise – and here we see the inner coherence of Bloy's equations: "It needs all the sufferings of Jesus and all ours, to reconstitute Paradise."[2]

It is at this point that Bloy's theories regarding the invisible world connect with the mystical economics in the light of which he interprets history and the conversation of his grocer.[3] For the sufferings that will reconstitute Paradise and pay for Mary are specifically the sufferings of the poor. These sufferings are, of course, expressed in terms of money, and money has therefore a transcendent importance. Money is the blood of the poor, which is the blood of Christ: eucharistic money that you eat and drink.[4] The words, "word," "flesh," "money," "poor," are "consubstantial words," synonyms of Christ. In the sufferings of the poor the crucifixion still continues: this is the secret of the financial successes of the Jews who are doomed still to crucify "money," holding it high above the "poor" whose substance it is.[5] The poor are creditors of the Jews, on foot of their sufferings, but, strangely, the Jews are creditors of the Holy Ghost, who is, in reality, the

[1] *L'Invendable.*   [2] Ibid.
[3] "I'll show you my books," said the grocer, when Bloy disputed an item. "Sir," said Bloy, "I will read your books when you have read mine." This was more than a quip: Bloy would have seriously maintained that the grocer could not understand the true and terrible significance of his own books until he had read Bloy's.
[4] *Le Sang du pauvre.*
[5] *Le Salut par les Juifs.* This was Bloy's principal exegetical work: I attempt to give its principal ideas in the passage which follows above. "It seems," writes Adolphe Retté ("Léon Bloy," 1923), "that at certain times, and especially when he composed *Le Salut par les Juifs*, he was haunted by the error of those who expect an incarnation of the Holy Ghost, immediately preceding the end of the world." This was the heresy of Vintras – a "sacrilegious farce" according to Retté. Jacques Maritain, Bloy's godson, warned that Bloy's writings should be taken as "mystical hyperbole," not scholastic truths. (*Quelques Pages sur Léon Bloy.*)

The Paradise of Léon Bloy 199

"Messiah" whom they expect and without whom they cannot release Christ from the cross. The Holy Ghost is *misère* (absolute destitution) and the cross, which is Israel and the Jews, is his image and infinite resemblance. "The Jews" can therefore only return "money" to "the poor" – and thus recapture the earthly Paradise – when "absolute destitution" has made itself known. This will occur amid devouring flames, and the Holy Ghost will be persecuted by the Church as Christ was persecuted by the Synagogue – Church and Synagogue being "the two harlot sisters" of whom Ezekiel speaks. Until this "burning solstice of the summer of the world," the crucifixion is the daily business of civilization and the especial care of the Jews:

> For *the SALVATION of the world is nailed on me, ISRAEL* and from me He must "descend."[1]

Bloy himself admitted the obscurity of his prophecies, and ascribed it to the inadequacy of human language: "When one speaks, with love, of God, all words become like blind lions seeking a spring in the desert." But dark and sometimes confused as the words are, the intuitions behind them are very real and unshakable in him. His thought is consistently "amphibological" – a favourite word of his, referring to the perception of the multiple supernatural symbolism of actual events and the supernatural repercussions of human language. All history is "an immense liturgical text," so Napoleon is "the Face of God in darkness" and the Battle of Waterloo may still be going on.[2] More vividly, the conversation of the man in the street takes on apocalyptic overtones in the ears of one who believes that "all talk of money, currency and trade relates to God and man."[3] In one of his best books, *L'Exégèse des lieux communs*, irony seems to find in "amphibology" a new dimension:

> When the midwife announces that "money doesn't give you happiness" and the tripe merchant knowingly replies "all the same it helps," these two augurs have the infallibile presentiment that they have exchanged precious *secrets*, unveiling before each

[1] Conclusion of *Le Salut par les Juifs*.
[2] *Quatre Ans de captivité*, II. [3] *L'Invendable*.

other's eyes the inmost shrines of eternal life, and their attitudes correspond to the inexpressible importance of their transaction.

Bloy does not add – he does not have to, if he has succeeded in involving the reader in his amphibological net – that what the midwife "really" said was, "Christ crucified has nothing to do with comfort," and that the tripe merchant replied: "You can make yourself fairly comfortable by crucifying Christ."

5.

Most Catholics, not possessed of the subtlety of a Maritain, would regard all this – if they read it – as "unhealthy," shot through with personal revelations, blasphemy, and a suspect excitement. Fortunately they are prepared to take Bloy, like most of the other "great Catholic writers," on trust. The bourgeois materialist would regard it as a clot of illusions, the result of burdening a hysterical brain with metaphysical rubbish: a haemorrhage of personal troubles in the form of grandiose generalities. But there is, I think, an approach that would reveal that Bloy's world is not as closed as it seems, is in fact relevant in rather an unexpected way to the external historical realities of his time.

The starting point is to regard Bloy's theory of "eucharistic money" as *a statement in mystical terms of the Labour Theory of Value*. *The poor* are the working class: *money* (meaning capital, prices, and wages) is their blood, i.e. is the expression of their toil. It follows that *the cross* represents the means of production, which at a given time both sustain capital and necessitate the oppression of the working class (crucifixion of *money* and *the poor*). *The Jews*, being the capitalist class, may be partly identified with the means of production (*the cross*) during the period of high capitalism (*the crucifixion*). Eventually, however, the last stage of monopoly capitalism is reached: the working class having touched its lowest depth of destitution, *la misère* – the *Holy Ghost* – makes his appearance: he has a distinct affinity to both *the Jews* and *the cross*, since he comes as the final result of capitalist operation of the means of production, which has sucked up all the produce of labour (consummated the crucifixion). Only then is the working class (*Christ, the poor*) able to take revolutionary

The Paradise of Léon Bloy

action: the descent *from the cross* means at the same time the general strike (dissociation of the working class from the means of production) and the final break with the capitalist class (taking *the cross* as *the Jews*). This cannot be accomplished without violence (*fire*) and in the final conflict the Church will be opposed to the working class (will persecute *Christ*). Yet, from the time of monopoly capitalism and the appearance of *la misère*, final victory is assured: only thus can we attain the classless society (*the earthly Paradise*).

Like most allegories this one should not of course be pressed too far, but the points of correspondence between Bloy's private myth and the central myth of Marxism – with which he was certainly not familiar – are surprisingly numerous. It is true that the two systems of prophecy have a certain common basis. Marx himself belonged to a Rabbinical family, steeped in Biblical exegesis; the Messianic aspect of his doctrine has been rightly stressed. There was, after all, also a common basis in objective fact: both Bloy and Marx perceived more clearly than their contemporaries the sickness of their society, the provisional nature of capitalism, and the historical importance of economic power: "Money more formidable than prayer and more conquering than fire."[1]

But to underline the similarities is to become all the more conscious of the gulf that separates the two men: Bloy, for all his historical perceptions, utterly committed to supernatural interpretation and aloofness from the battle; Marx, for all the element of poetry and myth in his system, equally committed to a practical and revolutionary role. Christopher Caudwell, most subtle of Marxist critics, defined religion as "a reality, but a *fantastic* reality." He would certainly have claimed that Bloy was expressing in fantastic terms – and so evading – the realities with which Marx

---

[1] *Le Femme pauvre*. Bloy, like Péguy but with less reason, prided himself on a revolutionary past. "I believe," he wrote to a friend in 1876, "that Society is stricken unto death, stricken in head and heart irremediably . . . I was too much of a *communard* before becoming a Christian to have any illusions on that score," If he ever was a *communard* it was not at the period of the Commune. "It is clear," he had written in 1871, "that any social innovation is the greatest possible outrage [*attentat*] since it implies the non-infallibility of God, and the authorities should suppress such things with the utmost vigour." (Letters quoted in Bollery, op. cit.)

grappled scientifically. Such an antithesis would be rather too neat – it is a question, for example, whether the earthly Paradise is any more "fantastic" or less "scientific" than the classless society – but it does force us to ask what there is left out, what there is of importance in Bloy which such an analysis ignores. This more than half-crazed man, who sometimes thought he was God, who made a Paradise out of his longing for death and his mother, and then twisted all history and the Catholic religion into a high fantastic road to reach that Paradise – why should anyone read him except for clinical purposes?

The first answer and indeed the last – although it requires qualification and analysis – is that his style is unique. Of that style he himself has left us a loving description which is at the same time a magnificent example.

> His violent colouring, his cautelous and alembicated barbarism; the giratory emphasis and stubborn winding of certain cruel images constantly twisting back on themselves like convolvulus; the unheard-of audacity of the form, as numerous as a horde and as rapid, although heavily armed; the sober tumult of the vocabulary, plumed with flames and ash like Vesuvius in the last days of Pompeii, slashed with gold, encrusted, crenellated, denticulated with ancient gems like the reliquary of a martyr; but above all the prodigious enlargement which such a style conferred at once on the least ambitious thesis, the tiniest and most acclimatized hypothesis; all this appeared to Leopold a magic mirror in which he could decipher his own soul, with a gasp of admiration.[1]

The style here is the man in a fuller sense than usual: the baroque ebullience of the decoration is at its best when the subject is Bloy himself: "They saw his soul moving about in him as one might see some great imprisoned Infanta come and press her face at the stained-glass windows of the burning Escorial."[2]

As the splendour of this image corresponds to the crazy splendour of Bloy's conception of himself – "they do not know who I am" – so do each of its parts refer one to an aspect of his prophetic work. *Infanta* and *Escorial* recall his Spanish mother and the in-

[1] *La Femme pauvre.* Marchenoir, whose style is here described, is Bloy himself. So is Leopold, who is lost in admiration at his own soul and Marchenoir's style.   [2] Ibid.

The Paradise of Léon Bloy 203

transigence of his Catholicism: the Escorial being *in flames* conveys his sense of his own martyrdom and his emphasis on pain (supported by the plan of that gridiron palace); the *fire* also suggests that apocalyptic vision of the "burning solstice of the summer of the world" which never ceased to haunt him: the fact that the soul is an *Infanta* rather than a Prince hints at the femaleness of his interior image and the *burning house* has of course a sexual connotation: the idea of an *imprisoned heiress* suggests his conception that the tribulations which were heaped on him had something to do with his being in some unrevealed way elect: the idea of an *imprisoned woman* suggests irresistibly the tragedy of Anne-Marie and this impression is heightened by the fact that we see her through stained glass ("The Church is shut up in a hospital for madwomen") in the light of flames, a frequent symbol of madness: the curious, vaguely sinister, sense of impassivity we get about the Infanta (she *presses her face against* the windows but we are not told that she makes any attempt to open them) accords with the atmosphere of insanity, but also carries those ideas of mystery and the acceptance of predestined suffering which are so essential to Bloy. Furthermore, a very strange and moving perspective in time is opened up by an ambiguity in the French. The adjective *incendié* applied to the Escorial can mean either *burning* or *burned-out*. Burned-out is indeed normally the primary meaning, but here one is likely to reject it after a little consideration because of the presence of the *windows*, which would have melted in the completion of the fire, and also because of the unlikelihood of imprisoning someone in a burned-out building. Yet common sense cannot altogether expunge from the mind the half-formed vision of the great Princess moving like a ghost, imprisoned by her own will or some obscure sentence, through some abandoned gallery or chapel which the flames had partly spared in the ruined building. This survives as a shadow-meaning and deepening of the image. We feel that the Infanta goes on living in the Escorial after the fire is over: *just as Anne-Marie lives on in Bloy after the conflagration of her reason.* Bloy seems both still obsessed by the vision of Anne-Marie *in the flames* of her madness and also aware that her visions (the face at the window) still continue in what, after the disaster, remains of him (the ruined building): she *is his soul.* There is also the twist – which would be characteristic of Bloy – of the possibility that the burned-out Escorial, with its single august and enigmatic inhabitant, *is the Church:* which again brings us back to Anne-Marie, about whom the whole image turns, from whatever point you choose to contemplate it.[1]

I do not claim of course that this rather elaborate structure was consciously worked out and intended to appear in the simile. But Bloy could not help writing with the full weight of his unique experience and prophetic intuition. The author of *L'Exégèse des lieux communs*, aware of very remote reverberations in ordinary speech, almost never uses words with a flat literalism: his metaphors vibrate in a prophetic air. This is so even when the metaphor is apparently trivial or frivolous, like the endless zoological figures of speech which lie in wait for his personal enemies and literary rivals. A few of these might perhaps be taken at their face value: the epigram on Gautier and his impeccable verse – "Theophile Gautier? An oyster in a pearl"[2] – needs no exegesis. But when he says that the vices of Catulle Mendés would "make a black bison go white with horror";[3] or that a disillusioned bourgeois would be comparable to a winged hippopotamus;[4] or that the perpetual goings and comings in Zola's novels would make an albatross sea-sick[5] – his hyperbolical humour has a special significance. These creatures – which teem in all Bloy's polemical work – serving as foils to the incomparable vileness of his victims, seem themselves to have the endearing innocence of beasts in a drawing by Thurber or Jean Effel. But the importance of animals, their innocence, and their sufferings are serious components of Bloy's prophecies. The beasts, suffering through man's

---

[1] In analysing the *Infanta* passage I have applied as best I can the "exhaustive" method used with such brilliance and verve by Mr. William Empson in his study of compressed meanings in the English poets (*Seven Types of Ambiguity*). The method is, I think, well suited to the highly charged, obsessed, and "amphibological" writings of Bloy. One is, at least, not open to the charge that it is "far-fetched" to read a plurality of meanings into his language.

[2] *Belluaires et porchers.*   [3] *Propos d'un entrepreneur de démolitions.*
[4] *L'Exégése des lieux communs.*   [5] *Je m'accuse.*

fault, have not lost the power of seeing what is invisible to man: "a simple restoration of the earthly Paradise which, for the last six thousand years, exists only in the anxious and suffering retina of these unconscious ones."[1] So that even in the tumult of controversy the metaphor seems to twist upwards: unnoticed, a Dutch mirror concentrates the image of that Paradise which is never out of his thought.

Similarly the monotonous torrent of scatology, which made his name a scandal to the *bien-pensants*, has its significance in the general scheme. It expresses his humiliation at his exile and his contempt for the condition of fallen man as well as for those who believe that that condition is the natural and only possible one. If he plastered his opponents with dung, covered them over with what Mr. Flann O'Brien has exquisitely described as "a thin layer of buff-coloured puke," it was because

> *The Vision of Christ that thou dost see*
> *Is my Vision's Greatest Enemy.*

The enemies are those who believe in progress, who think that the earth can again be turned, by material means, into some kind of Paradise[2] – what he savagely calls "the shitty Paradise of the Republicans."[3] And he feels himself befouled by them, and by having to work in this odd medium, to the point of martyrdom, the point where filth achieves a kind of apotheosis: "I shall ascend to Paradise with a Crown of Turds!"

* * *

The great feature of the work, then, is its integrity – the same sort of integrity that one finds in one of the great French cathedrals, where every detail, quaint, exuberant, or obscene, is yet conceived in the same spirit and executed with the same verve as the great motifs of the Crucifixion or the Last Judgment. By sheer passion Bloy succeeded where since the pre-Raphaelites so many wistful archaizers had failed: he wrote a medieval work about the nineteenth century. Yet integral and medieval though it is, and though it revives the symbolism of the Scriptures in the days of the symbolism of the *décadents*, the work is modern in

[1] *La Femme pauvre.*   [2] *Le Symbolisme de l'apparition.*   [3] *Le Désespéré.*

one very important respect: it is, as well as being a *Summa*, an immense self-portrait. It is a poem in which the mystical interdependence of all life – the "reversibility of the Communion of Saints" extended – is always implied and therefore there are no absolute lines of demarcation between the personal, the historical, and the religious. Bloy's private agonies, the progress of the nineteenth century, the preparation for the Second Coming: these can be fused into one work because they are felt to be the same; *felt*, and in a very real way, for the agent of fusion is pain. Pain is the very stuff of history, religion, and consciousness itself.

"Pain," wrote Bloy in one of his first works, "is everything in life and, because it is everything, we draw from it, as from the inexhaustible bosom of God, all the types of our thought."[1]

Because of its very anachronism, its extension in time and eternity, the work seems to accumulate a superhumanly vast charge of suffering: to be a hymn of all the inarticulate pain of Christendom, from the lazar-houses of Saint Louis to the factories of nineteenth-century England. And all this pain, for which Bloy's own sufferings are the "medium," calls with a tremendous voice for the recovery of the earthly Paradise. If Bloy was mad – and it would seem that he was at least very near madness at the time when, with Anne-Marie, he evolved the categories of thought on which his work is based – his madness was capable of picking up and re-transmitting, in a kind of code, the radiations of a collective mind, itself not so very sane. Moreover that very sensitivity, that "communion of pain," may have made him aware, as he claims to have been, of the trend of future events: the events that were already in his time being shaped by forces whose existence Marx had plotted in prose and he himself had transfigured in ecstatic poetry. He constantly spoke of impending terrible events, the coming of "the Cossacks and the Holy Ghost," and thought that humanity's sense of the nearness of doom was responsible for its aimless and insane conduct. "Could it be that we are approaching some divine solution, the prodigious proximity of which is sending the needle of the human compass spinning crazily on its axis?[2]

It had some cause to spin.

[1] *La Méduse Astruc.*   [2] *Le Désespéré.*

IX
MARIA CROSS

Was Catholic criticism deeply unjust towards my books? It certainly detected an element of corruption in them: but am I sure that I, too, cannot detect that element prowling over my work, in the way it prowls over cemeteries which are nevertheless dominated by the cross?

MARIA CROSS

THE question with which Mauriac simultaneously attacked and defended himself in *Dieu et Mammon* is both useful and misleading. It is useful in that it brings out the two essential elements in the work of a Catholic imaginative writer: the "element of corruption" and the cross. It is subtly misleading in suggesting a radical mechanical dichotomy between the two elements. The "element of corruption" here is something that "prowls," like a demon or a ghoul, not only the actual ferment of decomposition; it is active and alarming, down among the graves, in them, and over them. The cross, on the other hand, merely "dominates"; it is on a height, a little remote and above the battle: one senses a rhetorical marble, inert, moonlit, and expensive. The promise held out by such a monument is vague and sentimental, like that of

Clochers silencieux montrant du doigt les cieux.

At the same time – and this effect is only slightly less misleading – we feel that there is something dubious about the presentation of the Christian symbol presiding over orgies of corruption. The word *dominer* carries only a very faint suggestion of harrowing hell: its most obvious meaning in the context is to "overlook," to "command" in the purely topographical sense. "Nevertheless" is a verbal shrug of the shoulders. "I know the ghouls are eating the corpse, but the fact remains there's a cross above the grave."

Now this infused suggested contrast between the inertia of the cross and the activity of evil has a peculiar limited significance for Mauriac's own work. The accusation of blending pornography with pietism was not altogether unfounded, and the metaphor here does more to admit than to rebut it. There was a tendency in Mauriac – no one who has read *Le Flueve de feu*, for example, can doubt it – to use religious symbols and religion generally in a specious and impure manner, as a defence against criticism and a refined means of sexual stimulation. The cross on the ghoul-haunted hillside is also a crucifix in a plunging neckline, and the "element of corruption" evokes those gentlemen who on hearing Bossuet's sermon, "A grave opened before the court," anticipated in a sexual mode the posthumous activities of the ghoul: "with what increased frenzy must certain courtiers, leaving the chapel, have hurled themselves on a prey destined to perish and – for so short a time – still beautiful, living and full of blood!" (*Souffrances du pécheur*).

It is also true, I think, that this cross of *Dieu et Mammon*, standing as it does at the turning point of Mauriac's life, represents not only what was past for him but also what was to come. Under the influence of Maritain and physical decay he was about to "put his house in order," which meant that as well as abandoning the crucifix-*décolletée* – certainly no loss – he was to relax forever the tension between flesh and spirit which had been the life of his best work. He was now to accept, along with the strict application to his work of Catholic moral precepts – not to give scandal, not to be an occasion of sin – the bourgeois moral conventions – not to disturb "the neighbours," to idealize stasis and the sanctity of the family. What more fitting symbol for this bourgeois Christianity than the cemetery cross, the florid marble effigy which gives promise not of a glorious but of a respectable resurrection?

In both these meanings the cross is a hollow symbol, standing for something important to Mauriac himself but not for any vital principle in his work, still less for anything of general significance. In both meanings also, and in the nature of the metaphor, the cross is set apart from and contrasted with the "element of corruption"; although in the first meaning the contrast is, at a low level, a kind of link. Yet corruption and the cross are for the Catholic the two central facts: the point where they come together is the Redemption, when Christ on the cross bore the sins of the world. We should expect, therefore, to find, in an imagination permeated by Catholicism, that the two ideas would be related in a far more fundamental sense than they are in Mauriac's suggestive but histrionic image of the cemetery. To what extent do we find such a relationship in the work of the eight Catholic writers whom we have been considering?

Before beginning to answer this question we may do well to pause for a moment on the words "an imagination permeated by Catholicism." I am not attempting to define "the Catholic imagination" any more than I am presuming to conduct an inquiry into the nature of faith. What I have done is to consider, in turn, the work of eight writers who are Catholics, and to attempt in each case to follow the central imaginative pattern of the work. The relation this pattern bears to Catholicism is inevitably complex and variable; a concept may be ostensibly wholly Christian and yet reveal itself, on closer inspection, to be a technical term, the key to the whole pattern and containing much that is at least non-Christian – for example, Péguy's "hope" or the "pity" of Graham Greene. This equivocal relation between imagination and Catholicism has been a source of division among Catholic writers. Bloy contemptuously dismissed the idea that there could be such a thing as Christian art, and Mauriac, as we know, at one time accepted the Gidian doctrine of the necessary "collaboration of the demon." The poets and the novelists were naturally disposed to fall in with this view, but the philosophers were of a different opinion. Maritain formally condemned the idea of demoniac collaboration: Evil could not create, for it was of its nature sterile and negative; the devil was nothing. This seems an absurdly linear method of confuting Gide, who spoke not of *creation* by the demon, but of *collaboration*, a very different thing. A profound American critic, Mr. R. P. Blackmur, has drawn attention to the essential role of negation – parody and critique – in modern literature, and what is this if not the dialectical "collaboration of the demon"? However, our Catholic poets and novelists, for obvious reasons, have not explicitly contradicted the Maritain doctrine. One of them has silently refuted it by obeying its imperative and never again writing anything of importance. The others have not been visibly affected. We have seen no examples of a "purified" art that was not also a sterilized art. Even Claudel's work, the most integrally Catholic that we have considered, is filled with carnal passion, flouting the Maritainian law of "non-connivance." In theological terms it would seem that man's imagination, being the expression of his whole nature, cannot, since the Fall, be pure: an attempt to "purify" an imaginative work must therefore be an attempt to make it express less than the imagination urges. We shall not, then, speak of "the Catholic imagination." Even the phrase "imaginations permeated by Catholicism" is a little loose; "permeated" is too weak a word for Claudel and Bloy – "saturated" for the one and "blasted" for the other would be better – and yet probably too strong in the case of the English converts, for whom "tinged" would almost suffice. Yet "permeated" does, I think give the correct over-all impression: of something foreign having established itself and lodged in every part of the system of its host, without destroying that system yet profoundly modifying it, dwelling with it in an uneasy and unstable tension. In each case that we have examined, the imaginative pattern has naturally been different and the "permeation" has taken place in a different way. I have not attempted to impose on them any external unity, but have followed the pattern of what seemed to be important for each of them. I have also, provisionally, sketched the apparent relationship between each individual pattern and Catholicism. But the time has now come to see whether we can establish, apart from these "vertical" lines of connection, "convergent" lines, linking the patterns of the whole group with their religion. If we can do so, we may be able to shed a certain amount of light not on "the Catholic imagination," but on an imaginative pattern which is peculiarly receptive of Catholicism. We must remember that almost all these writers at some time deliberately *chose* Catholicism; it was something that their natures required, not something inescapably imposed on them. I propose, then, to examine, first, what these patterns have in common, and, later, what the significance of that common system is. In this inquiry we shall seem, at times, to be far away from the idea of the cross. It is well, however, to bear in mind that that idea can never be wholly absent from the imagination of a Christian writer; we shall return to it.

2.

The most striking common feature of all the patterns is a sense of exile. Tony Last and Captain Ryder cannot find their way back to their "enchanted garden," their "Gothic world"; Mauriac's hero struggles in vain to reach again the point of departure, the "kingdom of love and silence where his mother was an altar"; Scobie, symbolically exiled on the edge of Africa, is forced to plunge on into exile from his God; the saints of Bernanos are exiles from Christendom in the horrifying decay of the modern world; O'Faoláin's typical heroes – Leo Donnel, Corney, and even the unheroic St. John – are exiled from their country by their country's religion and spend their lives in an endless tortuous quest for a passage back; Péguy, an exile in the Bernanosian sense, is also, and more profoundly, an exile from "night," creature of "hope"; Claudel is not far in exile, only just beyond the frontier, at Coblenz as it were, but his lovers, Rodrigue and Prouhèze, are exiled from each other by the width of the Atlantic Ocean and by its depth from love itself, that subaqueous treasury; as for Bloy he openly proclaims himself – what in a sense each of the others is also – an exile from Paradise.

The foreign shore on which these exiles find themselves is known by various names. Of these the most current, because the most consciously accepted, is modernity. Each writer expresses in his own way that sentiment which Hugo, with intelligent antipathy, ascribed to Vigny: "Dans ce siècle où votre cœur se serre...."

It is the choked lost feeling of being astray in the century like a small child in a strange alley. The "modern world" is not, of course, the same in each case. For Bloy, for Péguy, for Bernanos even, this "preposterous pig of a world" is the bourgeois epoch: when they look back it is to the Crusades, to Saint Louis, although they can – Péguy most vividly – discern a reflection of this glory in the time of their own childhood. For O'Faoláin, too, it is a bourgeois time: the prosaic world ruled by the small farmer and the small shopkeeper, contrasted with the past heroic age of insurrection. For Mauriac, Waugh, and Greene, however, the world resented is that of the bourgeois breakdown, our own sour world; Mauriac and Waugh look back nostalgically to that very world which Bloy rejected, concentrating their gaze on the comfortable periphery of the landed bourgeoisis. Greene seems apathetic about the historical past; he is, historically speaking, an exile who has lost even the sense of home. Claudel is, as usual, less easy to classify. The agony of exile is there from the beginning, in *Tête d'or*, and the trilogy – *L'Otage, Le Pain dur, Le Père humilié* – expresses the idea of historical decline and degeneration:

> *aetas parentum peior avis tulit*
> *nos nequiores mox daturos*
> *progeniem vitiosiorem.*

Yet, unlike the others, Claudel does not abandon himself to mere nostalgia. He gently ridicules those who would resist all change, in a dialogue in *Le Soulier de satin*. Two Spanish grandees, setting out across the ocean, are discussing the craving for change and one of them is horrified to find the other claiming that people should be prepared to welcome *du nouveau*, something new. But when he protests, the other solemnly defines his term:

Du nouveau . . . mais qui soit exactement semblable à l'ancien!

The grandee's doctrine is near enough to the historical philosophy of, say, Péguy, but Claudel accepts even change for the worse not with mere resignation, but with positive *élan*. In the great hand of God he stands, and history is the unfolding of the will of God. This is the meaning of *L'Otage*; Sygne de Coufontaine loves, as Claudel loves, the *ancien régime*, personified for her in her cousin Georges. But the *ancien régime* has lost the mandate of heaven, and Sygne must come to terms with the new bourgeois world, Turelure. It is Claudel's criticism of her that she fails to do this, that although she marries Turelure she cannot overcome her personal feelings sufficiently to accept and "use" him, as Claudel has accepted and "used" his own time. His acceptance combines teleological assent with the dramatist's gusto in the grandiose historical spectacle. He is an exile who is not unmanned by the homesickness he feels.

This adaptation to exile, so marked in Claudel, is present in the others also, at least to the degree of a critical interest in the distasteful environment. Criticism, and hostile criticism at that, with the loveless lucidity of the immigrant, is the most clearly valuable result of this sense of exile. When a Bernanos, with his heart in the past, speaks of the "unemployment of the heart" in our world, he is pointing out a real lack; by a check against a not wholly imaginary past he shows us a crucial point where our culture has gone wrong. If Mr. Waugh turns the knife in Forest Lawn, or if Bloy, overhearing the conversation of his grocer, lights up the savagery which our clichés are organized to convey discreetly, it is that as "time-foreigners" they do not love us enough to be blind either to our cruelty or to our weakness. The considerable satirical power that all these writers possess, and use in varying degrees, derives in part from their underlying sense of discrepancy – the discrepancy between the modern world, seen coldly, and the past, so warmly felt. And in the degree to which they use this sense of discrepancy they are themselves escaping from the mere acquiescent wistfulness which Mr. Stephen Potter has called "Ah, the Past!" They are turning what might have been merely a lachrymose retreat into a point of vantage.

3.

The place of exile is not just a historical period; it is also a mental atmosphere, what we may call provisionally the rational element in society. Bernanos' termite-intellectual – Ouine, Guérou, or Cénabre – corresponds to Péguy's professors, *nos maîtres avides*, and the monstrous literary dinner guests of Properce Beauvivier in *Le Désespéré*. Certainly *odium theologicum* is at work here and also – at least in the case of Péguy and Bloy – professional jealousy. But there is also, I think a residue, of pure dislike of reasoners, a dislike seen more clearly in Péguy's hostile portrait of Eve as the manager, the "tidyer", and Greene's Louise, who is both manager – her vain attempt to make a European bathroom in the tropics – and literary intellectual. Such anti-rationality as shows itself in Mauriac's carefully devised humiliation situations – the Nietzscheism of Jean Péloueyre, the mocking of the student by Thérèse Desqueyroux – is not yet the bitterness of defeat, the feeling of the exile towards the government which has banished him; for him in his sentient universe "exile" in this aspect is little more than a threat. For Mr. Waugh, however, this exile is a reality. Hooper is in power: the death of an upper class has made things "safe for the travelling salesman with his polygonal pince-nez, his fat wet handshake, his grinning dentures" – characteristics which bring to mind the "obscene lips" and "clammy hands" of Péguy's pedants. Hooper and the travelling salesman are not, of course, intellectuals but they are "the enemy" in a more immediate sense: the male housekeeper, the practical, low-level, anti-imaginative reasoner. This is the class of person by which, in another guise, Mr. O'Faoláin also is banished. In this aspect, as in others, his case is useful in saving us from too simple an antithesis between "the Catholic" and "the non-Catholic" or rationalist, for his "Hoopers" are Catholics. They are symbolized by the Irish Censorship of Publications Board, a body which – contrary to a general belief – is anti-imaginative rather than anti-intellectual: it has no power to exclude the most corroding heresies or the blackest atheism provided these express themselves in abstract terms: its power in the literary field extends only to what is "in general tendency indecent and obscene" – the very words in which an adversary, an accuser, would frame the indictment of the human imagination. The people whom Mr. O'Faoláin loves, the "full" people – like the earthy, obscene, myth-making cobbler in *The Silence of the Valley* – seem to him to have become, in Mr. Waugh's phrase, "vermin by right of law" – not, however, of a godless socialist law such as destroyed Lady Marchmain's relatives but of the strict and pedantic application by Catholic people of a Catholic principle. In both cases there is a real enemy which is the same: the modern Philistine who applies such principles as he possesses in a rigid, mechanical, and linear fashion, the man for whom imagination is always irrelevant to reason, the man who, when he thinks he has spoken most reasonably, has invariably

> *Salué l'âpre Bêtise*
> *La Bêtise au front de taureau.*

In denouncing this enemy our Catholic writers are humanists

in the best sense, defending the terrible and glorious complexity of human nature against those who would reduce man to the level of an ersatz angel. Yet there is something in the proceedings that makes us a little uncomfortable. Surely all this violence, this intensity of rhetoric, are disproportionate to Hooper and his kind: powerful though these are, a little low-pressure irony would serve better against them. Behind the attack on them, and on their betters, the Renans and the Lavisses, something more important is going on. One is reminded of those revolutionary orators in the Convention who directed a furious barrage against the discredited person of the King, not that they cared about the King, but in order to force Danton to ruin himself with a "royalist" speech, or a suspect silence. *Derrière le roi on visait Danton.* Such a comparison would imply too great a degree of volition, of planning, on the part of our writers, but it is true to the extent that the attack is mounted on a scale to go far beyond its avowed objective. Who then is Danton?

We have already had more than a hint of the answer, but I think it can be made explicit through consideration of a crucial historic period, the last years of the nineteenth century. The English writers we have considered, born at the end of that period, were formed by its intellectual radiations: we are fortunate in having the direct experience of it recorded by an English imagination of a similar quality, that of G. K. Chesterton:

*A cloud was on the minds of men and wailing went the weather
Yea a great cloud upon the mind when we were boys together.*

The cloud was the oppressive domination of the rational faculties over the passions. "About 1870," according to Chesterton, "the force of the French Revolution faltered and fell." The passion of emancipation – the liberal passion – and passion sustained by religion – "the freedom of Wilkes and the faith of Dr. Johnson" – had destroyed each other. Thereafter: "These years that followed on that double disillusionment were like one long afternoon in a rich house on a rainy day."

Chesterton was aware that the passions repressed or alienated in the age of scientific puritanism were not solely "the liberal" and "the religious." His tentative explanation of the Victorian sex struggle – which he saw chiefly in terms of female refusal – was curious and significant. The refusal might be, he thought, "due to the great neglect of the military spirit by the male Victorians." The women would not accept the sexual wager, would not willingly risk having children, because the men would not willingly risk being killed. The argument may have some basis in fact – and Giraudoux's phrase, "faire la guerre c'est la façon d'aimer des impuissants," is a little too neat – but what is interesting, and apparently vital, is the tendency to identify repressed sexuality with repressed violence. "I feel a movement of the blood," he wrote in 1898, when he was twenty-four, "which declares that perhaps there are worse things than war." And in *The Napoleon of Notting Hill* (1904), having again evoked the atmosphere of the time – " 'Terribly quiet'; that is in two words the spirit of this age as I have felt it from my cradle" – he proceeds to the fantasy of his desire, bloodshed in the city:

> Down the steep streets which lead from the Waterworks Tower to the Notting Hill High Road blood has been running and is running in great red serpents that curl out into the main thoroughfare and shine in the light of the moon.

There is in this same novel a very interesting parallel with a modern work. The first touch of violence that breaks the "terrible quiet" in *The Napoleon of Notting Hill* is the apparently gratuitous action of the President of Nicaragua, who suddenly "stabbed his left palm." Precisely the same action is accomplished by a young philosophy student in a novel of M. Sartre, in order to "exist." M. Satre's novel, which deals with the period before the 1939 war, is called *The Age of Reason*.

In Ireland it was a poor house that experienced the "rainy day," and the "reasonableness" that prevailed was not in philosophy but in politics. These differences apart, the situation was the same. We have seen in the case of Mr. O'Faoláin – whose retroprehensive imagination makes him almost an exact contemporary of Chesterton's – the same convergence of repressed sexuality and repressed violence towards the overthrow of a "reasonable" policy:

the double emancipation of the boy Denis in the insurrection of 1916: as Yeats made Pearse declare:

> *There's nothing but our own red blood*
> *Can make a right Rose Tree.*

In France, where the long Victorian peace had been broken by war, defeat, and counter-revolution, the "terrible quiet" was not a suet-pudding depression but a still and gnawing despair. The courtiers in the opening scenes of Claudel's *Tête d'or* are oppressed not by external peace – their country is being defeated – but by a kind of internal peace, the lack of the will to fight. Their philosopher Eumère expresses the meaninglessness of existence as exposed by reason. No one can refute him until Tête d'Or arrives, having vanquished the external enemy. Tête d'Or kills the aged King, and proposes to carry on the war to the ends of the earth. He is accepted as the answer, and all will follow him to the end:

> *O Espérance d'or: très chère violence arrivée à*
> *la fin de notre journée lugubre*
> *Comme le soleil fait paraître plus douce sa potion,*
> *Quand il inonde les vieux toits après des siècles de suie!*
> *Laisse-moi te toucher! O notre très splendide automne,*
> *guide nous!*

The sexual element in this play we shall try to explore later; for the moment it is enough to note the name of the God who steps from the "machine" of this "lugubrious day": violence, the destructive, the anti-rational principle. This was the principle which Bloy also invoked – "I am awaiting the Cossacks and the Holy Ghost" – and Bernanos knew the enemy: "All the harm comes from the brain, always at work, the soft, shapeless, monstrous animal, like a worm in a cocoon, pumping tirelessly away." But it is a vibration in Péguy's eloquence, demanding the blood of the peacemaker Jaurès, which completes our symbol and reveals the true Danton. "The policy of the National Convention," wrote Péguy, meaning a revival of the Terror, "is Jaurès on a tumbril and a roll of drums to cover that great voice." The roll of drums in all their eloquence is intended to drown a greater voice which they fear may have too much power over them: the voice of Reason itself.

4.

Danton of course *had* been conspiring with the King. Reason, as used by the best reasoners, had been the aggressor in the struggle against imagination, had sustained the forces of science and puritanism in their struggle to make a world drab enough for Hoopers to live in. Reason had subdued love itself into a reserved conditional benevolence: Chesterton fancied that the great Whig philanthropists "loved the Negro for his colour and would have turned away from red or yellow men as needlessly gaudy." The levelling rational men sought – and still seek, although with different weapons and on a different terrain – to curb the imagination, limit its field, lower its prestige, destroy the institutions to which it clung. In England the Whigs had clipped the wings of the Church and the army: they were obliged, however, fortunately for the adventurers, to recognize the utility of that marvelously equivocal element, the sea. In Ireland it was the existence of the nation itself that was in question – the Whigs hoped to rationalize it out of existence with a restricted form of Home Rule. In France, too, as Péguy believed, the nation was under attack: the rationalists were exploiting the genuine scandal of the Dreyfus case in order to discredit first the army and then the idea of the nation. The Goddess Reason had become incarnated as science; imagination was something residual, dangerous, and operable, like a perforated appendix. Only one kind of fantasy was permissible: the so-called scientific fantasy in which the imagination became just and pure by extrapolating the achievements of contemporary science in a kind of prophetic hymn or *Carmen Saeculare*. The trouble with that was that this fiction had a strong tendency, when it was most powerfully imaginative, to be "unhealthy" and actually antiscientific, like H. G. Wells's *The Island of Dr. Moreau*, in which a scientist's attempt to turn beasts into men ends in horrible failure: this novel was greatly admired by Léon Bloy. On the other hand, the scientific Utopias with their diffused light and absence of all contrast, discrepancy, and struggle were unspeakably dull. And not dull merely but, to the imaginative, actually frightening: the peace-through-reason world at which the *Zeitgeist* was aiming was to be a world from which imagination would have been drained away.

To this situation the imaginative – if we may use for a moment the simplification of a class – responded in various ways. The milder or less positive spirits became, like Mallarmé, hermits for art's sake; they accepted the domination of reason in the external world, and merely withdrew within themselves: strictly non-political exiles. Others, among whom we may range, in one way or another, all those whom we have been considering, responded by conspiring to overthrow the regime. These Catholic writers are or were all in some degree "practical men" in a sense that the symbolists were not: they are not only imaginative writers but also pamphleteers, journalists, propagandists, politically minded people. It was natural that men of this stamp should respond combatively, even violently, to the attack on their imaginative world. It was natural also, since they were not, with the exception of Claudel, men with any great taste for abstract argument, that their counterattack should be not a reasoned attack on an abuse of reason, but an attack of the forces of imagination, with the weapons of eloquence, metaphor, and the artifice of situation, on the whole "reasonable" position. This counterattack did not, could not, declare itself as being against reason itself: the philosophy of Saint Thomas Aquinas, which the Church accepts as orthodox, would forbid explicit anti-rationalism. But it is certainly not the "reasonable", the "Thomistic," element in the Church that attracts these writers, and their Thomistic shepherds have had trouble enough with them – we have seen Maritain rebuking Mauriac for "collusion" and giving Bloy, rather dubiously, a licence for "mystical hyperbole." The Péguy of *Eve*, the Bernanos who saw, in M. Ouine, intellect devouring itself like a fabulous beast, the Claudel who exalted pure violence in *Tête d'or*, were as anti-rational as they could possibly be without drawing down the censure of the Church. The others, and these writers themselves in other works, were, if not so far advanced, unmistakably of the same tendency. They were obeying the call which they could not repeat, the call which Jules Laforgue had voiced without obeying:

Aux armes, citoyens, il n'y a plus de RAISON!

5.

We have seen, so far, that they are exiles in a double sense: exiles in the world both in so far as it is "modern" and in so far as it is "rational." In the middle of the twentieth century this combination has a sinister ring. "Reactionaries" who "think with their blood" and have a cult of violence are likely to horrify us as we look at them across our knowledge of what was done at Maidanek. Sorel's *Reflections on Violence*, so akin to those of the young Claudel and the young Chesterton, are a part of the history of Fascism. It is natural, then, that the question should suggest itself: is the imaginative pattern which runs through the work of these writers the same as the pattern which ran through the thought and actions of the Nazis?

Thus stated, the question does not permit an easy answer. It is not enough to answer that none of them ever actually became Fascist, or even that they opposed or fought Fascism; since they were deeply rooted in their own countries and their countries did not become Fascist or Nazi, it was inevitable that they should regard Fascism and Nazism as alien and unacceptable creeds. The "Western" Fascists were mostly men of a different stamp from the ordinary German Nazi: they were internationalists, even rationalists of a kind, and above all they prided themselves on being modern, on meeting the crisis of the time – Communism – with a fully contemporary reaction transcending old outmoded loyalties. Our Catholic writers could have little in common with these intellectual exotics. But the question is really whether they are mentally akin to the Italian and more particularly the German Fascists, whether they represent, in their own countries, the germ of a genuine growth of Fascist type, awaiting a favourable turn in the weather to spring from the native soil.

Four seem to me to have certain unmistakable Fascist affinities. Péguy's neo-Jacobinism, with its compulsive war drive and its appeal to tradition, investing political assassination with the aura of the sacred, was, I think, an adumbration of what would have been a characteristically French type of Fascism, had France, with its falling population and failing power, been capable of generating enough current to sustain the original impulse. The extent to which Bernanos expressed the urges of the Nordic form of Fascism we have already considered. Claudel's affinity is with the Mediterranean forms, with political Catholicism, "order," and the combination of inner traditionalism with exuberant experiment in certain externals: verse-forms or engineering. Unlike Mauriac and Bernanos, he supported Franco, and he wrote, and later retracted, an ode to Marshal Pétain, in whom he discerned "golden" attributes. The Jacobite melancholy of Mr. Waugh's maturity is a late phase in an evolution that has also included the racialistic "pistol-gang" of his boyhood and the strike breaking of his youth. If England had developed a Fascism of its own, a "Cavalier" type as distinct from the "Jacobin" type of Péguy, this Fascism would have had no more fanatical supporter then Mr. Waugh.

The other four, except in so far as they share in the double "exile" which I have described, have much less in common with Fascism. Bloy's passion for the destruction of the bourgeois order is an anarchist rather than a Fascist impulse – although the two are not necessarily distinct, as the case of Sorel shows. At the other extreme Mauriac's involvement with the bourgeois order is not, like Mr. Waugh's, violently defensive, but lucid and unhappily secure, distinctly pre-Fascist in tone. Mr. O'Faoláin's "Delphic Nationalism" might have brought him to strange places had he not been prevented, by the strain of mockery and caution in the Irish character, from taking it altogether seriously. As for Mr. Greene, the nearest he comes to the Fascist mentality is in his idealization of policemen and particularly in the ambiguity with which, in *The Heart of the Matter*, he treats the connivance (?) of sanctified policeman in murder.

It is perhaps necessary to emphasize that this is not a literary Nüremberg trial for "dangerous impulses," with half the accused convicted and the other half dubiously acquitted. The relation between the imagination and moral guilt is not as simple as that.

The guilty are, perhaps, not those who are shaken by the same demon as possesses the criminal, but those who "can't imagine" what it is all about:

> *Those passing with eyes closed*
> *On the other side of the day's quiet crime.*

The men with whom we are concerned are pre-eminently men who *can* imagine and it is through this faculty that they touch Nazism, which was, in one of its aspects, the great and long-awaited insurrection of the imagination against reason. The music, the banners, the marching, the "blood-and-honour" daggers, the high lights, and the great rhetorician's voice were the historical answer to the private invocation:

> *O Espérance d'or; très chère violence . . .*

About fifty years before Hitler, *Tête d'or* had wakened a people from despair only to carry them across a hundred victories to a last battle in the Caucasus. Yet the Nazi "insurrection of the imagination," which struck the Church only less than it did the Jews, those hostages of reason, had, unlike the world of our Catholics, a modern and progressive tendency. It appealed certainly to atavism and the ancient blood but only in order to derive from these the force to form a certain kind of future, a planet for supermen. This world, with a debased and yet ingenious experimental science in the service of omnipotent imagination, this world in which the vast plans finally and horribly go wrong, is something which we have glimpsed already: the territory of the "unhealthy" scientific romances, *The Island of Dr. Moreau*. Now this strange and terrible region lies, as we have seen, close to, but is not the same as, the country which we wish to explore. We have so far surveyed the border districts between the two, where the landscape is of similar character, and there is even a certain amount of suspect traffic; our further explorations will take us deeper inland, nearer the heart of the country of exile.

6.

The third exile, the exile from childhood, is in itself ambiguous. The simple longing for the conditions of the womb plays its part in it, as we have seen in Péguy, Bloy, and Claudel; there is also the nostalgic narcissism we find in Mr. Waugh's hero who was "in love with his own childhood," and the incestuous drive which dominates Mauriac's work appears inverted in Scobie's "children," and even rears from time to time in Claudel's verse its spray-drenched head. And the attempt to withdraw into childhood is sometimes, as one feels it is in certain of Mr. Greene's short stories, an attempt to fit together the broken pieces, to see what went wrong; sometimes, as with Bernanos' Steeny, it is the attempt to behold the reality of adult corruption through an innocent corruptible eye; or it can be what it is with Mr. O'Faoláin, an expression of the will to unity, rejoining through childhood memories the community from which the adult finds himself cut off. We need not here concern ourselves with these differences so much as with the common fact: the fact that these writers do, in a remarkable degree, turn back towards their childhood. This backward look is indeed their most obviously important common posture, and illuminates all their exiles. For if the land of the living, of the born, is a place of exile, is it not natural that the exile should be most keenly felt in the most sharply living region, the conscious present, and that mirage-homelands should appear in the historic past or the irrational instinct? More, is not this unappeasable conviction of exile, combined with the feeling of going home backwards, the very ground of the religious sense, the ground to which Abelard diverted the swing of the march of the legions:

> *Nostrum est interim mentem erigere*
> *et totis patriam votis appetere*
> *et ad Jerusalem a Babylonia*
> *post longa regredi tandem exsilia.*

Yet it is the ground only, a vague terrain of potential religion, an imaginative region susceptible of being haunted certainly, but not necessarily consecrated. What is there, in these imaginations, and not in those of so many other exile-artists, which is ready, in a hostile age, to accept Catholicism? How, in short, does this cemetery come to be "dominated by the cross"?

This question exceeds the bounds of criticism on all sides, yet the critic must attempt to answer it. The possibility of confusion is very great: the field is not the human soul, but profane written work and the writer's imagination, in so far as it appears in the work, and the critic is capable of perceiving it. We are several steps removed from a direct inquiry into religious experience, and not less remote from the sort of direct inquiry that a psychologist conducts. It is certainly tempting to the critic whose mind has been enfeebled by the fumes of romanticism to think of himself, concentrating on his chosen field of certain works of literature, as an astronomer who watches through his powerful glass the flight in space of a group of asteroids, and deduces from certain irregularities in their motion the presence and influence of great hidden suns, the Dialectic, the Unconscious, God. The comparison holds good in so far as it recognizes the elements of the remote and contingent in the critic's activity, but breaks down on the important matter of precision. The critic is really more in the position of one who would conduct an autopsy on the contents of Mahomet's coffin: his foolhardy but interesting enterprise will irritate all the specialists concerned, the medical profession, the holy Imams, and even the aviators. And not least will he irritate the section who maintain that the coffin is not there at all, and furthermore that it is empty.

The degree, then, in which we can try to answer this question is only the very limited degree in which we can see the work answering it for us. Wherever in the work of these writers we can see the idea of the cross, of crucifixion, used not merely as a pious external, but as an integral part of the pattern, we shall have a seamark to contribute to the charting of this obscure coast.

7.

At the end of Claudel's *Tête d'or*, the Princess, daughter of the Emperor whom the golden-haired hero has murdered, is wandering a refugee in the area of his last battle. A deserter confronts her and demands her last crust of bread; she must obey him as she would have to obey bread itself if it became "someone with a nose" and ordered her; he is a poor man. Because she has been rich and because she represents joy he nails her by the hands to a tree and leaves her there to die. To the same spot the wounded hero Tête d'Or is brought by his soldiers, and, by his own orders, also left to die. He rouses himself from his coma when he hears the Princess groan, goes to the tree, plucks out the nails, and collapses. She, unwilling to let him die on the ground like an animal, carries him as far as the bier which his soldiers have prepared: there he regains consciousness and addresses her in sacred language:

> *Voilà le courage du blessé, le soutien de l'infirme,*
> *La compagnie du mourant.*

She forgives him for the wrongs he has done her: she says she is glad that he killed her father and took her throne; she only regrets that it was not he who nailed her to the tree:

> *Et j'aurais voulu que ce fût toi aussi*
> *Qui m'eusses clouée à cet arbre,*
> *Et j'aurais fermé les yeux pour mieux sentir.*
> *Et en t'aimant je serais morte en silence.*

For him she is "Grace with pierced hands . . . Benediction." Yet he rejects her efforts to console him, he rejects her as a woman:

> *Non, femme! Tu ne peux*
> *Prendre cette vie-ci dans tes cheveux.*

He leaves her everything, she will be Queen, but as a female she is repellent; the carnal disgusts him:

> *L'homme humain,*
> *Comme un voyageur isolé, par un très grand froid, se retire dans les entrailles de son cheval,*
> *Se blottit en grelottant dans les bras de sa femelle.*
> *Mais leurs serrements de mains, comment! leurs tâtonnements électriques, leurs petits cris dans la chambre noire,*
> *J'appelle cela bêtise puérile, un inutile remède.*
> *Et toi, quand tu serais l'hymen même je ne veux pas de toi.*

He will die alone: he will be his own mother and give birth to himself, a comet-haired soul:

> *Mais, maintenant, moi, mère meilleure, moi-même comme un fils rigide, je vais naître une âme chevelue!*

And so, turning to the sun, he dies. He had, in the Princess's words, "forgotten everything except the paradise of himself." As for the Princess she is recognized as Queen by the soldiers, and is solemnly invested; then, kissing the dead lips of Tête d'Or, she dies.

One lover is crucified in *Tête d'or:* in *Le Soulier de satin* the two are crucified together. The nuptial night of Rodrigue and Prouhèze is spent physically apart, but on the same cross, as the Moon explains:

> "*Sœur pourquoi pleures-tu? n'est-ce point ta nuit nuptiale aujourd'hui? regarde le ciel et la terre illuminés! et où donc pensais-tu la passer avec Rodrigue autre part que sur la croix?*"

Prouhèze herself knows both that she is the cross for Rodrigue –

> "*Si je ne puis être son paradis, du moins je puis être sa croix*" –

and that he is her cross –

> "*Rodrigue est pour toujours cette croix à laquelle je suis attachée.*"

The whole play indeed is a commentary – and perhaps all the work we are considering is no more than a commentary – on the simple statement by Prouhèze:

> *La passion est unie à la croix.*

This, in deadly earnest, is the essential pun, which connects the Passion of Christ in a special but ambiguous way with human passion, romantic love. Pun-linking – *kenyôgu* – was for Claudel almost a form of revelation, as the casting of lots is for certain sectaries, and this particular pun represents the junction, clash, and embrace of the carnal emotions with the mysteries of the Christian religion. Furthermore the pun, with its inherent shiftiness, is probably the best way to symbolize a state of mind torn by contradictions, yet desiring unity. In the case of Claudel, the desire for unity dominates: the context of *Le Soulier de satin* expounds "passion" as desire exalted, by being held in check, into a suffering which purifies:

> *Le bien que désire mon âme est mêlé à ce corps interdit.*

But in other writings, where the contradictions are stronger, the element of the "forbidden" tends to recede under cover of the duplicity of the pun. It is so in Claudel's own *Partage de Midi*, in most of the earlier novels of Mauriac, and in Mr. Greene's *The Heart of the Matter*. Sometimes the idea in the pun descends to the level of a sort of quietistic three-card trick, expressible in the pseudo-syllogism:

Passion is the name of the sufferings of Christ on the cross;

Passion is the name of a certain kind of sexual desire;

Ergo a certain kind of sexual desire is the same as the sufferings of Christ on the cross.

Between this shakily blasphemous proposition and the orthodox rigour of *Le Soulier de satin* there is, theologically, a very wide gap: in terms of the emotions, however, and of emotional language, the gap is easily crossed and re-crossed. It is not always easy to distinguish, through the clouds of metaphor, on which side of the gap a given Catholic writer is standing. Is, for example, the Mauriac of *Le Désert de l'amour*[1] developing the same idea as the Claudel of *Le Soulier de satin*? Many people would say that he was, that Mauriac is concerned precisely to illustrate Claudel's point: "The good my soul desires is involved in that forbidden body." In this case the "forbidden body" which is the instrument of salvation is Maria Cross, that lazy and romantic woman whose name yet symbolizes doubly the supernatural forces which move through her, without her knowing it, to shape the destinies of the Doctor and his son; *Maria* to the Doctor, who saw her with simplicity as a mother sorrowing for her son's death: the *cross*, for Raymond, on which his youth suffered and died. And certainly, we are near the world of *Le Soulier de satin* in the scene where Maria comes to glimpse the meaning of her own existence: "Not loves but only one love in us. . . . We take the only road we can, but it doesn't lead towards what we're looking for." Yet coming so near, we realize all the more clearly that it is not the same world: the Claudel of *Le Soulier de satin*

[1] Analysed on p. .28–30.

is illustrating the doctrine of "only one love," but he believes that the road does lead "towards what we're looking for" – provided that we follow the sign of interdiction and not the sign of permission. Mauriac, with his theological pessimism and his "collusion" in practice, is very near the spirit of our syllogism, delicately poised on the strong side of the gap, with Mr. Greene squatting unhappily at his feet, peering into the depths.

For our purpose it is not necessary, and it would be both tedious and a little absurd, to attempt to assess the exact theological implications of the passion-pun in each of the writers with whom we are concerned. We shall consider, a little later, the extent to which the root idea of the pun exists in each writer, and it is of course present in some of them much more strongly than in others. As for the theology of the matter, it is enough to note the plain fact that a relatively small movement near the emotional centre may trace a wide arc at the intellectual circumference, where propositions emerge to be condemned, perhaps, by authority. We have considered the circumference long enough; let us consider now certain of these movements at the centre for what they are in themselves.

8.

"Woman is the cross." Bloy's equation provides, I think, the key to much that is otherwise hard to understand in these writers. Yet it is not in Bloy himself that we find the richest development of the idea; his suggested identification of the sexual act with crucifixion seems to be little more than a passing fancy or mechanical corollary, and he is in any case always more interested in bare assertion than in development. It may be rewarding, however, to examine in the light of Bloy's idea the implications of the works of Claudel and Mauriac which we have just been considering.

Maria Cross – the name itself is a significant development of Bloy's idea, for the name *Maria* in the context of Mauriac's work evokes special emotions which colour the abstract idea of woman: it suggests motherhood and holiness, ideas which are then immediately rendered equivocal by the character of her who bears the name – the kept woman of Victor Larousselle. "Was he not both a child of guilty love and son of a holy woman?" Maria Cross is surprisingly near to Margaret of Cortona. With this clue in mind, and with the background of *Le Rang* and *Génitrix*, the feature of *Le Désert de l'amour* we shall find most striking is the "absence" – through the colourlessness of the character – of Raymond's real mother. The mother characteristics are transferred to Maria Cross, not as seen, initially, by Raymond, but as seen by his father. The dramatic crux occurs when Raymond approaches her as a lover, and she, in repelling him reveals herself in the character of the woman his father loves; in effect she turns into his mother. This is the moment which, as we are told, will poison his whole life and all his future relations with women. Here the proposition "woman is the cross" can be expanded into: " 'The woman' turns into 'the mother' and *that* is the cross." To this cross Auguste Duprouy, Jean de Mirbel, Fernand Cazenave, and many another Mauriac hero are nailed. But the restatement of the proposition tends to conceal a very important aspect of Bloy's equation; the cross is in itself sentient, the crucifixion is always a double one. Thus the idea of suffering is conjoined to the idea of punishment. The whole of *Le Désert de l'amour* rings with the vibrations of its opening sentence: "For years Raymond Courrèges had cherished the hope of meeting again that Maria Cross upon whom he ardently desired to revenge himself."

Raymond's ardent desire was never to be satisfied; the revenge he might have wreaked upon Maria appears not in *Le Désert de l'amour* but in another work by another author. The crucifixion of the Princess in *Tête d'or* is, ostensibly, a revenge, not for an emotional but for a social wrong, yet it is clear, I think, that a substitution has taken place. In the Princess's own wish – and we are in the land of wishes – her decrucifier, Tête d'Or, was also her crucifier:

> *Et j'aurais voulu que ce fût toi aussi*
> *Qui m'eusses clouée à cet arbre.*

Her language leaves no doubt about the erotic significance of this crucifixion. As for Tête d'Or, he makes it very clear that it is only her "pierced hands" that make her tolerable to him; as a wife or mother – two categories not clearly distinguished – she is abhorrent, and, triumphantly, he does not need her:

> *Mais maintenant, moi, mère meilleure, moi-même comme un fils rigide, je vais naître une âme chevelue!*

He will be his own mother and give birth to himself. It is impossible not to admire this great act of *autarkie*, this emotional *coup d'état*, this unique seizure of the means of production. When one thinks of the terrible figure of *Génitrix*, the Moloch-mother who devours her children, the declaration of the Claudelian hero calls to mind Gide's Prometheus wringing his vulture's neck or, Henry James chasing his nightmare down the Gallery of Apollo. But there is an important difference. Prometheus-Gide and the sleeping James were preparing a new attitude to life; Tête d'Or is simply preparing to die. Only thus can he "become" his mother, descend from his cross. In life his only possible relationship to the Princess is that of crucifixion, inserting and extracting nails, giving and receiving pain.

In *Le Soulier de satin*, where this relationship is explicitly stated, the mutual crucifixion of the lovers, in an equilibrium of pain and punishment, is a conscious substitute, believed to be salutary, for sexual enjoyment. "Si je ne puis être son paradis," says Prouhèze, "du moins je puis être sa croix." The whole context makes it plain that "paradise" is used in the sexual sense which Bloy also gives it; indeed the sentence concisely expresses Bloy's conception of woman. So when Tête d'Or came to die, and became his own mother, he had "forgotten everything except the paradise of himself"; he had abolished women by assuming all the female sexual functions. Similar language is used, even more explicitly, in the passage already quoted from *L'Esprit et l'eau;*

> *C'est la mère, je dis, qu'il me faut!*
> *Possédons la mer éternelle et salée, la grande*
> *rose grise! Je lève un bras vers le paradis!*
> *je m'avance vers la mer aux entrailles de raisin.*

It seems necessary and right, following this passage, that the poet should imagine himself as the crucified sea (–mother):

> *Si j'étais la mer, crucifiée par un*
> *milliard de bras sur les deux continents.*

Maria Cross 233

Man remains nailed to his mother. When he seeks to break loose, to find "paradise" in loving another woman, he becomes aware of his crucifixion. Crucifixion, in which the cross suffers equally with the sacrifice, is punished for being the cross, is the only form of love. This balance of pain and punishment subsists until death. It can, but will not necessarily, reach the point of ecstasy where man the crucified identifies himself with his female Cross. Death then is the triumphant and paradisiac hour when the dying hero gives birth to himself. But even where there is no such ecstasy, death is always the longed-for consummation of the terrible exchange.

In this pattern, as it appears in the work of Mauriac, Claudel, and Bloy, a conception of Christianity and an emotional dilemma blend and interact in such a way that it is scarcely possible to separate the two.[1] The concept of woman as the cross is here the focus round which the imagination Christianizes itself. The question remains: how far does this pattern extend? Is it simply a matter of similar freaks of fancy in these three men, or can we perceive the same pattern in the work of the other writers with whom we are concerned?

9.

Here it is particularly necessary to be on guard against the temptation to prove too much, by laying undue emphasis on details in the other writers which correspond to what are certainly central preoccupations for the three whom we have been considering. This imperialistic method of criticism would certainly establish a kind of order, but not one that would be faithful to the underlying facts. What is required is not an attempt to establish uniformity but simply to see where and in what shape the group of ideas which seem to be important for each of the other writers overlaps with the pattern we have built up from the marked overlapping of certain ideas in the work of Mauriac, Claudel, and Bloy.

The female cross is, I think, clearly to be seen in the central preoccupations of Péguy, of Mr. Greene, and also, in a peculiar

[1] Bloy in fact did not separate them but identified, apparently in a literal sense, his own "crucifixion" to Anne-Marie with the actual crucifixion.

form, of Mr. O'Faoláin. Péguy's *Eve*, with its mother-martyr axis, the manner in which its images of suffering and death are grouped, alternately in attitudes of hostility and tenderness, round a central maternal figure, reveals a way of feeling which is very close to that which we have tried to describe. The teetering equilibrium of pain and punishment, the sense of being fixed to something – revealed here in the style – almost all the elements in our pattern are present. Even the element of direct, thwarted, sexual love is here, and the single verse that touches on it overtly associates it with a tree and with thorns:

> *Un autre effacera de nos livres de peine*
> *La trace de la ronce et de la fleur de mai.*
> *Un autre effacera de l'écorce du chêne*
> *La trace du seul nom que nous ayons aimé.*

The theme of *The Heart of the Matter* is similar. Scobie is a crucified man: he sees himself, as he saw Pemberton, as Christ on the cross. And the cross for him is female and sentient – Louise – Helen – and we have the equilibrium of pain inflicted and endured, the longing for death. In one interesting particular, however, the pattern is different: it is not to a mother but a to a child that Scobie's pity nails him. Are we to take this as equivalent to Tête d'Or's heroic act of becoming his own mother? There is certainly an identification with the cross, but – if my analysis of *The Heart of the Matter* is correct – it is of a different kind. What Scobie "pities" – what he is nailed to – is his own childhood: that is the cross into which his wife and his mistress have to turn. We note here a difference from our previous pattern but not, perhaps, a very fundamental one; the difference between a "mother-cross" and a "childhood-cross" is probably a difference in expression and in degree of self-consciousness rather than in the underlying emotions.

In Mr. O'Faoláin's work we see the pattern again, showing its versatility in abstraction and elaboration. His heroes – Leo Donnel, Corney, St. John – are nailed to an ambiguous but definitely maternal cross. The characteristic divided feelings towards the dominant mother polarize in two unreliably distinct figures:

Mother Church, who is to be for a time at least rejected, and Mother Ireland, who is loved. It is, of course, Mother Ireland who catches the hero, when he turns to living women; the tragedy is that she, the elemental, the kind, the permissive, turns back into the other aspect of the mother, the stern and intransigent Church. The characteristic result – frequent in all the writers with whom we are concerned – is suicide. In *Bird Alone* it is the woman Elsie Sherlock, in whom the two mothers converge, who kills herself; here as elsewhere the cross is sentient. In *Come Back to Erin* it is St. John, tied to a living woman yet realizing that "he could not have Ireland until he had paid the last penny of her price," who pays with his own death – like Elsie's a death by water. The escape was an illusion, the nails are the reality. The mother was the same mother all along, no more two beings than was that Mme Dézaymeries, mother of Mauriac's Fabien, whose kiss "had a taste of church, a smell of fog."

So far, the overlapping, the repeated occurrence of certain key ideas, is fairly conspicuous and extensive. In the remaining two writers, Bernanos and Mr. Waugh, it is less complete, but it does, I think, exist in a sufficient degree to point to the emotional kinship of the whole group: they are members of the same family in more than a formally religious sense. Sebastian Flyte spanking his teddy bear is nearer to Scobie with Helen Rolt than one might think, and not only because each hero is really, to quote again Mr. Waugh's words, "in love with his own childhood." This kind of love, on both cases, is close to cruelty; one does not need to take Sebastian's punitive action against his furry fetish very seriously, but delight in cruelty, and particularly "the spectacle of women at a disadvantage," is one of the most obvious characteristics of Mr. Waugh's work. The eating of Prudence, the incineration of Aimée Thanatogenos, and, most recently and horribly, the roasting alive of the luxurious Fausta in *Helena* – these punishments are more promptly destructive than the wounds inflicted by Scobie's "pity," and no doubt less sophisticated than the vengeance Raymond would have wreaked on Maria Cross, but they reflect the same longing and come, I believe, from similar sources. The "Gothic world" of childish fantasy, in which Tony

Last lived with Brenda, came to grief when Brenda showed too plainly that she was not willing to live in it; "Si je ne puis être son paradis," she could say in a different sense from Prouhèze, "du moins je puis être sa croix." The fate of Prudence, Aimée, Fausta is the punishment inflicted on the cross; the crucifixion itself, for the two tragic heroes, Tony Last and Captain Ryder, takes the form of accepting a kind of death-in-life. Our pattern does not exist in any single work of Mr. Waugh's; for example, the two aspects of the double crucifixion, the punishment of the woman and the protagonist's own suffering, are usually presented as quite separate things, not closely conjoined as in, say, *The Heart of the Matter*. Yet, once we have seen the pattern itself, in those works where it appears integrally, we can hardly fail to recognize its chief elements in the work of Mr. Waugh; they are not scattered very far apart.

With Bernanos we seem, at least at first, to be in territory of a quite different kind. Sexual love plays little part in his novels and takes the form of a rather abstract parade of perversion. The figures that obsess his imagination are almost all male and predominantly intellectual: Cénabre, Ouine, Guérou. Insistence on suffering and interest in cruelty are the only obvious emotional links between this world and the crucifixion pattern we have described. But are there any less obvious links? As we found the elements of the pattern scattered in the work of Mr. Waugh, can we find them buried in the work of Bernanos? I think that the degree of similarity we have found in the imaginative outlooks of all these writers, in other respects, justifies us in asking these questions; it is well to be clear, however, that we are here entering the realm of conjecture, and not, as with the others, simply noting the relation between rather obvious facts. It is, however, probably necessary, by the very nature of Bernanos' work, that this should be so. Bernanos is an abstract writer, not in the sense that he is cerebral or unemotional – he is the reverse – but that his characters are usually not felt as men and women; they are the symbols he uses to convey the violent emotions with which his conception of the world fills him. It would, for example, be a great mistake to regard his diabolic male figures as counterparts

Maria Cross 237

to the dominating female characters of Mauriac. They are not father-images – indeed the father is oddly unimportant in all the work we are considering – they are abstractions to convey the horror of "curiosity." This curiosity "has such *élan* that it might be mistaken for love," and it is like love also in its span, from the holy, a passionate interest in the spiritual, to merely carnal sexuality and even sadism. It is indeed love gone bad, and it is perhaps in this sense that we should understand the saying of the Abbé Chevance: "The blood that flows from the cross can kill us." It seems, then, that there exists a kind of black cross to which these spiritual thieves are nailed, suffering and inflicting pain. To the nature, in personal terms of this cross, we have, I think, two important clues. The heroine of *Un Crime*, the nun's daughter, is a being who could be described almost in the same terms as the unfortunate offspring of Margaret of Cortona: "a child of guilty love and son of a holy woman." She is a son in imagination if not in fact, this Lesbian who pretends to be a priest and relives the images of her mother's remorse; she is also – with her impure and almost insane curiosity – love, her bad vocation, a being akin not only to the poor friar of Cortona but to those more abstract figures, Cénabre and Ouine.

But it is strangely and movingly in the last and most shadowy and confused of the novels that we catch our nearest glimpses of the black cross. Mme Alfieri, the "flawed saint" of *Un Mauvais Rêve*, is, like the heroine of *Un Crime*, devoured by curiosity and a *hantise des prêtres:* she is therefore in the line of the Faustian arch-villains. But also she bears, to the two principal male characters in the book, a relation somewhat comparable, in a darker mode, to that between the heroine of *Le Désert de l'amour* and the two Courrèges. For old Ganse, the literary figure who presides over this Sabbath, she is an invaluable helper, in fact the real writer of all his last books, and spiritually so like what is alive in him that she may be called his soul; at the same time he feels obliged to humiliate her and even make her the silent victim of brutally sadistic attacks. For Olivier, Ganse's degenerate pupil, she is a sinister protectress who supplies him with drugs, understanding, and a kind of home: the two subsist in an uneasily inert, mutually torturing sexual relation. Olivier, who hates Christianity, sees her as its perverse embodiment. "Love," he tells her, "in your language means, 'Help me suffer, suffer for me, let us suffer together!' You hate your pleasure: you hate your body with a sly bitter hate. You've hated it from childhood. Only a child's hate has that character of mean artless ferocity. Your body is the little frog a boy pricks with pins, the captured cock-chafer, the stray cat. Christianity is in the marrow of your bones."

From this system of torments exchanged, Mme Alfieri attempts to break away, not by suicide like Maria Cross, but by murder. Or is her murder of the old lady who had been for Olivier a mother a form of suicide? In any event, without pushing the analogy too far, we can see clearly in *Un Crime* and *Un Mauvais Rêve* the same imaginative pattern that we have recognized in the other writers. And this pattern is closely related, as we have seen, to the "Faustian" pattern, dominant in all Bernanos' work.

That "curiosity" which for Bernanos represented the devil might be defined as the criticism of love by the conscious intellect. May not the growth of despair and especially the broken "nightmare" of the last work be related, as well as to events in the external world, also to the success of this criticism, the emergence into consciousness of an unbearable pattern of love?

If I am right, the shadow of Maria Cross lies over all this work.

10.

The "triple exile" and the "female cross" are more or less cumbrous intellectual approximations to an emotional truth, which is not to be pinned down by words. At the same time it is only by the attempt to pin it down, by the continual reshuffling of that greasy pack of cards, our vocabulary, that we have a chance of consciously apprehending something of this truth. In the present case if the reader perceives, through what has clumsily been stated, a certain marked community of feeling in these writers – the socket ready to receive the cross – the approximations have served their purpose and the scaffolding can be removed. Nor, once we are aware of this community of feeling, is there much need to attempt a detailed reply to a question which answers itself: why, admitting that they are disposed to be Christians, should such writers as Mr. Waugh and Mr. Greene choose to be Catholics rather than Protestants? Modern Protestantism, which is dead from the waist down, which conceals the cross, refuses devotion to the Mother of God, ignores the Communion of Saints, lays its emphasis on the reasonable rather than the mysterious, has obviously nothing to offer to imaginations like these.

It is the community of feeling that is important. Through their acceptance of the holy mysteries, of the cross, they turn what might have been – what is, perhaps, in many – a private and incommunicable suffering, into public utterance and communion with others. This sense of communion varies in intensity and in expression; it can take the form of an overwhelming and painful sense of solidarity with a particular class – as in Mauriac or Mr. Waugh – or with a particular nation – as in Péguy or Mr. O'Faoláin. Yet, without excluding violent patriotisms and class loyalties, it can ascend to a majestic and vividly present conception of the community of all mankind. For Bloy and for Claudel, Christ's blood is streaming in every human transaction. Once money, the blood-stream of our society, is seen as *le sang du pauvre*, communion and crucifixion become inseparably part of our daily lives:

Ce qu tu nommes échange je la nomme communion.

Pain, the basis of this currency, is also the language of historical change and it is not surprising that a Bloy or a Bernanos should speak that language. We have seen – in the individual essays that make up this book – many examples of the Delphic utterances of the historic sense. It is not only at that border of Fascism which we have surveyed that such utterances are heard; they come from a level at which political definitions do not yet apply, a level at which the cry of pain has not yet been articulated into a slogan. This cry, this revolutionary urge, can take different and apparently quite opposite forms of words. For Claudel, the revolutionary class – the poor – is the man, "bread with a nose," who crucifies the Princess for the joy he has not had. Bloy, to whose mind all history is the crucifixion, sees destitution, *la misère*, as the man who takes down the victim from the cross. The difference is less important than that which is common: the idea that history explains itself in terms of crucifixion. They hear, as Péguy did, the cry of Jesus on the cross vibrating through all history:

> *Clameur qui sonne au cœur de toute humanité:*
> *Clameur qui sonne au cœur de toute chrétienté;*
> *O clameur culminante éternelle et valable.*

In this conception of crucifixion, this intersection of pain, the individual's private suffering partakes of, is the same, as, the general sufferings of humanity. The sense of history reaches the writer not intellectually, through the acceptance of a programme – as with a Stalin prizeman – but from below, through all the deepest feelings which animates his work. That the pattern of these feelings cannot be identified with Catholicism, of which it uses the language, is something that has been stressed. It is well to stress also how natural it is that such feelings should find expression in that language which alone can carry them with conviction. Community of pain, community in the acceptance of pain, has been the very substance of Christendom; there is still enough of that substance left to make intelligible the Catholic language, the *lingua franca* of suffering. More than this, the moral and emotional style of our suffering has been so formed by our Christian history that the distinction between "feeling" and "language" is not absolute; the "language" has formed the "feelings" to such an extent that it can convey, from the deep levels of one mind to those of others, whole systems of emotion which might astonish their conscious hosts. The power of conviction which the best in these writers has over others, who are not conscious of sharing either their religious outlook or their pattern of feeling, comes, I think, from this intuitive harmony of mystery and suffering, the reverberation, even at the oblique touch of a fingernail, of the great Catholic bell. However much we may disclaim the tie, we are all related, like Raymond and his father – through Maria Cross.

APPENDIX

1. A PILLAR IN THE CLOUD

THE great man who is dead was more a prophet than a poet; more a poet than a dramatist; in his late years a vociferous, dogmatic old zealot, turning the moral creditors of the Left, with rhymed abuse, off his estate:

> *Robespierre, Lénine et les autres, Calvin, ils n'ont pas épuisé tous les trésors de la rage et de la haine!*
> *Voltaire, Renan et Marx, pas encore ils n'ont touché le fond de la bêtise humaine!*

Zeal, prophecy, castigation are not, however, congenial to the intellectual Right, which likes cynical prose, Byzantine verse, the unanswerable and impregnable. Paul Claudel was not a man of the Right in the sense that he loved the *status quo* or desired a return to the *ancien régime*. He had a powerful historical imagination, lit, not by any political theory, but by the concept of the Communion of Saints. He was – and this set him apart from other Catholic writers of our time – a Counter-reformation Catholic. Where many Catholic intellectuals today try to recapture something of the largeness and generosity of the Medieval Church, to think and feel as if neither Reformation nor Counter-reformation had happened, Claudel thought and felt as a Catholic warrior, an old heretic-fighter, a man not of the thirteenth but of the seventeenth century. By no accident, it is a Jesuit who speaks the prologue, and defines the rules, of Claudel's most ambitious play, *Le Soulier de satin*.

The Spanish War of 1936–9 was, for Claudel, primarily a great new chapter in the Counter-reformation. Where other Catholics – Mauriac, Bernanos, Maritain – were troubled by the crimes of those who took "the Catholic side," Claudel preferred to sing the glory of his own side and the crimes of the other:

[1] Reprinted, with permission, from *The New Statesman and Nation*, 30 April, 1955.

Quarante secondes c'est trop! sœur Espagne, sainte Espagne, tu as choisi!
Onze évêques, seize mille prêtres massacrés et pas une apostasie!

Reading *Aux Martyrs Espagnols* and certain other "political" poems, one might fancy that for Claudel, as for so many others, history was no more than a grandiose game of cowboys-and-Indians. But the passionate partisanship of the occasional poems, real as it is, is only a surface, a result. The depth is in the historical trilogy, *L'Otage*, *Le Pain Dur*, *Le Père Humilié*; in the vast charade, *Le Soulier de satin*; in the obscure myths *Tête d'Or* and *La Ville* and in that drama of spiritual economy *L'Echange*.

The key to this literature is acceptance; not passive resignation but joyful acceptance, despising what is less than total. History is – as Léon Bloy taught – the crucifixion, and the art of this dramatist was to make us conscious, through the crucifixion, of the redemption also, in history and in certain chosen lives. The plays are full of pain and mockery and triumph, expressed in the buoyant recurrent paradoxes of one whose imagination is divided between two orders of reality. All the Claudelian lovers – Prouhèze and Rodrigue, Mésa and Ysé, Pensée and Orian – are destined for each other, and to be thwarted. This thwarting of predestined lovers is the "Beatrice" phenomenon which Dr. Ernest Beaumont has described;[1] the reference to Dante is less helpful than the connection, which Dr. Beaumont also makes, with *l'amour courtois*. These lovers are literally star-crossed, destined in the mysterious order of the universe to represent for each other the cross of salvation:

Salut, grande Nuit de la Foi, infaillible Cité astronomique!
C'est la Nuit et non pas le brouillard qui est la patrie d'un Catholique!

The whole Claudelian drama takes place under this participating sky, serene and even smiling, over human suffering. There is a total absence of human pity in the famous words of the Moon to Prouhèze:

[1] *The Theme of Beatrice in the Plays of Claudel*, by Ernest Beaumont, (Rockliff).

Sœur pourquoi pleures-tu? N'est-ce point ta nuit nuptiale aujourd'hui? Regarde le ciel et la terre illuminés! Et où donc pensais-tu la passer avec Rodrigue ailleurs que sur la croix?

Prouhèze, of course, is saved and therefore, we are meant to feel, celestial sympathy would be out of place. The weakness in this, and of much else in these plays, is that Claudel was not God. Claudel's Moon sounds not like the voice of God, but like a demented Reverend Mother; it is a dramatic effect, but hardly what was intended. The absolutism of the priests, saints, Popes and heavenly bodies who appear in the plays chills us, not by its theology, but by what it contains of ordinary human arrogance and a certain gusto in taking extreme attitudes about suffering. "Dressing-up" and cruelty have long historic associations and there is a great deal of both in *Le Soulier de satin*. "Give a man a mask and he will tell you the truth," said Wilde; "Give a man a mask and he will give you hell" is more applicable here.

A seemingly cruel extremism rules also the most dramatic of Claudel's works, *L'Otage*. This play is set in Napoleonic France; the Pope has been kidnapped, then rescued, and is again in danger. Sygne de Coufontaine, a noble woman orphaned by the Revolution, is told by the priest Badilon that in order to save the Pope she must accept in marriage the cynical ex-revolutionary and murderer of her people, the prefect Turelure. Sygne assents, death in her soul, breaking faith with her cousin Georges de Coufontaine, a Royalist officer, and bringing death on them both in the end. "*Hélas!*", cries the priest Badilon, "*je n'avais qu'un seul enfant et voilà qu'on me l'a égorgé!*" The sacrifice demanded by Badilon has long embarrassed and annoyed Catholic critics. "Sacerdotal idolatry," said Péguy, and that in effect is also the judgment of Dr. Joseph Chiari in his new assessment of Claudel's poetic drama:[1] "the priest's arrogant dogmatism in compelling her to this most inhuman sacrifice appears to us as repellent and unacceptable on the Christian plane." One may share this indignation and yet consider that after all there may be more than one "Christian plane." There is, I think, an element of symbolism in *L'Otage*, and this, if felt, makes Sygne's sacrifice more moving and less incomprehensible.

The Poetic Drama of Paul Claudel, by Joseph Chiari (Harvill Press).

When *L'Otage* appeared in 1909, the Papal policy of the *Ralliement* – the acceptance by French Catholics of the Republic – was nearly twenty years old, but there were many Frenchmen to whom the words of the Encyclical *Inter multiplices sollicitudines* still sounded not less outrageous than the words of the priest Badilon urging marriage with Turelure, *le boucher de 93 tout couvert du sang des miens*. There were many Frenchmen also who felt the *Ralliement* to be a personal betrayal, as Georges de Coufontaine felt the marriage of Sygne. Nor was this just an abstract historical situation; Claudel himself was professionally involved. Sygne wedded Turelure, *l'homme du possible*; and was not Paul Claudel to be Ambassador of the Third Republic? These tensions, aggravated by the dramatist's need of an extreme situation helped, I believe, to produce the fanatical rigidity of *L'Otage*, the vertigo of the sublime:

> *Les choses grandes et inouies, notre cœur est tel qu'il ne peut y résister.*

The words of Sygne are true for Claudel himself, as a dramatist; the difficulty for his critics – a difficulty not overcome by Dr. Chiari or Dr. Beaumont – is to discriminate: to know when it is relevant to discuss a situation literally in terms of Christian doctrine, and when one is in the realm of things that are irresistible, simply because great and astonishing. The difficulty, we may suspect, existed also for the prophet-dramatist himself whenever he created characters who allowed themselves to sound like mouthpieces of God.

Presumption, the central defect of Claudel's work, is the product of a firm faith and an undisciplined power of projection. It is, therefore, the besetting sin of the Christian dramatist. But the aberrancies of faith illuminate the imagination; confidence among mysteries and equanimity in the presence of suffering permit distinction of style. There is room to be great and room also to make a great fool of oneself; Claudel took advantage of both.

Yet, it would be wrong to think of the dramatist's faith as only stimulus or armour; it is the drama itself, it is history, it is human relations. For Claudel, the significance of our lives is recorded by a vast system of double-entry book-keeping, in the two orders of reality; the poet and historian attempt to reconstruct a section of the great accountancy. The drama itself, therefore, irrespective of any religious content, and simply as an expression of human interaction, is inescapably religious, in so far as it is faithful to life itself. The Biblical undertones in Claudel's writings belong to this total concept, tinged by presumption. Properly understood all history is Sacred History; what is true in all writing is Holy Scripture; the physical market is an expression of the Divine Economy.

> *Comme l'or est le signe de la marchandise, la marchandise aussi est un signe,*
> *Du besoin qui l'appelle, de l'effort qui la crée*
> *Et ce que tu nommes échange, je la nomme communion*

That fishy millionaire, Thomas Pollock Nageoire, in *L'Echange* offers Louis Laine money in exchange for his wife; Louis accepts and proves to have bought his own death; as for the millionaire, he finds that he has bought, not Marthe, but his own soul. (Curiously, Dr. Chiari in his otherwise full summary of this play omits the essential transaction – which gives the play its title – although he later quotes a relevant letter from Claudel.) The idea of money as a means by which the supernatural interpenetrates the natural order – "eucharist money" – belongs also to Léon Bloy, but in Bloy the debtor on earth is the creditor in Heaven, and a most vindictive creditor he is. In Claudel, the millionaire gets value for his money, even though it is not the value he expects. What the two writers, as writers, have in common, is a self-coherent formula wherewith they can revive in us the unappeasable conviction that our actions are not less but more important than they seem.

He prophesied in long irregular lines of exalted everyday speech; with *élan* unpredictably checked in mid-air by peasant shrewdness and mockery; sometimes with a word thrown accurately and cruelly, like a stone at a cat. Often enough the responses "Biblical" and "inspiration" seemed too complacently expected, but almost always – except in certain State odes and certain work of his extreme old age – a sting of precision, a whip-back in the line, would restore the sense of an identity amid so much conviction, a pillar in the cloud. So, with a shade of difference, Prince Wronsky, the doomed Polish exile in *Le Père Humilié*, thinks of Rome:

> *Voilà ce qu'est Rome pour moi, quelque chose de solennel et de sous-etendu, la majesté en silence de quelque chose où nous sommes, qui n'est pas de nous et qui ne dépend pas de nous.*
>
> *Et l'on sent que si l'on rouvre les yeux, ce ne sera pas pour se voir emporté les pieds en l'air par le tintamarre d'une rue comme une eau de moulin, une furibonde et vaine bousculade de morceaux coloriés qui sont les voitures et les passants fracassés contre les glaces des boutiques.*
>
> *Mais ce qui s'offre au regard, c'est une colonne de porphyre entourée d'une guirlande d'or qui s'élève parmi la fumée des sacrifices.*

To a Puritan, especially with sacrificial smoke in his eyes, the contrast between a *vaine bousculade* and a gold-garlanded porphyry column will seem less than perfect. But plays are not for Puritans; certainly not plays from that side of French Catholicism that looks towards Spain.

2. MR. GREENE'S BATTLEFIELD[1]

The End of the Affair was, we are now given to understand, aptly named. "Religion," Mr. Greene's publishers assert with ill-suppressed elation, "plays little or no part" in a new series of novels, of which *The Quiet American*[2] is to be considered as the first. This idea strikes one at first as odd: one can hardly imagine, say, Léon Bloy changing the subject in quite that way. When we read the book we find, of course, that the subject has not been changed at all, only the method. The themes are those we know: guilt and innocence, loyalty and treachery, hopelessly confused in the world of appearances. It is not true to say that religion "plays little or no part" in a novel which works to its concluding sentence:

> Everything had gone right with me since he had died but how I wished there existed someone to whom I could say that I was sorry.

The narrator, Fowler, is an English reporter with long experience in Indo-China, separated from his wife and living with an Annamite girl, Phuong, who leaves him for the greater security which she hopes for from "the quiet American," Pyle. Pyle is that venerable character, the transatlantic innocent, but with the twist that it is his own well-meant activity and his "innocence" itself, not the wickedness of Europeans, that brings about his own destruction and that of many others. When Fowler is questioned by Vigot – one of those melancholy and upright policemen of whom Mr. Greene has always been so fond – he gives us our definition of Pyle:

> "... He's a good chap in his way. Serious. Not one of those noisy bastards at the Continental. A quiet American." I summed him up precisely as I might have said "a blue lizard, a white elephant."

[1] Reprinted, with permission, from *The New Statesman and Nation*, 10 December, 1955.
[2] Heinemann, 1955.

Vigot said "Yes." He seemed to be looking for words on his desk with which to convey his meaning as precisely as I had done. "A very quiet American."

We are made to realize that Pyle is by now "a quiet American" in the sense in which a frontiersman, we are told, used to speak of "a good Indian." Death is the fourth character in the story. It is to work, in one sense or another, with war and terrorism that Pyle and Fowler are both in Indo-China. *It's a Battlefield* – the title of one among Mr. Greene's earlier novels which this most closely resembles – is a literal description of the setting of this novel, whether the action is in the guerilla-haunted rice-fields or in the uncertain streets of the city. "The horrors of war" have grown stale enough in print, but Mr. Greene's dry and casual prose brings them sickeningly home:

> The canal was full of bodies. I am reminded now of an Irish stew containing too much meat. The bodies overlapped: one head, seal-grey and anonymous as a convict with a shaven scalp, stuck up out of the water like a buoy. There was no blood: I suppose it had flowed away a long time ago.

The observation of the reporter Fowler is precise and unsentimental; indeed, it is one of the novel's great merits that its narrator is a professional reporter and knows how to behave like one. "I am a reporter," writes Fowler proudly. "God exists only for leader-writers." This is, in other terms, what Albert Camus claims as the essential of the writer's code: "the reserve that befits a good witness." Those who admire Mr. Greene's great talents, and have been alarmed at the use he made of them in his last two novels, will welcome the re-emergence of the reporter and the quiescence of the leader-writer. The ingenuity which produced the strange devices of *The Heart of the Matter* and *The End of the Affair* – with their accumulations of "proofs" planted there by their creator, like fossils in Brighton rock – is in *The Quiet American* turned entirely to the telling of a story. In his narration Mr. Greene knows how to move backward and forward in time with the minimum of effort and show and the maximum of impact, as a boxer moves in the ring. His style has shed most of its trials and flourishes and clipped off those luxuriant bunches of similes.

Mr. Greene's Battlefield

Indeed, the old characteristic Greenery has grown so sparse that it is with positive, though morbid pleasure that one encounters an occasional patch:

> Even their [American] lavatories were air-conditioned and presently the temperate tempered air dried my tears as it dries the spit in your mouth and the seed in your body.

Anyone who has read Ford Madox Ford's *The Good Soldier* will be likely to think of it on reading this novel. Ford, too, had his quiet American and his telling mobility in time – indeed, thinking also of Henry James, one almost comes to regard an innocent American as the necessary rabbit in a display of narrative conjuring. But Ford's narrative was all concerned with a small group of people and their relationships; Mr. Greene is only partly concerned with his human characters and handles them rather sketchily. Pyle is an angry though effective caricature, Phuong an opiate fantasy; two things are alive, the consciousness of the reporter and the war. The awkward American and the birdlike Annamite are little figures in the foreground, placing the war in human perspective. All modern tragedy, Napoleon told his marshals on the morning of Austerlitz, must be a political tragedy, for modern man's conception of Necessity is political. In this sense *The Quiet American* is a political tragedy. Yet the limitation which is the novel's strength – the reporter's restriction to direct personal experience – does not allow it the full scope and complexity of a political tragedy – if we think of that as involving a great mesh of many varying human purposes and decisions. On a more routine political level one must add that bitter anti-Americanism, defensive discomfort about colonies and apathetic anti-Communism – "leader-writer" themes, but part of Fowler's mental furniture none the less – make up together a cumbrous and confusing equipment. The war, as seen, comes horrifyingly alive for us; as thought about – in dialogue asides – it remains dark.

The Quiet American, whatever else one may say about it, is an exciting book. It is also the best novel for many years – certainly since *The Power and the Glory* – by one of the best living English novelists.

3. OUR MEN IN AFRICA

Doctor Colin examined the record of the man's tests – for six months now the search for the leprosy bacilli in smears taken from the skin had shown a negative result. The African who stood before him with a staff under his shoulder had lost all his toes and fingers. Doctor Colin said, "Excellent. You are cured".[1]

QUERRY, the great architect who comes to live in the leper colony, feels himself to be, like the African, cured and mutilated. The nature of his disease is mysterious. He himself sometimes identifies it with Catholicism, and is dismayed when he finds priests and nuns at the leper colony. "He blamed himself for not realizing that the area of leprosy was also the area of this other sickness." At another level he thinks of his disease as having been self-expression which "eats everything, even the self." Religion and self-expression were indeed part of the one disease, for Querry had been a religious architect, who lost his faith and his art, his love and his vocation. To Marie Rycker, a planter's wife who persuades herself that she loves him, he tells a fable of a master jeweller who

> had believed quite sincerely that when he loved his work he was loving the King and that when he made love to a woman he was at least imitating in a faulty way the King's love for his people.... But when he discovered there was no such King as the one he had believed in, he realized too that anything he had ever done must have been done for love of himself.

At the same time the jeweller wonders, as the architect clearly does also, whether this unbelief is not really a proof of the King's existence. This would mean that the "cure," like the mutilation – the end of sex and of vocation, was simply another phase of the disease.

At the leper colony, two stupid men, a spoiled priest and a priest,

[1] *A Burnt-Out Case*, by Graham Greene (Heinemann, 1951).

Our Men in Africa

take Querry for a saint. Although both are disillusioned – the spoiled priest Rycker finally kills Querry, in the mistaken belief that he is Marie Rycker's lover – a reader might be left with the impression that they had been right originally. Father Thomas, who suggests that Querry has been granted "the grace of aridity" and is "walking in the steps of St. John of the Cross, the *noche oscura*," is represented as a fool, and Querry rejects his interpretation. Yet the interpretation fits well enough the jeweller-architect's own conception of unbelief as a proof of the King's existence. A much more perceptive observer than Father Thomas, Dr. Colin – who bears a strong family resemblance to the hero of Camus's *La Peste* – finally pronounces Querry "cured." He diagnosed the disease, not as Querry had done in terms of religion and self-expression, but as "a form of frigidity," going through "the motions of love." He was cured of this through learning "to serve other people and to laugh." (His laughter, indeed, was the immediate cause of his death, since Rycker imagined that Querry was laughing at him; there is a distant scent of martyrdom.) Although Dr. Colin, as an atheist, rejects the idea that Querry had recovered his faith, the wise and gentle Father Superior reminds him of Pascal's saying, that a man who starts looking for God has already found Him.

There are differences between Querry and Scobie, between Marie Rycker and Helen Rolt, between Wilson and Rycker, between the Father Superior and Father Rank, between the devoted boy Ali, who is killed by Scobie, and the devoted boy Deo Gratias, who is saved by Querry. There are even some differences, though not very many, between the West African colony of *The Heart of the Matter* and the Congo of *A Burnt-Out Case*. The two novels are, however, very much alike, not only in characters, setting and structure – both are very short novels with a strange proliferation of parts and chapters – but above all in their central theme, the progress of an ambiguous pilgrim. Does he in fact progress, or is he standing still in a complicated posture to which clever lighting imparts an illusion of movement? Is he a pilgrim, or a conjurer? Is his ambiguity a device to conceal a lack of meaning under a plurality of possible interpretations? The answers to these questions, in the order given, are, I believe, "standing still," "conjurer" and "a device."

Standing still. There is certainly an apparent progress from Scobie to Querry. Scobie was a mechanism, seeking objects of pity as certain missiles are said to seek heat, and with much the same results. Querry has some human attributes, including intelligence. Scobie could never have analysed his failure as a policeman as Querry analyses his failure as an architect and lover. Querry also moves in a more convincing way; he is not forced, like the unfortunate Scobie, through a succession of improbable theological hoops. There is nothing improbable in his actions, yet he himself remains theoretical, like Scobie: a set of propositions clipped together with mannerisms and bundled, more expertly now, towards a predictably ambiguous conclusion. The standard of play has improved; the game remains a game. It is much the same game that we follow with delight in Mr. Greene's "entertainments," but with a rather more complicated code of rules, and a higher proportion of snakes to ladders. Querry and Scobie are counters in such a game: our men in Africa.

A conjurer. The patter is first-class, the audience is put in its place:

> "Of course she loves him, he's her husband."
> "Love isn't one of the commonest characteristics of marriage, father."
> "They're both Catholics."
> "Nor is it of Catholics."

Very well, better than patter; this magician can tell fortunes, is often frightening. As often, the conversation itself is much more interesting than the illusion which it is intended to foster, and also than the deft movements which it masks. Yet why should we say that Querry, more than any other fictional hero, is an illusion, or that the plot of *A Burnt-Out Case*, more than other fictional plots, is a trick? Mr. Greene himself provides a large part of the answer in his preface-dedication, where he says that the novel is "an attempt to give dramatic expression to various types of belief, half-belief and non-belief in the kind of setting, removed from world politics and household-preoccupations, where such differences are felt acutely and find expression." This discrete setting is in the Congo, and if the newspaper-reader jibs at such a description of the Congo he is told, "This Congo is a region of the mind." It is not surprising that we scarcely believe in Querry, himself a dramatic expression of some kind of belief, half-belief or non-belief, or in his relation to this carefully painted back-drop called the Congo.

A device. The ambiguity and the severance from reality are perhaps allied, and both devices to the same end. People involved in "household preoccupations" and – whether they like it or not – in politics may not feel differences of belief "acutely," but if the differences are important they will surely find expression, and often unambiguous expression, in the preoccupations, and in the politics. Divorced from these realities, and bathed in the local colour of a mental colony, amid "the innocence and immaturity of isolation," these differences find a free play, a freedom which is play. In that freedom there is no obligation to choose. Querry the non-believer may or may not be a believer. There is no pressing need to grow up: most of the priests, all the blacks, both the Ryckers, are markedly childish. The characters are in a state of weightlessness; the novelist-God can move them without resistance, or much relevance to the earth. The question of relevance to heaven and hell is left open.

The most striking passage in *A Burnt-Out Case* is that in which Querry tells the story of the jeweller who worked so long making intricate gold-and-enamel ostrich eggs:

> Everyone said he was a master-technician, but he was highly praised too for the seriousness of his subject-matter because on top of each egg there was a gold cross set with chips of precious stones in honour of the King.

The architect's parable about a jeweller will be generally taken as referring to the novelist, and it would indeed be artificial to take it in any other sense. Querry's story, in tone and content, is not unlike that of Jean-Baptiste Clamance in *La Chute*: he is a *romancier-pénitent*, or he seems to be one. The puzzle is that, while putting into the mouth of his chief character a devastating criticism of the previous works of Mr. Graham Greene, Mr. Greene has written a novel which, except for this passage, very closely resembles these previous works; he has produced, in fact, another egg, complete with gold cross. The "penitent judge" did not go on to try another case, in the same style.

This is not a religious age, except in the sense in which we say that "following the French Revolution the early nineteenth century witnessed a revival of religion." They were frightened and we are frightened. Like them we seek distraction, and often dignify this search into a quest for faith. The success of such novels as *The Heart of the Matter* and *The End of the Affair* – and what will certainly be the success of *A Burnt-Out Case* – seems to be related to this need for dignity in distraction. Some people can find that satisfactorily in Barchester – another "region of the mind" – but many now need the flattering illusion of "facing reality." Mr. Greene's Africa seems rigorously unpleasant, but we know in our hearts it is harmless, because it has no economics and no politics. It has only a theology, of which – unlike economics and politics – we can all make exactly what we like.

INDEX

Abelard, Peter, 225
Ame de Napoleon, L', 197n
Anges noirs, Les, 11, 18, 21, 26, 32
Asmodée, 33
Aurevilly, Barbey d', 193
Aux Martyrs Espagnols, 244
Aymé, Marcel, 40

Bady, René, 6
Baiser au lépreux, Le, 3, 5n., 9, 18, 24n., 26
Basement Room, The, 80
Baudelaire, Charles, 185
Belluaires et porchers, 204n.
Bernanos, Georges, 37–54, 131, 209–40 *passim*, 243
Bethléem, Father Louis, 5
Bird Alone, 88, 90–95, 97, 102, 104, 235
Black Mischief, 111, 112, 114, 122
Blackmur, R. P., 211
Bloy, Léon, 49, 62, 189–206, 209–40 *passim*, 244, 247, 249
Bollery, Joseph, 193n., 194n.
Bonheur du chrétien, 31
Bossuet, 31
Brideshead Revisited, 109–11, 113, 114, 115–17, 123
Brodrick, Father, S. J., 52n.
Brown, Father Stephen, S.J., 103
Burnt-Out Case, A, 252–6

Camus, Albert, 33–34, 250
Cantate à trois voix, 160, 165n.
Caudwell, Christopher, 201
Celle qui pleure, 197n.
Ce qui était perdu, 14, 19n.

Charles, Father Eugène, 5
Chemins de la mer, Les, 11, 17, 32
Chesterton, G. K., ix, 217–18, 220
Chute, La, 255
Claudel, Paul, 157–86, 192, 209–40 *passim*, 243–8
Come Back to Erin, 99–101, 102–3, 105, 235
Commencements d'une vie, 12, 13
Connaissance de l'Est, 160, 164, 167, 169
Conte de noël, 25n.
Coups de couteau, 17
Crime, Un, 46, 237, 238

Decline and Fall, 111–12, 113, 114
Désert de l'amour, Le, 4, 5, 7, 8, 28–30, 31, 163, 229, 230–1
Désespéré, Le, 189, 190, 193 and n., 195, 197n., 205n., 206n., 215
Destins, 4, 5, 9, 10, 18, 31
Dieu et Mammon, 6n., 32, 209, 210
Drumont, Edouard-Adolphe, 51
du Bos, Charles, 27
du Passage, Father Henry, 52n.

Echange, L', 160, 164, 247
Ehrenburg, Ilya, 52
Empson, William, 204n.
End of the Affair, The, 46n., 249, 250, 256
Enfant chargé de Chaînes, L', 9, 18, 25
Esprit et l'eau, 169, 170–1, 232
Eve, 128, 139–51, 234
Exégèse des lieux communs, L', 199–200, 204 and n.

257

Femme pauvre, La, 189, 191, 192, 196n., 201n., 202n., 205n.
Feu sur la terre, Le, 33
Feuilles de saints, 160
Fils de Louis XVI, Le, 196n.
Fin de la nuit, La, 11, 17, 32
Fleuve de feu, Le, 5, 18, 163, 209
Forster, E. M., 81
France, Anatole, 33, 45
France contre les robots, La, 52
Fumet, Stanislas, 194

Gardiner, Father H. C., 109
Gautier, Théophile, 204
Génitrix, 5, 7, 11, 12, 15, 20, 21, 24, 34, 231, 232
Gide, André, 6, 32, 45, 49, 211, 232
Giraudoux, Jean, 218
Grande Peur des bien-pensants, La, 51
Grands Cimetières sous la lune, Les, 51, 131
Great O'Neill, The, 98
Greene, Graham, 57–84, 209–40 passim, 249–56
Gun for Sale, A, 62

Halévy, Daniel, 183n.
Handful of Dust, A, 110, 117, 123
Heart of the Matter, The, 57–84, 223, 229, 234, 236, 250, 253, 256
Helena, 123, 235
Hello, Ernest, 195n.
Hemingway, Ernest, 26
Hugo, Victor, 154, 213
Huxley, Aldous, 122

Imposture, L', 37–39, 41–43, 47
Invendable, L', 190n., 196n., 197n., 198n., 199n.
It's a Battlefield, 62, 250

Je m'accuse, 204n.
Jeanne d'Arc, 131–2, 134, 152
Jeudi saint, Le, 25n.
Jeune Fille Violaine, La, 168, 176
Joie, La, 39, 41, 42, 47

Journal d'un curé de campagne, 47, 48
Joystone, Emil, 178

Kelleher, J. V., 94n., 103
Keun, Odette, 119
King of the Beggars, 98–99, 100, 103

Labels, 112
Laforgue, Jules, 9, 222
Lawrence, D. H., 5, 30
Lettres à sa fiancée, 191
Lettres aux Montchal, 190n.
Loved One, The, 119, 120–2, 123

Madaule, Jacques, 11, 157, 161n.
Mal, Le, 13
Mal Aimés, Les, 21n., 33
Marcel, Gabriel, 27
Margaret of Cortona, 22
Maritain, Jacques, 6, 32n., 77, 103, 189, 198n., 210, 211, 221, 243
Martindale, Father C. C., S.J., 77
Marx, Karl, 201–2
Mauriac, François, 3–34, 63, 103–4, 115, 163, 209–40 passim, 243
Maurras, Charles, 51
Mauvais Rêve, Un, 237, 238
Méduse Astruc, La, 206n.
Mendés, Catulle, 204
Mendiant ingrat, Le, 196n.
Midsummer Night Madness, 95–96, 102
Moidrey, Abbé Tardif de, 194
M. Ouine, 39, 40, 41, 43–49 passim
Muses, Les, 160
Mystère de la charité de Jeanne d'Arc, Le, 129–30, 134
Mystère des Saints Innocents, Le, 135, 136
Mystère Frontenac, Le, 10, 13–14, 16

Nest of Simple Folk, A, 88–90, 93–94, 95
Nœud de vipères, Le, 7–8, 10, 11, 17n., 20, 21, 26
Nouvelle Histoire de Mouchette, 48

Index

O'Brien, Flann, 205
O'Connor, Frank, 102, 115
O'Faoláin, Seán, 87–105, 209–40 passim
O'Flaherty, Kathleen, 157n., 163n.
Oiseau noir dans le soleil levant, L', 165n.
Orages, 27, 31
Orwell, George, 81
Otage, L', 182, 214, 244, 245–6

Pain dur, Le, 214, 244
Partage de Midi, 162–3, 175, 229
Pascal, Blaise, 23n., 31, 253
Passage du malin, 33
Péguy, Charles, 63, 78, 127–54, 178, 179–81, 182–3, 192, 201n., 209–40 passim
Père humilié, Le, 176, 214, 244, 248
Peste, La, 33, 253
Pharisienne, La, 11, 18–20, 21, 32
Porche du mystère de la deuxième vertu, Le, 135–6
Potter, Stephen, 215
Power and the Glory, The, 62, 251
Préséances, 8, 9
Propos d'un entrepreneur de démolitions, 204n.
Proust, Marcel, 6n., 21, 116–9
Purse of Coppers, A, 97, 102
Put Out More Flags, 112, 114n.

Quatre Ans de captivité à Cochons-sur-Marne, 199n.
Quiet American, The, 249–51

Racine, 30
Rang, Le, 15–17, 34, 231
Renan, Ernest, 42
Repos du septième jour, Le, 173
Retté, Adolphe, 198n.
Rideau, Father Emile, 26
Robbery under Law, 113
Robe prétexte, La, 18n., 23n.
Rolland, Romain, 125, 132n.

Romains, Jules, 34
Rossetti, 110
Route interrompue, La, 173

Sagouin, Le, 11, 21, 32
Sainte Marguerite de Cortone, 22
Sainte Thérèse, 171
Salut par les Juifs, Le, 196n., 198n., 199n.
Sang du pauvre, Le, 198n.
Sartre, Jean-Paul, 32–34, 40, 218
Scoop, 111, 112
Scott-King's Modern Europe, 119–20
Sheed, F. J., 181n.
Sorel, Georges, 222, 223
Souffrances du pécheur, 31, 210
Soulier de satin, Le, 160, 163, 170, 173, 183, 214, 228, 229, 232–3, 243, 245
Sous le Soleil de Satan, 40, 45, 47
Suite d'Eve, 129, 147n.
Summer in Italy, A, 105n.
Symbolisme de l'apparition, Le, 205n.

Teresa, 101
Tête d'or, 157–9, 161–2, 165n., 170, 171, 172, 175, 214, 219, 221, 226–7, 231–2
Thérèse Desqueyroux, 5

Valéry, Paul, 184
Vers d'exil, 164, 176n.
Vile Bodies, 111, 112, 114, 115
Ville, La, 159, 170, 171

Waugh, Arthur, 114
Waugh, Evelyn, 109–23, 209–40 passim
Waugh in Abyssinia, 112
Wells, H. G., 220
Wilson, Edmund, 113

Yeats, W. B., 76, 78

Zola, Emile, 34, 204